D0849875

ESSAYS IN
SOUTHERN
LABOR HISTORY

ESSAYS IN SOUTHERN LABOR HISTORY

Selected Papers,
Southern Labor
History Conference,
1976

EDITED BY GARY M FINK
AND MERL E. REED

CONTRIBUTIONS IN ECONOMICS AND
ECONOMIC HISTORY, NUMBER 16

 **GREENWOOD PRESS**
WESTPORT, CONNECTICUT • LONDON, ENGLAND

196191

 8

Library of Congress Cataloging in Publication Data

Southern Labor History Conference, Atlanta, 1976.
 Essays in Southern labor history.

 (Contributions in economics and economic history ;
no. 16 ISSN 0084-9235)
 Includes index.
 1. Labor and laboring classes—Southern States—
History—Congresses. 2. Strikes and lockouts—Southern
States—History—Congresses. 3. Trade-unions—Southern
States—History—Congresses. I. Fink, Gary M.
II. Reed, Merl Elwyn, 1925- III. Title.
HD8083.S9S66 1976   330.9′75   77-85
ISBN 0-8371-9528-4

Library of Congress Catalog Card Number: 77-85
ISBN: 0-8371-9528-4
ISSN: 0048-9235

First published in 1977

Greenwood Press, Inc.
51 Riverside Avenue, Westport, Connecticut 06880

Printed in the United States of America

Contents

Tables

Preface

The essays presented in this volume were selected from the papers read at the Southern Labor History Conference held in Atlanta, Georgia, April 1 to 3, 1976. Each of the papers was read and evaluated by at least two referees. Based on those evaluations, the board of editors made its selections. Quality, of course, was the prime consideration in selecting essays for inclusion; but the editors were also interested, as far as possible, in having the volume reflect the spirit and character of the conference. Labor activists, friends of the labor movement, established scholars, graduate students, and high school teachers participated in the program; they are all represented in this publication.

The essays that follow, with a few exceptions, are identical to the papers read at the conference. They were, of course, edited; and passages peculiar to an oral presentation were eliminated. Our authors would no doubt have appreciated more time to revise and refine their essays, but considerations of time and circumstance did not permit extensive revisions. In a few instances, the authors, due to the limitations of time, read only portions of their essays at the conference. In these cases, we have elected to reproduce the essays in their entirety.

We would like to express our appreciation to those who served on the board of editors and to those who read and evaluated papers for us. Joseph Y. Garrison and Seth Wigderson made a preliminary evaluation of the papers, and James W. May, Jr., wrote the synopses of the commentators' remarks. Mary B. Fink assisted in editing and proofreading the manuscript. Our typist, Pauline Pullen, labored valiantly in the face of time restrictions and difficult copy. Financial assistance from the Rockefeller Foundation and the Organized Labor and Workmen's Circle Awards Banquet Committee of Atlanta covered

the costs of manuscript preparation. Finally, our special
thanks to the contributors whose prompt response to inquiries
and requests greatly facilitated the editing of this volume.
Whatever contribution this volume makes to the study of labor
in the South is a tribute to their scholarship.

Gary M Fink
Merl E. Reed
  Georgia State University, Atlanta   November 1976

Introduction

The Southern Labor History Conference, planned by a committee representing both academe and organized labor, reflected the spirit embodied in the Southern Labor Archives from its inception. The concept of the archives began as a joint project of the Department of History, Georgia State University,* and organized labor in Atlanta; the continuing cooperation of these two groups has assured its success.

THE SOUTHERN LABOR ARCHIVES

The movement to establish a labor archives in Atlanta was initiated in late 1968 when Merl E. Reed suggested such an endeavor to Atlanta labor leaders. Through contacts with E. T. (Al) Kehrer, Southern director of the AFL-CIO Civil Rights Department, Reed learned that local labor groups were seeking a way to honor long-time Atlanta labor lawyer Joseph Jacobs. They already had formed an awards committee consisting of representatives from organized labor and Workmen's Circle. Reed, with the strong support of Joseph O. Baylen, head of the Department of History, unofficially proposed the establishment at the university of an archives for the records of organized labor in the South; and the awards committee enthusiastically endorsed the proposal. Quantities of labor union records already had been discarded in Atlanta, a city that had witnessed labor union activity almost since its founding. There was no doubt that similar circumstances existed throughout the South. The history of labor in Atlanta and the South might never be written unless considerable source material from the trade unions and their leaders could be preserved.

---

* Georgia State College until fall 1969.

The historians were especially anxious to see the establishment of an archive. With a labor history course already
being offered by the Department of History and a labor field
being considered as part of an impending Ph.D. program in
history, faculty and graduate students needed a ready source
of primary material. The labor leaders were urged to expe-
dite the program with an initial endowment of $5,000 to be
matched in various ways by the university and its history department. Once an archive was operational, contacts with
labor organizations could begin in the Atlanta area and expand to include Georgia and the Southeast. Collecting would
stress general source material, oral history, case records,
and lawyers' briefs. Within a short time, university officials had approved the archives proposal and forwarded it to
the board of regents.

The awards committee proceeded with its own plans to honor
Jacobs and support the archives. It decided to hold a Labor
Awards Banquet on May 1, 1969, and to donate the proceeds "as
seed money" for the Southern Labor Archives. With an attendance of over 600, the affair was a great success and produced a surplus of nearly $3,800. Soon thereafter, the com-
mittee decided to hold an annual Labor Awards Banquet to
honor outstanding leaders of organized labor and to secure
funds for the archives.**

In just six months, much had been accomplished; but more than
two years were to pass before the collecting of labor records
actually would begin. In the meantime, the ad hoc arrangement existing between Atlanta labor and the university had to
be formalized. Drawing upon the experience of the Archives
of Labor and Urban Affairs at Wayne State University, university officials prepared an agreement that was submitted to
the Labor Awards Committee in August. It stipulated that
Georgia State University would provide the operational neces-
sities -- space, staff, supplies -- and that labor would con-
tribute the records and the proceeds of the annual banquet.
One feature of the agreement provided for participation in
archives activity by both labor and academe through a Southern Labor Archives Council and a Southern Labor Archives Advisory Committee. These two groups, respectively, provide
assistance in obtaining material for the archives and consult
with the archivist on policy matters as need be. Approved by
the board of regents in March 1970, the contract was formally
signed during a Southern Labor Archives celebration at
Georgia State University on April 28. The archives now existed on paper and had a fund of $3,800 at its disposal.

After determining to place the archives administratively and
physically in the library, the university, in June 1970,

_____

** By the end of 1976, over $19,800 had been raised.

retained a consultant to view the library's physical facilities and advise on the next steps in the development of the
archives. Philip Mason of Wayne State University was impressed with the progress already made and advised the immediate preparation of a budget. He estimated that 1,000
square feet in the library, properly arranged and partitioned
for access and security, would be adequate for three to five
years. The new archivist should be selected from as wide a
field of applicants as could be generated by advertising the
opening. By fall, 1970, the search for a full-time archivist
was under way.

David B. Gracy II, a recent Ph.D. in history from Texas Tech
University and archivist of the Southwest Collection, was
hired. A crucial decision for the future of the archives was
made within a few months of his arrival. Archives' directors
decided to decline the offer of an insurance company's records, although an attractive collection. This action established firmly a policy that the Southern Labor Archives would
be only what its title specified, a labor repository that
would accept no business, urban, or other archival material
unrelated to labor history.

The new archivist's first chores consisted of preparing a
policy statement elaborating and implementing the contract
and laying the groundwork for both the collecting program and
the processing enterprise. The first major collection -- the
records of the Atlanta Typographical Union -- was received in
September. The records had been discovered in the basement
of the Labor Temple by fortuitous accident while searching
for another collection which was never found.

Collecting and processing began in earnest with the hiring of
two staff processors in March 1972. The first collections
were largely local union records and dated since the 1930s.
To announce these new holdings to the research community and
to express gratitude for those attending the annual Labor
Awards Banquet, the archives published for initial distribution at the 1972 banquet a list of materials received and
processed. Thereafter, a similar list has been prepared
annually.

The archives received a significant boost when the Georgia
and Florida AFL-CIO bodies endorsed the repository and named
it the home of their official records. In subsequent years,
the South Carolina and Virginia AFL-CIO bodies followed suit,
making the Southern Labor Archives one of the most exten-
sively endorsed labor archives in the nation.

By the third year of operation, the number of new accessions
gradually diminished; but the size, complexity, and historical value of the collections received grew notably. As
knowledge of the archival enterprise spread from Atlanta and

Georgia, the archives, in addition to local material from
various states, obtained files from regional offices, including those of the Woodworkers, Communications Workers, and
United Textile Workers (UTW). Indeed, the UTW named the
archives the repository for its noncurrent materials and
shipped 1,610 pounds of records from the international office
in Massachusetts for preservation and research. The archives
staff had determined that the archives would consider accept-
ing any labor-related material from within and about the
South. But it realized, too, that the South in some ways
could best be studied only within the context of the labor
movement in other sections and in the country generally. Re-
ceipt of the UTW records led to active collecting in this
broader context of "the South."

Reflecting the growth of the holdings, in October 1975, three
and one-half years after the archives began full operation,
the original temporary quarters had been filled to overflowing; and the repository was moved to much larger quarters in
the adjacent Urban Life Center. By the fall of 1976, the
Southern Labor Archives held more than a half-million leaves
of processed material ready for study.

As one means of encouraging use of the holdings and study in
the field of labor history, in 1976 the Southern Labor
Archives, in cooperation with the Labor Awards Banquet Committee, developed a "Labor in the Modern World" lecture
series. This series brings to the Georgia State University
campus noted labor leaders and experts in labor relations to
speak on the labor scene. In a somewhat different vein but
for similar purposes, the archives worked with both the Labor
Awards Banquet Committee and interested historians to establish the Southern Labor History Conference.

THE SOUTHERN LABOR HISTORY CONFERENCE

Organizers of the conference were very conscious of previous
work of the Association of Southern Labor Historians (ASLH).
The ASLH had been developed by a group of scholars interested
in the study of the labor movement in the South, who met during the Southern Historical Association (SHA) convention in
Memphis in November 1966. William G. Whittaker, then of the
University of Mississippi, had called the meeting; and those
in attendance warmly endorsed his proposal to create a formal
organization. Wayne Flynt of Samford University in Birmingham agreed to issue an annual newsletter to keep association
members informed of research in progress, publications, and
other activities related to the study of labor history in the
South.

The ASLH met concurrently with the SHA between 1967 and 1972
and at times sponsored sessions on the SHA program. After

the SHA eliminated special sessions proposed by subfedera-
tions, the ASLH's continued existence was evident mainly in
the columns of Flynt's Newsletter.

Scholarly output in the field of Southern labor history, however, increased; and this, with the development of the Southern Labor Archives, inspired renewed interest in the ASLH.
In the spring of 1975, a group of scholars and labor leaders
closely associated with the archives met in Atlanta to discuss the feasibility of organizing a conference devoted to
Southern labor history. The success of labor studies conferences elsewhere in the nation augured well for the undertaking. The suggestions most consistently received by the
Atlanta group were to involve trade unionists and others interested in the study of organized labor in the South and to
avoid confining the conference to academicians. Agreeing,
the labor awards committee responded enthusiastically, offering to cosponsor the conference with the Southern Labor
Archives. The conference was scheduled to coincide with the
Seventh Annual Labor Awards Banquet.

The conference formally convened on April 1 in the Urban Life
Conference Center on the campus of Georgia State University.
Besides the formal papers, a number of which are reproduced
in this volume, three panel discussions were held. The pan-
els endeavored to identify the relationship between Southern
labor and the national labor movement and the role of women
and blacks in the labor force.

At a business meeting held during the conference, the group
decided to organize a Southern Labor History Association "to
encourage the study and understanding of the rise and development of organized labor in the South and to promote the
dissemination of that knowledge." An executive director and
treasurer were appointed and provisions made for the creation
of steering and program committees. The steering committee
is charged with coordinating the organization of the new
association, and the program committee will plan the next
Southern Labor History Conference, scheduled for the spring
of 1978.

Shortly before the conference convened, it was learned that
the Rockefeller Foundation had extended support through a
financial grant. This money, among other things, made possible the videotaping of all conference sessions. Five edited
videotape presentations (one of which is also available on
16 mm. film) were prepared from these tapes and are available
on loan from the Southern Labor Archives.***

*** The program and list of available videotapes are provided
    in the appendix.

ESSAYS IN
SOUTHERN
LABOR HISTORY

CHAPTER I

THE SOUTHERN KNIGHTS:
Discord and Accommodation

The Knights of Labor began attracting a following in the South relatively late in that organization's existence. Yet as black and white Southerners joined its ranks, most of the problems that the order faced elsewhere also plagued the Knights in the South. Melton A. McLaurin discusses these "Internal Dissensions of the Southern Order" in an essay that focuses primarily on its Southern leadership. The most common Southern problems, as elsewhere, grew out of its diverse membership, ineffective leadership, confusion over goals, internal feuding, lack of funds, and the self-serving attitudes and ambitions of many of the leaders. Two problems, however, which seemed to be particularly troublesome to Southern Knights, according to McLaurin, were the race issue and the scarcity of native-born leaders.

In an essay which concentrates on race and class consciousness in the West Virginia coal fields, Stephen Brier also deals with the Knights along with two other unions, the National Federation of Miners (NFM) and the United Mine Workers (UMW). During the Knights' 1886-1887 drive, Brier found race to be a significant barrier to organization. So also were certain structural forces within the region, especially its domination by the coal operators and the absence of any miner or working class tradition. Being sparsely populated, the area attracted numerous outside workers, including blacks from eastern Virginia who had experienced social and political organization during Reconstruction. Brier found that contrary to general belief, blacks in southern West Virginia joined labor unions more readily than whites, developed strong leaders, and were most important to the Knights, the NFM, and the UMW between 1880 and 1894.

Melton A. McLaurin received the Ph.D. from the University of South Carolina in 1967 and is currently Associate Professor of History at the University of South Alabama. He is the author of Paternalism and Protest: Southern Cotton Mill Workers and Organized Labor, 1875-1905 (1971); Mobile: An American River City (1975); and several articles. McLaurin is presently completing a book on the Knights of Labor in the South.

Stephen Brier served as Research Coordinator for the American Labor History Film Series at Station WGBH-TV, Boston, and is finishing a dissertation on "The Formation of Multi-Racial Coal Mining Communities in West Virginia, 1880-1920," for presentation to the Department of History at the University of California-Los Angeles. The research and writing of the article herein was supported by a United States Department of Labor Manpower Administration Doctoral Dissertation Grant.

Knights of Labor: Internal Dissensions of the Southern Order

Melton A. McLaurin

When the General Assembly convened in Richmond on October 4, 1886, even to its opponents, the Knights of Labor appeared as a formidable advocate of the Southern worker. The Knights had locals in every Southern state and were establishing state assemblies in North Carolina, Florida, and Alabama. The order was active in congressional and municipal elections throughout the region and was then conducting at Augusta, Georgia, the largest strike in the history of the Southern textile industry. The fact that the national convention of the country's largest labor union was held in a Southern city indicated that the Knights might, indeed, sweep the "producers" of the region into one organization which would possess the power to drastically alter the region's political and economic establishment.

The Knights' outward appearance, however, belied the actual state of the order. Rather than a vital, powerful, expanding organization, the Knights of Labor was a dying institution, already on the decline nationally. Although not at peak numerical strength, the Southern order, too, was floundering. Built on the hopes and dreams of the economically powerless, lacking a solid foundation, and plagued by internal weaknesses, the Southern Knights were on the brink of collapse. For the national union, internal problems, that is, those over which the order had some control, would soon lead to the order's rapid disintegration.[1] While the Southern order also faced some internal problems like those encountered by the order nationally, some were unique to the region.

Ironically, the Southern Knights' large membership, which so alarmed industrialists in 1885 and 1886, led the list of the order's internal difficulties. Because of the virtual absence of membership requirements, the Knights had a polyglot mixture of rural and urban, black and white, male and female,

laborers and white collar workers, salesmen and small businessmen. Large, mixed, urban assemblies frequently contained
representatives of numerous occupations, social classes, and
religious and political persuasions. Farmers (both land own-
ing and tenant), day wage workers, and "mechanics" comprised
most rural assemblies. Coming from such disparate backgrounds, members had little in common except the desire to
improve their economic standing. The order's liberal membership policies created confusion among local officials as to
who could join the union. Wage laborers in Richmond resented
efforts to organize city officials. The secretary of a Danville local requested Grand Master Workman Terence V.
Powderly to define the term wage worker because, he wrote,
"we have men in our midst who are engaged in a small business
on their own account. Such as bakers, merchants, sewing machine agents ... contractors ... etc."[2] Such diversity of
membership and confusion about eligibility made specific,
tangible goals difficult to define, let alone achieve.

Most of those who joined the order were ignorant of the principles of the Knights of Labor in particular and organized
labor in general. White collar members knew little more than
wage workers. Both barely understood the vague programs proposed by the national order. A contractor, for example, was
so poorly informed about the concept of cooperation that he
asked Powderly to explain the 1885 General Assembly's decision that contractor members share their profits with member
employees. Should he share profits before or after the payment of wages? If the latter were the case, he wrote, all
contractors would be forced to depart the order's ranks.[3]
John Power of Mississippi informed Powderly late in 1885 that
"there is a great need of a speaker who would instruct in the
principles of our Order." Nearly two years later, he wrote
Powderly that "the great majority of those composing the
order here are very illiterate and many of the organizers
have been little better, knowing but little of the organization they were spreading and but imperfectly explaining the
objectives of the order."[4]

The task of molding such a diverse membership of persons
largely unlettered in the concepts of organized labor into a
viable union capable of sustained growth would have been difficult under the best leaders and the most favorable circumstances. The South of the 1880s hardly presented a healthy
environment for an institution dedicated to changing the region's economic and political structure; and the Knights were
woefully short of able, experienced leadership. Lack of effective leaders, in fact, ranked as one of the Southern
order's most serious internal weaknesses.

Leaders of the Southern order fell into three major cate-
gories -- politicians or the politically ambitious; professional and small businessmen; and the true believers, those

who felt a need to devote themselves to the "cause" and can
be called martyrs. Most influential within the order were
the politically ambitious, many of whom attempted to use the
Knights to advance their political careers. Among this group
were C. B. Pendleton of Florida, John Nichols of North Carolina, and William Mullen and Samuel Hopkins of Virginia, each
of whom entered congressional campaigns in 1886.[5] Lesser
figures used the order in an effort to obtain election to municipal and county offices and are typified by J. J. Holland
of Jacksonville, a major personality behind the scenes in
that city's 1887 municipal election.[6] No matter how genuine
his concern for the worker, the politician ultimately failed
as a labor leader because the American laborer, especially in
the South, was not prepared to seek political solutions to
economic problems. Political activity by the leaders caused
dissension within the ranks and diverted energy from more po-
tentially productive pursuits, especially economic ones. On
the other hand, undoubtedly the Knights' refusal to endorse
economic actions against capital led some of its members to
experiment with political activity.

The second major category consisted of professional or small
businessmen and merchants who understood the inequities of
the distribution of wealth within their society and sought
ways to remedy the situation. Typical of this group was
J. Melville Broughton of Raleigh, who was convinced that cooperation held the answer to the economic problems of the
day. His work within the order demonstrated this belief, for
he served as a director of a tobacco cooperative in Raleigh
and as a member of the national cooperative board. John J.
Power, state master workman of Mississippi, also fit this
category. Like many of the order's national officers, Power,
manager of a gas company in Natchez, believed that education
and cooperation could lead to a workable accommodation between capital and labor. A reformer to the core, he was involved with a number of causes, including the Irish-American
Land League.[7]

The third category of leaders can be labeled the martyrs.
Neither ambitious politicians nor contemplative professionals
or businessmen, members of this group were totally dedicated
to the "cause" of labor. John Ray of North Carolina and the
Reverend Simmions Meynardie of South Carolina are typical of
this group. Ray, who helped introduce the order to North
Carolina and served as a state officer, worked himself into a
state of nervous exhaustion trying to build the order. "I
walked over a greater portion of this State," he wrote to
Powderly, "and have gone nearly two days and nights without
tasting food; have stood up before mobs congregated to take
my life, and have had to flee for my life and sleep in the
mountain forests alone for the cause."[8] Meynardie, who led
the 1886 Augusta textile strike, collapsed under the burden
of leadership. His letters to Powderly during the strike

reveal the same frantic dedication to the order as that expressed by Ray. Nicholas Stack, state master workman of Alabama, wrote Powderly in 1889 that "I have travelled the Alabama labor field & counseled with & encouraged to the best of
my ability some of the most oppressed people on the continent.
So long as I had a dollar of my own to travel with.... Now my
race is run."[9]

The Knights' leadership shared certain characteristics which
handicapped their efforts to organize and lead Southern laborers. Most significant was the fact that most were not laborers; rather, they were small entrepreneurs, businessmen,
printers, contractors, teachers, but not wage laborers.
While printers might have been wage laborers, that is, employed by a press, most who obtained positions of leadership
within the order owned their own printing firms. Among those
in this category were William Mullen of Virginia, John
Nichols of North Carolina, C. B. Pendleton to Florida, and
T. M. White and M. A. Thomas of Alabama. John Power managed
a gas works at Natchez, and Nicholas Stack was employed as a
superintendent by a Birmingham coal company.[10] J. J. Holland
of Florida owned a dray and contracting business. Emil
Lesser, prominent in the founding of Birmingham locals, operated a restaurant and boardinghouse. J. Melville Broughton
was a bookkeeper and merchant and in 1888 established one of
Raleigh's more successful insurance and real estate agencies.[11] At the 1887 General Assembly, only three of the ten
Southern representatives -- a nailer, a carpenter, and a
plumber -- could be considered wage workers; and the plumber
could have been a contractor rather than a wage laborer.[12]

Perhaps almost as detrimental to the efforts of the leadership to rally Southern workers to the cause was the fact that
many of the leaders were not natives of the South. Others
who were Southern born were not natives of the state in which
they served the Knights, a fault not quite as grievous as
being a Yankee. Nicholas Stack illustrates the "foreign"
origins of some of the Southern order's highest officials.
Born in Ireland, Stack immigrated to New York, then moved to
Ohio where, in 1870, he began mining coal. Bitten by the
gold bug, he traveled to the Rockies, eventually drifting
into Mexico by way of Tombstone, Arizona; and in 1884 he returned to the United States through New Orleans. There he
read of Alabama's booming iron industry and headed for
Birmingham. Obtaining employment at the Cahaba Mining Company, a year later Stack helped found the Anti-Convict League
of Alabama, serving as secretary of that organization until
it merged with the Knights.[13]

John Power's biography reads remarkably like that of Stack.
Born in Ireland in 1848, he came to America when a young man
and obtained employment as a railroad laborer. He later
secured a position as assistant superintendent of a gas works

at Middleton, Connecticut. Forced to resign because of ill
health, he went South and accepted a position as manager of
the Natchez gas works in 1884. Like Stack, Power had joined
the Knights in the North and continued his association with
the order when moving South. The growth of the order in the
mid-1880s allowed both men to renew their activities as
Knights.[14]

The career of J. J. Holland of Florida follows the same pattern. A carpetbagger and an ex-union officer, Holland
settled in Jacksonville. He became a contractor, a leading
citizen, and major figure in the Republican party. He served
as city clerk, alderman, fire chief, and sheriff of Duval
County.[15] Other men, like John Ray, brought the principles
of Knighthood to North Carolina from Massachusetts; and
William Oree, organizer in the Richmond area, was a native of
New York.[16] Lacking experienced Southern union members, the
Knights relied upon leadership from outside the region, which
made the order suspect to xenophobic Southerners. It also
afforded business and industrial spokesmen an opportunity to
denounce unionism in general and the Knights in particular as
both un-American and alien to the Southern way of life. The
Knights' opponents failed to allow such an opportunity to go
begging.

While Northerners played a major role in the organization and
leadership of the Southern Knights, there were too few to
provide all the leaders needed. The great rush of members
into the union after its initial success in 1885 compelled
the development of native leadership, which had to come from
persons almost totally ignorant of the most fundamental concepts of organized labor. As a result, leadership at the
local, and often district, level was frequently incompetent.
Ignorant of the Knights' structure, procedures, and principles, local officers deluged Powderly and other national officers with trivial procedural questions. Inexperienced
local leaders also encouraged rank and file members to pursue
their already unrealistic hopes and aspirations. Ignorance
and overoptimism led locals to adopt untenable positions and
to attempt projects far beyond their means. Locals plunged
into strikes with no preparation, to be humiliated by defeat.
Others sought to establish cooperatives with little or no
capital and even less managerial skill.[17] In the face of
harsh reality, local leaders frequently reverted to quoting
platitudes about the virtues of labor's cause. As a result,
they consistently relayed overly optimistic reports to the
national leadership until well into 1888.[18] By that time,
the deterioration of the order was obvious to all but the
most ardent true believers.

The order in the South also failed to prevent internal feuding or to suppress those feuds once they began. Southern
Knights shared this problem with their Northern brethren, for

interorganizational wrangling was the bane of the national
order. Except for the racial issue, Southerners argued over
the same issues as Northerners. Their interminable feuds involved petty personality conflicts, race, politics, procedural and jurisdictional disputes, and other matters, some
unbelievably trivial. Members invested considerable time and
energy in the most petty disputes, whether at the local, district, or state assembly level. So intense was this internal
warfare that from 1885 to 1890, Powderly received at least
thirty-one letters concerning feuds in Georgia locals alone,
despite the fact that many letters concerning procedural and
jurisdictional disputes were not usually sent to Powderly but
to the national secretary-treasurer.[19]

Bitter personal clashes rent the order in every Southern
state, and letters filled with invectives directed at fellow
Knights poured into Powderly's office. An Atlanta member
complained that a local organizer was spiteful, argumenta-
tive, jealous, and incompetent. John Ray described a foe in
the order as being "as selfish and hypocritical as it is possible for human [sic] to be." Florida Knights described
their colleagues as "arbitrary and dictatorial," "dead limbs
and trash," and "blackguards."[20]

Local, district, and state assemblies seemed incapable of
coping with procedural questions that varied slightly from
the order's constitution and bylaws. Instead, they forwarded
an endless stream of trivial questions to Powderly for his
decision.[21] Some of this squabbling was pathetically comic.
The recording secretary of a South Carolina local complained
that his master workman had requested him to notify a member
of his expulsion. This was an absurd request, the recording
secretary maintained, since the expelled member was in attendance when the local voted to expel him. Members of
Savannah District 139 spent hours trying to determine if
women would "spread broadcast" the order's secrets, should
they be organized. Failing to reach an agreement, the assembly sent a five-page brief of the case to Powderly, asking
his decision.[22]

Jurisdictional disputes raged between locals, between districts, between locals and districts, between districts and
state assemblies, and occasionally between locals and state
assemblies. Trade locals resented mixed locals which admitted members from occupations represented by organized
trade locals within a given area. An Atlanta local of railroad car builders felt it should have jurisdiction over all
carpenters, who frequently joined mixed assemblies. A carpenters' local in Birmingham complained when mixed assemblies
in that city accepted carpenters.[23] Most jurisdictional disputes, however, were over more mundane matters. Members of
Charleston Local 8225 "seceded" to form four other locals, an
action which Local 8225 protested to the General Executive

Board. The board upheld the local, allowing it to use its
own discretion in welcoming seceding members who might wish
to return. The board received similar protests from locals
in Lynchburg and Wilmington.[24]

Relations between locals and their district assembly were
often poor. Many locals resented the formation of districts,
since district assemblies reduced the ability of locals to
communicate directly with the national organization. Locals
resented per capita dues for district membership, assessments
levied by districts, and what they considered arbitrary
treatment at the hands of district officers. Such provocations, whether real or imagined, prompted aggrieved locals to
appeal to either Powderly or the General Executive Board for
permission to leave the district and affiliate directly with
either the state or the national assembly. Invariably, the
board denied the locals' appeals, replying that as long as
district or state assemblies were in good standing, permission for locals to disassociate must be obtained from them.
Among local and district assemblies involved in such disputes
were Local 722 of Macon and District 105 of Atlanta; Local
5431 of Atlantic City, Virginia, and Norfolk District 123;
Hephzibah, Georgia, Local 8979 and Augusta District 176;
Local 9095 of Brunswick and Savannah District 139; Local 6700
of Charleston and District 187 of the same city; and Local
6271 and District 139, both of Savannah.[25] District Assembly
193, Lynchburg, Virginia, found it particularly difficult to
control member locals and constantly appealed to Powderly to
restore order.[26] Jealous of their autonomy, locals paid
little attention to the nominal authority of district assemblies. In a plea to Powderly "to promote peace and harmony
where now exists discord," Victor St. Cloud of Savannah District 139 complained that members of an expelled local "don't
care a damn for D.A. 139" and continued to meet and initiate
members.[27]

Locals attached directly to state assemblies seemed no happier with this arrangement than those attached to districts.
Some locals, formed long before state assemblies were organized and originally attached directly to the national assembly, regretted ever joining state assemblies. Several, such
as Local 4106 in Durham, sought to disaffiliate from the
state assembly but were denied permission to do so by the
General Executive Board.[28] Powerful older locals, such as
Local 5009 in Birmingham, frequently challenged state assembly policies.[29] Many locals received few, if any, benefits
from state assemblies and yet were taxed by them. Members of
Huntsville, Alabama, locals lamented that they were "in the
worst condition you ever saw anything and it is all on the
account of being attached to the State Assembly."[30]

Once organized, state and district assemblies jealously
guarded their powers, seeking to stifle the development of

additional districts within the area of their jurisdiction.
Opposing the creation of new districts were state assemblies
dominated by locals of a single urban region, such as the
Florida Assembly, run by Jacksonville locals; the Alabama
Assembly, controlled by Birmingham area locals; and the North
Carolina Assembly, dominated by locals of the Raleigh-Durham
area. Since officers of state assemblies usually came from
the dominant urban locals, the urban assemblies controlled
the order statewide, especially in the years 1885 and 1886,
before the Knights began to recruit heavily in rural areas.
The creation of additional districts would have diminished
their control of the order within the state. Thus District
Assembly 84 in Richmond, which acted much as a state assembly
through 1886, sought to block the chartering of a district in
Petersburg and Lynchburg.[31] The Florida State Assembly prevented the creation of a district in Pensacola in 1888; the
North Carolina state assembly stymied efforts to establish
districts in Durham and Dallas; and District Assembly 105 of
Atlanta opposed the creation of a district in Macon.[32]

Political action also contributed heavily to the order's internal feuding. Fierce political conflicts erupted within
the Florida State Assembly in 1887 and finally led the General Executive Board to revoke its charter in 1892.[33] Politics prompted most of the chronic internal difficulties which
plagued Lynchburg District 193 and Savannah District 139.
Politics also accounted for much of the trouble encountered
by Charleston locals in District 187 and bedeviled the order
in North Carolina.[34] Many of the political difficulties
arose, as might have been anticipated, from the efforts of
politically ambitious Knights to use the order to further
their own ambitions.

The ever present racial issue, along with politics, contributed to the Knights' failure to achieve internal stability.
J. J. Holland of Jacksonville and W. P. Russell of Charleston
both sought to associate the Knights, especially black assemblies, with local Republican organizations; and their attempts were resented by white Democratic members.[35] Blacks
resented white dominance of state and district assemblies, so
much so that they attempted to form black districts in Virginia, Florida, and Georgia. Whites resisted these efforts,
just as they resisted attempts by white locals to create competing district assemblies.[36] Blacks also complained of
high-handed treatment by white members who visited black
assemblies; and whites expressed the fear that the relatively
liberal racial policies of the national order might promote
"social equality," despite the fact that nearly all local
assemblies were strictly segregated.[37]

In an effort to solve the order's internal difficulties, both
Powderly and the General Executive Board dispatched national
officers to the scene of particularly disruptive quarrels.

The South received its share of such visits. In 1887,
Mrs. L. M. Barry traveled to Lynchburg, T. T. McCartney
sought to smooth ruffled feelings in Wilmington, and Tom
O'Riley attempted to quell a dispute among the ranks in
Charleston.38 The following year, T. B. Barry journeyed to
Lynchburg, T. B. McGuire attempted to restore order among
black locals in Pensacola and Savannah, and William Bailey
sought to settle difficulties among the Knights of the
Birmingham area.39 In 1889, J. J. Holland traveled to
Birmingham on a second peace mission; and in 1890, A. W.
Wright went to Savannah, and John Devlin was to bring peace
to the conflict-ridden Florida order.40

The incessant internal conflict within the Southern order, as
within the order nationally, occasionally overcame Powderly's
patience, as revealed in his scathing letter to locals in
Lynchburg:

> For some reason or other, since the district was
> organized, it has failed to conduct itself as a
> District Assembly of the Knights of Labor. Bicker-
> ings, dissensions, and jealousies have characterized
> the actions of both officers and members, until it
> would be better to turn over the property of the
> entire District and cease to work than to continue
> in such a foolish manner.41

Powderly could have easily written such a letter to almost
every district and state assembly in the South.

Dissension in the South did not prevent quarrels between the
Southern order and the national leadership. From local master workmen to state officers, Southerners complained, at
times with some justification, that national officials and
policies "slighted" their region. Powderly treated such complaints seriously, and they were promptly and courteously
answered.42 William Mullen of Virginia wrote Powderly that
"I get hundreds of letters asking me why it is that the
Southern wing of the Order is entirely ignored by the Board,
while it is continually travelling, laboring, and calling for
assessments to sustain the Order in the North and West."
Powderly replied that the South had not and would not be
slighted.43 John McDonald, elected state master workman of
Mississippi in 1889, criticized the board for not sending
lecturers of national prominence to work in the state. Members in Alabama also chided Powderly for failing to assign
lecturers to that state, thus restricting the order's
growth.44

Such criticism led Powderly to appoint John O'Keefe a general
lecturer in the South in mid-1888. This action failed to ap-
pease Mullen, because O'Keefe was not from the South. Other
Southern Knights, however, found O'Keefe quite acceptable and

welcomed his appointment.[45] But O'Keefe's tour of the South
in the fall of 1888 did not end the sense of alienation felt
by many members in that region. At the 1888 General Assembly,
the Alabama State Assembly introduced a resolution calling
for the order to place at least one Southerner on the General
Executive Board. Although the resolution was rejected by the
assembly, J. J. Holland of Jacksonville was elected to the
board.[46] The resentment expressed by the Southerners also
probably led the General Executive Board to send Mrs. Leona
Barry on a tour of the region early in 1889.[47] Still, some
Southerners, including Nicholas Stack, complained that
Mrs. Barry, as head of the order's "women's work," lacked experience in the South, which had a high percentage of women
and children in the labor force.[48] Quite clearly, Stack
would have preferred the position to have gone to a Southern
lady.

Because the Knights never established a sound financial
structure at either the national or lower levels, the lack of
money was a constant problem. In the Southern order, the
situation was compounded by the financial irresponsibility
and outright dishonesty of leaders at all levels. Complaints
of theft and embezzlement by officers were numerous. The
financial secretary of a Macon local absconded with the
treasury, and a Birmingham local expelled a member for em-
bezzling funds. Locals in Richmond, Virginia; Waycross,
Georgia; and Dallas, North Carolina, also reported expulsions
of sticky-fingered officers.[49] N. B. Stack attributed some
of the financial woes of the Alabama State Assembly to the
"rascality" of the membership. A Mississippi master workman
accused his predecessor of making a $157.00 error in his
favor and discovered that "the financial secretary has robbed
us of about three hundred dollars, our treasurer of about
$150."[50] Charges of fraud against organizers were common and
often resulted in bitter feuds since locals organized by an
individual frequently defended the organizer against charges
of corruption.[51]

In undertaking to organize the Southern worker, the Knights
of Labor accepted a Herculean task. The Southern laborer was
impoverished, lacking in the most elementary understanding of
the concept of organized labor, and polarized by race. The
diversity of the order's membership defied any coherent approach to the laborer's practical problems. To build a successful union under these conditions would have required superior leadership, financial stability, and minimal managerial opposition; and even then, the chances for success would
have been remote. The Knights in the South were plagued with
poor leadership, financial instability, and incessant internal squabbling. They faced an environment hostile to the
development of any institution that threatened the almost absolute power of the region's new industrial elite. Under
such circumstances, the destiny of the Southern Knights was

all too predictable. By 1888, the order was in serious decline; within another year it had almost ceased to exist except among black day laborers of the rural South who still
hoped that Powderly and the Knights could provide some
miracle of economic salvation. The white urban laborers who
had given the order strength in 1885 and 1886 deserted its
ranks, disillusioned by the order's inability to address effectively their grievances. That inability resulted largely
from the internal dissension that the order proved unable to
either prevent or control.

Notes

[1] For a discussion of the national order's internal problems, see Gerald Grob, Workers and Utopia (Evanston, Ill., 1961), 43-59; and Norman Ware, The Labor Movement in the United States, 1860-1895 (New York, 1929), 103-16.

[2] R. J. Steel to Powderly, February 17, 1886, and R. P. Nicholas to Powderly, January 13, 1886, Terence Powderly Papers, Catholic University, Washington, D.C.

[3] J. T. Blackwood to Powderly, July 23, 1886, Powderly Papers.

[4] Power to Powderly, December 11, 1885, and February 13, 1888, Powderly Papers.

[5] Melton McLaurin, "Knights of Labor in North Carolina Politics," North Carolina Historical Review 49 (Summer 1972), 298-315; General Assembly Proceedings, 1886, 313-25, hereafter cited as Proceedings; Pendleton to Powderly, September 26, 1886, Powderly Papers; Richmond Dispatch, September 24-October 31, 1886; and Lynchburg Virginian, October 4-November 5, 1886.

[6] Jacksonville Times-Union, November 26-December 10, 1887.

[7] Journal of United Labor, July 19, 1888, 2665, hereafter cited as JUL; Power to Powderly, December 11, 1885, and Broughton to Powderly, November 28, 1887, Powderly Papers; and Proceedings, 1887, 1595, 1611-12.

[8] Ray to Powderly, November 9, 1886, Powderly Papers; Melton McLaurin, Paternalism and Protest (Westport, Conn., 1971), 94-110.

[9] Stack to Powderly, October 14, 1888, Powderly Papers.

[10] T. T. Allen to Stack, April 22, 1886, Nicholas Stack Collection, University of Alabama, Tuscaloosa, Ala.; JUL, July 19, 1888, 2665.

[11] Jacksonville Times-Union, November 26-30, 1887; Birmingham City Directory, 1887, 122; and Raleigh City Directory, 1888, 26.

[12] Proceedings, 1887, 1831-34.

[13] JUL, June 16, 1888, 2645; Birmingham News, July 29, 1931; and Stack to his son, February 10, 1914, Stack Collection.

[14] JUL, July 19, 1888, 2665.

[15] JUL, December 27, 1888, 2760.

[16] William Mullen to Powderly, October 30, 1884, Powderly Papers.

[17] Badger Terrill to Powderly, April 11, 1888, and Alex Anthony to Powderly, April 9, 1888, Powderly Papers.

[18] For examples, see JUL, April 21, 1888, 2616, and May 26, 1888, 2336.

[19] For examples, see M. E. Stone to Powderly, December 14, 1885; George Schall to Powderly, October 19, 1886; Ben Doster to Powderly, December 30, 1886; and T. P. Towns to Powderly, August 29, 1887, Powderly Papers.

[20] Ray to Powderly, November 9, 1886; Backenstoe to Powderly, August 14, 1891; W. B. Maston to Powderly, August 16, 1891; and Learing to Powderly, July 22, 1891, Powderly Papers.

[21] Henry Smith to Powderly, May 8, 1886; Invison Goodwin to Powderly, July 7, 1886; Gibbs Gardiner to Charles Litchman, February 16, 1887; Louis Du Brok to Powderly, May 10, 1887; and Powderly to George Schall, November 9, 1886, Letterbook 23, Powderly Papers.

[22] Victor St. Cloud to Powderly, December 19, 1886, Powderly Papers.

[23] M. E. Stone to Powderly, December 14, 1885, and C. H. Bowling to Powderly, August 3, 1886, Powderly Papers.

[24] Proceedings, 1887, 1364, 1375, 1439.

25 Proceedings, 1887, 1340; Proceedings, 1888, 58; George
Schall to Powderly, October 19, 1886, Ben Doster to
Powderly, December 20, 1886, James McGuin to Powderly,
January 22, 1887, A. C. Franklin to Powderly, January 29,
1887, and Victor St. Cloud to Powderly, April 10, 1887,
Powderly Papers.

26 John Crawford to Powderly, March 20, 1888, and Powderly to
Crawford, March 26, 1888, Letterbook 39, Powderly Papers.

27 St. Cloud to Powderly, April 10, 1887, Powderly Papers.

28 Proceedings, 1888, 24.

29 T. W. White to Powderly, August 1, 1889, Powderly Papers.

30 H. N. Moore to Powderly, April 15, 1888, Powderly Papers.

31 R. W. Kruse to Powderly, April 28, 1886, Powderly Papers.

32 Proceedings, 1888, 24, 107; Powderly to S. D. Brown,
February 23, 1888, Letterbook 32, J. L. Sanges to Powderly,
July 16, 1888, and Richard Bowen to Powderly, March 21,
1887, Powderly Papers.

33 Correspondence on this issue is abundant. See Powderly
to A. W. Fletcher, January 5, 1892, Letterbook 60; S. G.
Learing to Powderly, September 10, 1891; and John Devlin
to Powderly, January 21, 1891, Powderly Papers.

34 W. P. Russell to Powderly, November 17, 1886, Powderly
Papers; and The Messenger (Fayetteville, N.C.), November 9,
1888.

35 John O'Brien to Powderly, November 21, 1886; Powderly to
J. L. McGinn, March 28, 1887, Letterbook 29; and J. W.
White to Powderly, November 6, 1890, Powderly Papers.

36 JUL, November 10, 1886, 2000-2001; Proceedings, 1888, "Report of the General Executive Board," 107-108; and R. W.
Kruse to Powderly, April 28, 1886, Powderly Papers.

37 Alexander Walker to Powderly, May 18, 1886; Samuel Wilson
to Powderly, October 6, 1886; John Devlin to Powderly,
November 2, 1890; and William Mullen to Powderly, April 7,
1885, Powderly Papers.

38 Proceedings, 1887, 1364, 1582, 1439; and John O'Brien to
Powderly, March 12, 1887, Powderly Papers.

39 Proceedings, 1888, "Report of the General Executive
Board," 37, 50-53, 107-108.

40 Proceedings, 1889, "Report of the General Executive
   Board," 23-24; and Devlin to Powderly, January 21, 1891,
   Powderly Papers.

41 Powderly to John Crawford, March 26, 1888, Letterbook 39,
   Powderly Papers.

42 See, for example, John Andrews to Powderly, November 3,
   1887, and Powderly to Andrews, November 9, 1887, Letterbook 30, Powderly Papers.

43 Mullen to Powderly, January 22, 1887, and Powderly to
   Mullen, January 26, 1887, Letterbook 27, Powderly Papers.

44 McDonald to Powderly, September 11, 1889, and F. P.
   Singletary to Powderly, September 23, 1888, Powderly
   Papers.

45 JUL, September 13, 1888, 2697; September 27, 1888, 2705;
   October 4, 1888, 2712; and November 22, 1888, 2740.

46 Proceedings, 1888, 50, 52, 90.

47 Proceedings, 1889, 3-4.

48 Alabama Sentinel, December 15, 1888.

49 JUL, November 10, 1886, 2194, and April 16, 1887, 2357;
   Proceedings, 1888, "Report of the General Executive
   Board," 52-53.

50 Stack to Powderly, October 14, 1888, and John McDonald to
   Powderly, September 11, 1889, Powderly Papers.

51 For example, see H. F. Hoover to Powderly, May 22, 1886,
   Powderly Papers.

Interracial Organizing in the West Virginia Coal Industry: The Participation of Black Mine Workers in the Knights of Labor and the United Mine Workers, 1880-1894

Stephen Brier

In the preface to the new edition of Spero and Harris's <u>The Black Worker</u>, Herbert Gutman notes that

> Labor historians and others have spent much time disputing the intent of the national leaders of the A.F. of L. <u>vis a vis</u> the Negro, a dispute that has generated much heat, shed less and less light, and used up unnecessary energy. Much of this talent could have been used more fruitfully to explore in detail the confrontation of the black worker and industrial America in particular settings. Here a great gap still exists.

The focus on the relationship between race and class on a national level has tended to obscure significant developments in local industrial communities and urban areas, particularly in the late nineteenth century.* Where local studies have considered the question of the relationship between race and class at all, they have tended to do so in a static and isolated manner. Particular strikes, usually where black strikebreaking has engendered a racist response by white workers, have been described in some detail. Few studies have been made of long periods of interaction and struggle

---

* The paper printed herein was somewhat revised by the author following its reading at the Southern Labor History Conference, in answer to comments and criticisms of Professor Herbert Gutman, commentator on the session "Knights of Labor in the South." In addition to Professor Gutman, the author wishes to thank Jon Amsden, Pamela Brier, John H. M. Laslett, and Peter Rachleff for their critical comments on an earlier draft of this paper.

between black and white workers on a local level. Such
studies over time are essential, however, if we are to begin
to untangle the complex relationship between race and class
consciousness which has played such a crucial role in American working class history.[1]

The West Virginia coal industry provides a particularly useful starting point for a local, in-depth analysis because of
several general characteristics: (1) the relatively high
proportion of blacks employed in West Virginia coal mining in
comparison to other major coal fields; (2) the traditional
commitment (at least rhetorically) of national miners' unions
to the recruitment of all mine workers into a unified industrial organization, regardless of occupation or race; and
(3) the militant and sometimes violent confrontation between
mine workers and coal operators, often revolving around the
systematic use of black (and other minority) strikebreakers.

By the last quarter of the nineteenth century, the labor
force of the West Virginia coal industry was heavily populated by blacks who represented over 60 percent of the workers in the two largest coal regions in the state. Moreover,
after 1880, when high quality West Virginia coal began to
penetrate Eastern markets, replacing the production of older,
traditionally unionized coal states, a succession of Northern
based coal miners' unions were increasingly impelled to attempt the organization of the West Virginia coal fields in
order to survive as national organizations. In organizing
West Virginia, particular attention therefore had to be paid
to the race question. It is the confluence of these characteristics that makes the West Virginia "problem" central to
an understanding of the relationship between race and class
consciousness in the American working class.

This paper focuses on the growth of the Knights of Labor and
the early United Mine Workers of America (UMW) in the coal
fields of southern West Virginia, with particular emphasis on
the Flat Top-Pocahontas field, from 1880 to 1894. These
years encompassed the initial efforts of the Knights of Labor
and the UMW to bring West Virginia coal miners under the um-
brella of national organization. Their involvement in the
various forms of national trade union organization represents
only one aspect of this story, however. More significant is
the growth of militant, interracial local unions among southern West Virginia mine workers. While the relationship between West Virginia and national coal unionism has been analyzed, the history of local organization is almost entirely
unknown, especially with respect to the active participation
of black mine workers in local and district trade union organizations in West Virginia.[2]

Prior to 1900, the southern West Virginia coal industry was
comprised of two major coal regions: the Kanawha-New River

field, encompassing the counties of Kanawha and Fayette; and
the Flat Top-Pocahontas field on the West Virginia-Virginia
border, encompassing the southern West Virginia counties of
Mercer and McDowell and the northern tip of Tazewell County,
Virginia, at the town of Pocahontas. These two fields
followed very different patterns of development with respect
to the nature of coal resources and marketing, the growth of
the labor supply, and the emergence of working class activity.

The Kanawha-New River field, or at least that part of it near
Charleston, was the older, having shipped coal by river barge
for the Great Lakes market since the Civil War. In the
1870s, the mining labor supply in the Kanawha Valley was
drawn principally from the Charleston area and the neighbor-
ing coal states of Ohio and Pennsylvania. By 1880, 75 percent of the work force was native born, with an additional 20
percent being British or Irish. Although the Kanawha-New
River labor force would be supplemented (particularly in
Fayette County) after 1880 by a large influx of black workers, Kanawha Valley miners remained closely tied to their
Pennsylvania and Ohio counterparts throughout the late nineteenth century, sustaining trade union organization and working class political activity from the earliest years of the
area's development.[3]

Much of this early trade union and political involvement was
no doubt the result of the close proximity of the Kanawha
Valley mines to the working class movement in Charleston, the
state capital. The Greenback labor movement claimed a considerable following among the workers of Charleston and the
nearby coal camps and towns of the Kanawha Valley. Greenback
conventions and meetings held in Charleston were often attended by miners from these surrounding communities. In June
1880, the superintendent of a Charleston area mine was reported incensed because his miners had shut down the pit in
order to hear Richard Trevellick speak in the city. The existence of a strong working class movement in and around
Charleston in this period was reflected in the power and
militancy of local trade union organization among the Kanawha
Valley miners. These local organizations were sufficiently
strong to force major concessions from area operators. Aggressive trade unionism was probably based on the emergence
of local assemblies of the Knights of Labor in the Kanawha
Valley after 1882. In that year reports from the area indicated that the Knights were expanding rapidly with a majority
of the miners belonging to the organization. It should be
noted that the Knights of Labor in the valley elicited the
active support of black mine workers recently migrated from
the South. In the early 1880s, these black miners served on
integrated mine committees and helped persuade black strikebreakers to leave. This early black commitment to local
trade unions would bear fruit in the latter part of the

decade when national miners' unions made strong advances in
the Kanawha-New River field.[4]

The working class political traditions and vigorous trade
union organization existing among Kanawha Valley miners in
the early 1880s were not evident in the other major southern
West Virginia coal field, Flat Top-Pocahontas. In the latter
field, the growth of the coal industry after 1883 was the
motive force for the economic, political, and social development of the entire area. While mine unionism in the Kanawha
Valley had been built upon an existing organizational structure and a coherent worker ideology, the miners' struggle to
form unions in the Pocahontas field represented the first instance of self-activity of a newly formed working class. Established, independent working class traditions and organizations did not exist and could not be drawn upon by Pocahontas
miners in their drive to forge trade unions in the mid-1880s.

The delay in the development of the coal industry in the Flat
Top-Pocahontas field resulted from two related factors: the
slow construction and consolidation of the Norfolk and Western Railway (N&W) financed largely by Philadelphia and
English capital; and the limited ability of the local labor
supply to meet the burgeoning needs of the coal industry.
Although the town of Pocahontas, Virginia, was laid out in
1882, mining operations did not begin until the following
year when the N&W tracks finally made connections possible
with eastern Virginia and the tidewater coal trade. And unlike Northern coal fields (or for that matter, the Kanawha
Valley) which had been opened by individual coal operators,
the Flat Top-Pocahontas field was entirely the creation of
the N&W railway. In addition to holding an obvious monopoly
over coal transportation, the N&W owned all of the coal land
leases in the area and sold all of the area's output through
a sales agency.[5]

One overriding concern motivated the N&W management throughout the early period: the southern West Virginia coal industry would operate at a relatively low margin of profit because of the greater distances to Northern markets. Keeping
transportation costs and retail prices at a bare minimum was
therefore paramount. Despite the control exercised by railway management over all aspects of the coal industry, leases
were taken up rapidly. The original four operations in 1886
had increased to thirty-eight by 1894, employing approximately 6,000 mine workers. The leases were especially desir-
able since the coal was of exceedingly high quality, and a
relatively low initial capital expenditure was required.
Drifts and slopes could be utilized rather than the more expensive deep shafts prevalent in the North.

The N&W's concern for cost reduction was shared by the individual coal operators who secured leases from the railway.

Since the market price for Flat Top coal was established by
contract through the N&W sales agency, local operators were
impelled to maximize their profits by adopting various methods of labor exploitation. The most notorious of these methods from the miners' point of view was payment by the coal
car rather than by actual tonnage and the "slack dock" system,
whereby individual miners were arbitrarily penalized for mining "unclean" coal. In addition to these methods, Flat Top-
Pocahontas operators also relied on the traditional mecha-
nisms of economic and social control employed by their counterparts in the North: price gouging by the company store
and through company housing; the use of script; and irregular
payment of wages.[6]

This pattern of ownership and control gave class relations in
the Flat Top field an autocratic flavor. The local coal operators (several were former Pennsylvania and English miners)
ran their mines in the manner of feudal lords. Such men as
John Cooper, Lawrence Tierney, and Justus Collins created
local baronies which dominated the area not only economically
but also socially and politically. The town of Bramwell, in
Mercer County, arose in the late nineteenth century as the
seat of the operators' personal and social power; newly constructed and decidedly elegant Victorian homes stood as monu-
ments to the immense profitability of southern West Virginia
mining. The city of Bluefield (also in Mercer County) served
as both the administrative and political center of the operators' power.

By the mid-1880s, a well-financed Republican organization run
by the coal interests dominated local politics in Mercer and
McDowell counties. Trade union organization among Pocahontas
miners would thus emerge without the benefit of an extant
working class movement and in the midst of an economic and
political order controlled by the operators.[7]

The near totality of the operators' domination is suggested
by the problems faced by Flat Top miners in obtaining adequate meeting facilities during organization drives. This
problem was endemic throughout the late nineteenth century in
southern West Virginia and was yet another illustration of
the difficulties encountered in forging trade union organizations in an area which did not possess a working class tradition. Most meetings in Flat Top-Pocahontas had to be held at
railroad sidings, baseball fields, or simply in the woods.
The coal operators consistently denied the miners access to
company-owned churches, halls, and meeting rooms. In one instance, when an organizing meeting was scheduled in a black
church John Cooper, the local coal operator, insisted that
the miners be denied access to the church; when this failed,
he bought and padlocked the church.[8] The miners' movement
also faced the recurring problem of the huge influx of new
workers from outside the area as the industry expanded. By

the early 1880s, the railroad and the coal operators realized
that the indigenous labor supply, composed largely of native
white farming and mountain families, required constant sup-
plements from outside the field. The historian of the N&W
graphically described this situation, "Being a country extremely inhospitable to agriculture, it was but sparsely
settled: therefore much labor had to be imported and communities had to be organized in the wilderness."[9]

The major source of labor was the cities and farms of eastern
Virginia at the end of the N&W line. The vast majority of
new workers located by coal company recruiters were blacks
from Richmond, Lynchburg, and other tidewater cities, and
from contiguous agricultural areas. In addition, coal operators also brought in smaller numbers of newly immigrated
Hungarians and native whites, many of whom were apparently
experienced miners from strike areas in the North.[10]

The economic and political background of this newly formed
Flat Top-Pocahontas coal mining work force is of singular importance. The influx of Northern skilled workers with trade
union backgrounds was no doubt beneficial to subsequent union
organization among Flat Top-Pocahontas miners, providing a
base and a tradition on which to build. But what of the
newly migrated blacks, mostly young, single men from Virginia
and North Carolina? The standard view of these black workers
argues that they impeded trade union organization. Spero and
Harris, for example, noting the availability of a black labor
surplus in Virginia and other Southern states, argue that
this "industrial reserve army" could be used "to defeat the
purposes of unionism." The most recent monographic work on
the Flat Top-Pocahontas area concludes that "surely the great
majority of Negroes, coming out of southern agricultural
areas, had no concept of labor solidarity."[11] To the contrary, however, blacks became, in fact, the most stalwart and
consistent supporters of early trade union organization in
Flat Top-Pocahontas. How is this seeming contradiction to be
explained? If blacks were in fact the leading element in
local trade union development what in their previous experience made this political behavior possible?

At least in the case of eastern Virginia blacks, some answers,
albeit quite general, can be suggested. Blacks coming out of
eastern Virginia in the 1880s were not necessarily leaving a
political void. To the contrary, eastern Virginia, particularly the city of Richmond, but not excluding the country-
side, was a hotbed of political activity which took the form
of militant and widespread black support of the Republican
party during Reconstruction, a vital black-white political alliance in the 1879-1881 period which brought the Readjuster
party to power on the state level and the interracial organization of Knights of Labor local assemblies throughout the
eastern section of the state. Finally, in recognition of the

central role played by eastern Virginia in its Southern organizing strategy, the Knights of Labor held its 1886 national
convention in Richmond. At the meeting, questions of interracial cooperation received considerable attention. Although
the political activity of the 1880s in eastern Virginia
failed to consolidate these initial interracial organizational gains, the fact remains that extensive political and
organizational participation may well have been part of the
prior experience of many eastern Virginia blacks recruited
for the Flat Top-Pocahontas coal field after 1885.[12]

The year 1885, in fact, marked the formation of the first
secret Knights of Labor local assemblies in the Flat Top-
Pocahontas field. The secret local assembly was not only the
most prevalent form of organization in Flat Top-Pocahontas
until the end of the century, but it was the most defensible
in an area where the operators held nearly total political
and economic power and often discharged miners for merely
serving on committees. Open trade union organizations like
those in the Northern coal fields "will get [southern West
Virginia] men to have the heart to speak in defense of their
fellow men and oppose the wrongs that are perpetrated upon
this class of men," one miner noted, "but they will be sent
adrift."[13]

By 1886, four local trade assemblies of the Knights of Labor
were active in Pocahontas, two for white miners and two for
black. They included a majority of the mine workers in the
town. The rationale for the racial separation of these local
assemblies is not clear, although it is consistent with a
common pattern adopted by the Knights in this period of
Southern organizing. Also, the patterns of social development in Pocahontas indicate that segregation was common, particularly in schools, churches, and housing.[14]

The fact remains, nevertheless, that race did appear to be a
barrier to early trade union development in the Flat Top-
Pocahontas field. As early as 1883 there had been indications of racial divisiveness among Pocahontas miners; reports
in the National Labor Tribune on the growth of the Knights in
the town indicated that some Pocahontas residents even thought
that the Knights' purpose was to oppose the employment of
blacks in the mines. Probably much of this early hostility
and misunderstanding had to do with the fact that the work
force was almost wholly imported from outside the area. However, despite these indications of racial divisiveness and
the segregation of the Knights assemblies, evidence exists
that blacks did serve as representatives on integrated executive and mine committees in Pocahontas throughout 1885 and
1886. This fact suggests that the separation of local assemblies by race was not the only organizational solution to the
race question in the Flat Top-Pocahontas field. Apparently
black and white Pocahontas miners, like their counterparts

elsewhere, recognized and accepted the importance of having
black participation on committees which represented local
miners.[15]

Antagonism between the coal operators and the Pocahontas miners intensified in the summer and winter months of 1886. The
operators, in an apparent attempt to break the growing
strength of the Knights of Labor assemblies, resorted to outright repression. Committees of miners sent to the superintendent to complain about conditions were summarily dismissed
and blacklisted. The result, as one correspondent noted, was
that men were even afraid to serve on committees. The issue
was joined when the Pocahontas operators resorted to the importation of Hungarians to replace discharged Knights. A
mass meeting called in September 1886, to protest the employment of Hungarians, was described by one miner as "the meeting that decided the future of the miners here, as the men
were out to a man." Although understandably hostile to the
Hungarians, the black and white Pocahontas miners did not resort to nativist attacks against the new immigrants. The
meeting passed two resolutions which were forwarded to the
mine superintendent by an integrated committee: "That no one
be employed at the mines until the men now working receive
living wages; That all men of good repute discharged be restored to their work." The Pocahontas Knights were apparently unsuccessful in preventing the influx of Hungarians;
and by early 1887, the operators' efforts to destroy the
local power of the Knights of Labor were largely successful.
With the decline of the Knights in Pocahontas the impetus for
organization shifted both organizationally and geographically
to other areas in southern West Virginia.[16]

As indicated earlier, the organizational advances in the
first half of the 1880s were largely local in scope and
secret in form, although affiliated with the Knights of Labor.
With the formation of a series of national miners' unions
after 1886 (culminating in the United Mine Workers of America
in 1890), the struggle to organize southern West Virginia
entered a new phase. The spark of union organization was re-
kindled first in Kanawha-New River in late 1885 by the National Federation of Miners and Mine Laborers, a new national
trade union of coal miners.[17]

The creation and subsequent growth of the National Federation
elicited a strong response from Kanawha Valley black mine
workers. National Federation organizer T. P. Gray noted that
"the colored men seem to have organization at heart; they
have all joined us to a man." The importance of organizing
black mine workers in southern West Virginia was formally
recognized in a resolution passed at the founding convention
of the National Federation in the Kanawha-New River field
held in early 1886: "That we heartily recommend the speedy
organization and recognition of the colored miners and mine

laborers of this valley in the Miners and Mine Laborers Federation of West Virginia."[18]

This rhetorical promise to organize black mine workers was an integral part of a general commitment by union miners after 1886 to oppose privilege and favoritism in the work process. As in most coal fields, the southern West Virginia fields were plagued by what one miner called "the abominable robbing system called the free turn." Since miners were paid by the tonnage loaded each day, the supply of empty coal cars (or the "turn") was directly related to the daily wage they could earn. In most mines, both union and nonunion, the drivers (working for a daily wage paid by the company) who brought the empty cars to each miner's room were in principle required to distribute an equal number of cars, based on availability, to each miner. The free turn system, where an individual miner received additional coal cars out of turn, was particularly pernicious when the demand for coal was low since a lost turn meant a sharp reduction in pay. This grievance was endemic to the coal industry nationally, and the fight to eliminate the free turn was a principle to which all union miners were required to adhere. Obviously, abuse in the system of coal car distribution led to favoritism, dissension, and ultimately the undercutting of organization in the pit. In an area like West Virginia where divisive forces were already strong, the fight against the free turn was one important indication of the commitment of local unions to a broad-based, active organizing strategy. Writing to the National Labor Tribune, a Kanawha Valley miner suggested the link between the fight against the free turn and the strength of local organization:

> The free turn system is one of the most destructive
> agencies to unionism that can be devised and should
> be regarded as such by all miners that believe in
> union principles. Where the system is in vogue the
> many always suffer, while the few are feasting at
> their expense. No good feelings can exist where a
> few miners are allowed to take cars that rightfully
> belong to others. All are entitled to a fair share,
> and if our union miners would use their influence
> to abolish the system, instead of giving it encourage-
> ment in many places that we read of, the result would
> give a boom to organization in every mine where the
> free turn system has been in practice. Give every
> miner an equal turn in our mines and a feeling of
> friendship will be created that will soon ripen
> into the strongest ties of unity.

Another correspondent, widening his attack on the free turn to include the race question, lamented that in some Kanawha Valley mines the free turn had spawned a contract system whereby individual miners contracted with the coal company

for several rooms in a pit and had "two to ten colored men
working for them and they pay these poor fellows but from 50¢
to 75¢ a day." He concluded his letter with an attack on
this system of privilege, arguing that free turners and contract miners "are not fit members of any organization." Another NLT correspondent, who supported these attacks, hoped
that the day was near "when both colored and white men will
have price enough to make a living without hiring laborers."[19]

Despite the existence of this system of privilege, with the
upturn in coal production in 1887, the National Federation
made dramatic advances in organizing the Kanawha-New River
field. The National Federation commissioned an organizer,
H. W. Smith, who held meetings throughout the field. An interesting feature of this campaign was the commitment of
black ministers to the union cause. Smith, noting a large
turnout at a meeting in Fayette County, reported that two
black Baptist ministers "made some excellent practical remarks on organization." On June 25, 1887, a National Labor
Tribune report noted that at an organizing meeting in Coal
Valley, eighty-nine new men joined the Federation. The correspondent quoted the remarks of a local black preacher, who
addressed the meeting on the black commitment to unionism:

> unless the negro [sic] had justice done him he would
> turn out to be the yellow dog every time, and if the
> white brethren treated him like a man he would stand
> by them as long as there was a button on their [sic]
> coat, and when the buttons were all off he would
> still hang to the old coat; and it was only when they
> turned the coat inside out that the negro would go
> the other way.[20]

The growth of the National Federation in southern West Virginia led, in early 1888, to the founding of the first statewide miners' organization. The emergence of the West Virginia State Federation was part of the general development of
national trade union organizing in all coal fields in the
country after 1886. While the intricacies of national organizational politics need not concern us here, it should be
noted that in January 1889, discussion of merger on a national level between the Knights of Labor National Trade
Assembly 135 of coal miners and the National Federation resulted in the formation of the National Progressive Union
(NPU), the direct antecedent of the UMW.[21] The organizational successes of 1888 encouraged President Michael F.
Moran of the West Virginia State Federation (a white trade
unionist previously active in Alabama) to begin a vigorous
organizing drive in 1889, which included not only areas in
support of the State Federation, like Kanawha and Wheeling,
but also fields which had lagged in organization since 1886,
like Flat Top-Pocahontas.[22]

Success rewarded Moran's efforts as the first full-time state organizer, especially after the formation of the National Progressive Union in early 1889. By May, he reported that the NPU was growing rapidly throughout the state. Over the past year the West Virginia state organization had grown from two locals with 135 members to twenty locals with nearly 1,000 members. Moran made his first visit to Flat Top-Pocahontas in April 1889, which resulted in the formation of an NPU local at Simmon's Creek. Simmon's, the oldest mine on the West Virginia side of the field, had an active Knights of Labor local assembly as early as 1885.[23]

Moran acknowledged that black miners in the Flat Top would play a leading role in forging active local organization. His weekly reports in the National Labor Tribune continually stressed the commitment of black workers to trade unionism in general and to the NPU particularly, suggesting that the presence of blacks in the Flat Top was a positive factor in the organizing drive, rather than a hindrance. In April 1889, after his first trip to Mercer County, Moran wrote that the Flat Top miners "are used very near as bad as any mining district I have visited in the last 20 years." Yet he acknowledged that "if the white miners were possessed of half as much manhood [as the black miners] there would be very little trouble to help these men out of their present condition."[24]

In early July the Flat Top field received its first official organizing visit by a national union officer. Thomas W. Davis, a white Ohio miner and NPU vice-president, accompanied by State President Moran, held meetings across the field. The meeting at Cooper's mine in Mercer County, as one example, was an enormous success. "There was quite a large number of colored miners present," Moran reported in the NLT, "[who] came forward and added their names to the local union, which is already growing very strong in membership." "There is no cause to be the least despondent now," Moran concluded, "All the Flat Top region is moving for organization and the boys are in real earnest so it is only a question of a short time." These initial successes in the Flat Top were consolidated in the final months of 1889; eight Flat Top locals and over 500 members had enrolled in the NPU. Moran reported that the locals at Cooper's and Simmon's, with large black memberships, were the banner locals in the state. Thus, on the eve of the formal creation of the UMW in January 1890 and in spite of numerous obstacles, Flat Top miners had created a series of strong and viable interracial local unions in the field.[25]

The growth of the UMW in 1890 in the Flat Top-Pocahontas field reflected the heightened cooperation among white and black mine workers. President Moran reported in April that throughout southern West Virginia, he had "received very

kindly treatment from both white and colored miners and I
hope the friendly feeling will always exist." This interracial cooperation was formalized at the founding convention
of UMW District 17, held at Charleston at the end of April
1890. Three of the ten official delegates to the convention
represented Flat Top-Pocahontas local assemblies; one of
them, Horace Smith, a black miner from Pocahontas, Virginia,
had been an active Knight and National Federation member
since 1885. Smith was nominated for the vice-presidency,
running against an Irish miner from the Kanawha Valley, and
was elected by the convention to serve as the first UMW District 17 vice-president.[26]

Smith's election in 1890 was not merely a token gesture towards black representation, however. It also reflected his
strongly organized base of support among unionized black mine
workers in southern West Virginia. For example, the local
assembly at Freeman in Mercer County (with a 50 percent black
membership) was reported by President Moran to be "the
largest local in District 17 both in numbers and workmanship;
they own their own hall and it was [often] packed to overflowing." President Moran noted with some irony the results
of black participation in West Virginia organization: "The
colored miners have been in the lead in this district until
they have shamed their white brethren, and now the devil is
to pay. The white men all want in at the same time."[27]

Black West Virginia miners saw in the election of Horace
Smith as District 17 vice-president an important opportunity
to put an active black organizer into the field. President
Moran reported in June 1890 that "we have been told in very
plain language that Vice-President Smith must get out on the
road with us, and our [black] brothers seem to mean just what
they say." The results of this organizing drive were star-
tling, given previous periods of apathy. William Jewell, a
District 17 executive board member from the Freeman local,
reported that "there is a general stampede for membership in
all local assemblies in the Flat Top region." By July 1890,
President Moran noted that the increases in membership in the
Flat Top resulted in the building of a meeting hall at Freeman's. "One year ago we could hardly get a house of any kind
to hold a meeting in," he noted, "until the colored people
let the miners have the use of their place of worship, but it
was not long until the greedy coal corporation turned their
miners out of that by buying it out. Now [Local Assembly
10,138] has a home and a house of its own and can fill it to
overflowing." By September the Freeman mines with 335 workers were 100 percent unionized, first in the history of the
Flat Top field. At Bramwell, in Mercer County, the miners
were sufficiently strong to organize a cooperative supply
store in March to offset the worst effects of the local company store. One Pocahontas miner summed up the organizing
boom in 1890: "The steady increase of oppression upon the

miners has aroused them from a state of inactiveness, and
they are now making rapid strides towards organization."[28]

The organizing push was consolidated with the creation of a
Flat Top subdistrict of District 17. A mine delegate meeting
held in September 1890 voted to make the second Tuesday in
every month "a general labor day" with meetings to be held at
various mines across the field. President Moran noted that
one of these mass meetings in November was packed with 1,000
miners and local citizens. Held at the Bramwell Masonic Hall,
the meeting was racially mixed. An all black brass band from
the Simmon's Creek local provided entertainment, and Vice-
President Smith gave an address. Moran's report concluded
that "it may be that this is the turning point in the Flat
Top region."[29]

President Moran pressed on in his organizing work in southern
West Virginia at the beginning of 1891. Moran's District 17
reports in the NLT note that he received a great deal of support in his work in the Kanawha-New River area from John L.
Edmonds, a black miner and officer from a large New River
local assembly. Edmonds accompanied Moran on an organizing
trip through New River in March, giving speeches in support
of the UMW. Richard L. Davis, a significant black UMW
leader throughout the 1890s, noted the importance of Edmonds's
work: "This I am truly proud to see, not only because ...
Bro. Edmonds is a colored man, but because it shows that the
prejudice that once existed in West Virginia is dying out."[30]

Edmonds's work in support of District 17 organization was rewarded the following month by election as District 17 vice-
president, replacing Horace Smith. Edmonds's position, like
that of Smith in the Flat Top, was based on strong organized
black support in the New River field. A white miner from
Vice-President Edmonds's home local in a letter to the UMN
Journal indicated the practical results of the employment of
black officers and organizers. Noting that at the last organizing meeting twenty-three black mine workers had enrolled
in the UMW, he observed that

> We are made up of all races and colors [here]. The
> colored element are the majority and be it to their
> credit are mostly the best men to stick up for their
> rights. But allow me to say that the operators do
> not fail to try and keep up race dissensions when-
> ever they see the slightest opportunity. It is a
> natural feeling also, that colored people will listen
> with more confidence to one of their own race than
> they would to a white man. We have now to get at
> the dead-heads of white miners.[31]

Rapid organization of black mine workers into the UMW was
also occurring further south, in Pocahontas, Virginia. In

the organizing drive during the spring of 1891, President
Moran addressed large meetings of miners in the town. His
reports give an interesting insight into the dynamics of
racial division and class consciousness among southern West
Virginia miners in this period:

> At the hour of meeting I appeared and was agreeably
> surprised to find a large number of white miners
> present to take part in the meeting, this being the
> first time in six years that any white men have at-
> tended a meeting when organization was the topic of
> discussion. The cause for their absence in the past
> I do not wish to discuss in a newspaper as it would
> be of no benefit to our cause.

Moran's allusion to the previously recalcitrant attitude on
the part of white miners in Pocahontas toward interracial
organization is particularly important in view of the traditional analysis which has emphasized black unwillingness and
opposition to unionism as the cause of the failure to secure
permanent trade union organization in areas where the work
force was divided along racial lines. Quite clearly the history of black involvement in miners' unions in southern West
Virginia in this period suggests a radically different picture. William B. Wilson, then a member of the national UMW
Executive Board and later first secretary of labor under
Woodrow Wilson, confirmed this rather ironic difference in
black and white commitment to the UMW in southern West Virginia. On an organizing trip to Pocahontas, Virginia with
President Moran, Wilson noted: "To the honor of the colored
men, be it said they are the ones who are doing what they can
to help us in our work, while the English speaking white men
... lie back on their oars.... The truth is the most persistent unionists here are blacks." In addition to active support of the UMW, Pocahontas black miners, under the leadership of ex-District 17 Vice-President Horace Smith, founded
two cooperative stores in 1891 which were reported doing over
$100,000 in business annually.[32]

The black commitment to the UMW was sorely tested, however,
by a major strike which broke out in another area of southern
West Virginia later in 1891. In september, the miners
(nearly all white) at Raymond City in Kanawha County under-
took a strike for higher wages. The management immediately
determined to break the strike and the union through the importation of inexperienced black strikebreakers from the
Deep South. Raymond City, therefore, became a kind of litmus
test for the drive for interracial organization in southern
West Virginia.

The black strikebreakers had been duped through false statements made by recruiting agents. President Moran asserted
that "the majority of the colored men were deceived in coming

here and some refused to go to the mines when informed of the
condition and immediately left for other parts." The influx
of black strikebreakers apparently continued unabated, however, prompting a stern rebuke from R. L. Davis:

> I do think it about time colored men would stop
> running around breaking down the wages of their
> fellow-workmen and be men. I know that there has
> been a prejudice against [blacks] at Raymond, but
> two wrongs will not make a right. It is to be
> hoped that these men may be induced not to work
> and teach the tyrannical bosses that they will have
> to resort to some other source to get their tools.[33]

President Moran reiterated Davis's sentiments, although he
was careful to differentiate his critique of the black
strikebreakers from a more widespread criticism of black
workers: "Let the discussion about the colored men at Raymond City stop. There is nobody at Raymond City except
blacklegs of the most damnable type, both white and black,"
he said. "As it is, no renegade is a success, irrespective
of the color of his skin. A blackleg is a blackleg, no matter what his color."[34] Apparently the careful distinctions
drawn by Davis and Moran were lost on many of the white
strikers at Raymond, who vented their hostility and racism
toward the black strikebreakers in the pages of the UMW
Journal. One correspondent, for example, attacked blacks as
"the lowest class of renegades."[35]

Davis, again in measured words, rebuked the white miners at
Raymond for having excluded blacks from work in the past and
concluded that "the men of Raymond will now have to learn the
lesson that I have been trying to teach for some time, viz.
take down the [race] barrier." Despite Davis's anger at the
white miners over the race question he nevertheless canvassed
tirelessly throughout Ohio for aid to the Raymond strikers.
Davis's critical support suggests a complex relationship in
his ideology between race and class identity. While clearly
critical of exclusionary actions, Davis offered support to
white strikers because they were involved in a common struggle against coal operators. Nevertheless, situations like
the Raymond strike no doubt sorely tested the continued commitment of black miners to a common class identity with white
workers.[36]

Racial conflict, engendered in the Raymond strike, became an
issue once again in early 1892. R. L. Davis, writing on the
race question in West Virginia in the pages of the UMW
Journal, noted the absence of District 17 Vice-President
J. L. Edmonds from West Virginia and attributed it to the
failure of the district officers to pay the black leader as a
full-time district organizer. "Just such things as these is
what the negro [sic] is kicking against and we are not going

to have it. If your vice president is a negro," wrote Davis,
"he must be treated the same as a white man and unless you do
there is going to be a mighty earthquake somewhere." Henry
Stephenson, District 17's secretary-treasurer, denied Davis's
charge that he and other district officers failed in their
responsibilities to their black members. "I will say the officers of District 17 have in every respect treated the
colored members and officers just the same as the white members," he wrote, "and I defy successful contradiction." What
is interesting to note here is that both Stephenson and Moran
had developed long-standing reputations for encouraging,
rather than discouraging, interracial organization and cooperation.

Edmonds personally replied to Stephenson's letter and to
charges that he had shirked his duties as district vice-
president. In a letter to the UMW Journal in February 1892,
Edmonds argued that at the 1891 District 17 convention where
he was elected, the delegates had "endorsed unanimously" an
amendment to the District 17 constitution that "the Vice
President be commissioned and put on the road as [a paid]
organizer." "Everytime Stephenson, or any other man or set
of men, say that the executive officers have not discrimi-
nated against the colored miners of District 17," Edmonds
concluded, "they say what is not so.... the negroes of
District 17 have no rights that the officers are bound to
respect." Edmonds, obviously bitter at this treatment, reiterated a long-standing demand of black miners, namely, that
black district officials work as paid organizers in the same
way as the president and secretary-treasurer.[37]

While he voiced a major concern of West Virginia black miners, Edmonds clearly did not speak for all of them when he
attacked the white District 17 officers, especially President
Moran. In March, the Beury mine, with a largely black local
assembly in Fayette County, adopted unanimously a resolution
condemning Edmonds's "exaggerated attack." The resolution
stated that Edmonds had been recalled from the field because
of lack of funds in the District 17 treasury. Moran "has
spent the best days of his life in his endeavors to unite the
white and colored men," and the Beury miners unanimously
voted their confidence in their district president. The
Edmonds incident demonstrated both the sensitivity of black
miners to infringements on their rights within the union and
also an on-going sense that interracial cooperation had to be
defended.[38]

The consequences of the Edmonds incident became obvious at
the District 17 annual convention held the following month.
J. J. Wren, a black miner from Beury, was elected to succeed
Edmonds as District 17 vice-president. The principle of
black representation was preserved with Wren's election; he
was the third consecutive black elected to the District 17

vice-presidency. More important perhaps was the fact that
the Edmonds controversy had engendered a positive result --
Wren was appointed a full-time, paid organizer, marking the
first time that a black district officer served in this capacity. Wren functioned actively throughout 1892, accompanying President Moran and later, R. L. Davis, on major organizing trips in southern West Virginia. Moran, felled by ill-
ness from overwork, finally was forced to resign in October
1892, and was succeeded by Wren as District 17 president.
Moran died early in 1893. He had devoted his life, first in
Alabama and then in West Virginia, to the elimination of
racial divisiveness in the working class movement. Leaders
like him left an important, although unheralded, legacy of
interracial organization and cooperation. It seems appropriate that Moran's death had elevated a black man to the presidency of District 17.[39]

In the same month the national UMW Executive Committee decided to commit a full-time national organizer, W. C. Webb (a
white miner from Tennessee), to organize in the Flat Top-
Pocahontas field. Despite a two-month sojourn in October and
November 1892, Webb was unable to consolidate the impressive
organizational gains made in the 1890-1892 period. The problem, which seemed to exasperate both district and national
UMW leaders, was not racial divisiveness, however.[40] Webb,
reporting on his efforts in the Flat Top, noted the continued
commitment of both black and Hungarian miners to the union
cause: "I heard that the Hungarians and colored people were
a barrier to organization in the Flat Top region, but find
things different. They want to organize and I will surely do
my utmost." Webb succeeded in organizing a new local assembly in Pocahontas, Virginia, composed largely of Hungarians.[41]

The decline in local organization, which began early in 1893
and deepened the following year during the depression, seemed
to be the result of intensified economic and political repression on the part of the coal operators. Writing to the
UMW Journal in January 1893, "A Youth" lamented the inability
of local unions to secure new members and hold on to old ones.
Attributing this decline to overcrowding in the mine, low
pay, and the tyranny of the company store system, he wrote
that "the [pit] bank is so crowded that the turn don't run
but one or two to a man. The reason of that is so that the
miners draw all [of their wages] out of the pluck-me [the
miners' colloquialism for the company store]." By March,
S. F. Beckett, the Master Workman at the Simmon's Creek mine
in the Flat Top, reported the pit running about one-third
time. The local operator, in an attempt to take advantage of
the large surplus of miners and the slack work, demanded that
miners set up their own timber props in the mine and lay
steel rails for the mine cars without pay (these jobs were
normally done by mine workers paid a daily wage by the

company). When the Simmon's miners struck, their leaders,
including Beckett, were fired and blacklisted by the company.[42] By the end of the year, similar actions by other operators and the severity of the nationwide depression resulted in the dwindling of the important organizational gains
made between 1889 and 1892. "Observer," a Flat Top miner
writing to the UMW Journal in November, reported that the
local operators were "very thoroughly organized." Work was
very slow, averaging one to two cars per day at seventy-five
cents per car; the docking system which had been eliminated
in 1889 had been reinstituted; and prices at the company
store were exorbitant. He dejectedly concluded that "it is
as easy to organize a bible society in hades [sic] as to
organize the coal miners of this section."[43]

The decline of local organization in southern West Virginia
in 1893 anticipates, and in part explains, the subsequent
failure of West Virginia miners to support the national coal
strike called in April 1894.[44] The fact remains, however,
that for nearly a decade West Virginia mine workers, black
and white, had flocked to the banner of trade unionism.
Their participation in local, district, and national organizations occurred in the face of major structural forces active in the West Virginia coal industry which militated
against the creation of an interracial, industrial organization. These included the newness of the Flat Top-Pocahontas
coal field and the absence of an urban-labor tradition from
which mine workers could draw support; the colonial nature of
the southern West Virginia economy, with its near total reliance on the extraction of coal and the concomitant social,
economic, and political control exercised by coal operators;
a newly recruited, often transient and racial and ethnically
divided labor force; and a labor system structured by the
coal operators to maximize divisions among mine workers based
on race, skill and systems of work and payment.

Perhaps the most striking aspect of this episode in American
working class history is the fact that southern West Virginia
black mine workers, many recently migrated from the cities
and farms of eastern Virginia, came to view interracial trade
union organization as the vehicle through which they could
fight for their liberation both as workers and as black
people. In a largely Southern environment and in an increasingly hostile climate of racial and class repression, their
commitment to national trade unionism and the consequent
growth of interracial local organizations before 1894 represented an important illustration of the possibilities of cooperation between black and white workers. Despite the organizational decline after 1893, southern West Virginia miners
succeeded in leaving a legacy, "planting a seed" as one miner
put it, of interracial organization and cooperation that
would be regenerated in future struggles in southern West
Virginia.

Notes

[1] Sterling Spero and Abram Harris, The Black Worker: The Negro and the Labor Movement (New York, 1972), xi. Examples of the national focus include: Herman D. Bloch, "Labor and the Negro, 1866-1910," Journal of Negro History 5 (July 1965), 163-84; Gerald Grob, "Organized Labor and the Negro Workers, 1865-1900," Labor History 1 (Spring 1960), 164-76; Herbert Hill, "In the Age of Gompers and After: Racial Practices of Organized Labor," New Politics 4 (Spring 1965), 26-46; and Bernard Mandel, "Samuel Gompers and the Negro Workers, 1886-1914," Journal of Negro History 40 (January 1955), 34-60. An example of a static approach to local events is Robert Ward and William Rogers, Labor Revolt in Alabama: The Great Strike of 1894 (University, Ala., 1965). The best example of an in-depth local study is Paul Worthman, "Black Workers and Labor Unions in Birmingham, Ala., 1897-1904," Labor History 10 (Summer 1969), 375-407.

[2] The role of West Virginia in the drive to create a national coal union has been analyzed by Arthur Suffern, Arbitration and Conciliation in the Coal Industry (New York, 1915). See especially chapter 2, entitled "The West Virginia Problem." The description of union developments in southern West Virginia outlined in this paper was basically derived from the letters and reports from southern West Virginia which appeared between 1880 and 1891 in the pages of the National Labor Tribune (NLT), a national workingman's weekly published in Pittsburgh, and also the UMW Journal (UMWJ) from its founding in April 1891 to the end of the period covered in this paper. Professor Gutman's critique of this paper delivered at the Southern Labor History Conference noted the difficulties posed by overuse of the working class press in the writing of labor history. While I generally agree with Gutman's comments, there is an

extreme paucity of available primary source material on the
Flat Top-Pocahontas area before 1895. For example, the
only extant local newspaper, the Bluefield Daily Telegraph
(the local operators' organ), is not available before 1896;
existing county histories for this period are concerned exclusively with genealogy, and the few accessible company
records begin in 1898. Unfortunately the pages of the NLT
and UMWJ are almost the only sources which can be used to
re-create the history of the Flat Top-Pocahontas working
class before 1894. It is interesting to note that the most
recent study of the area laments the lack of written
sources on southern West Virginia, claiming that the operators were "much too busy" to leave personal accounts; and
"of course most miners in this period could scarcely write,
so the thoughts of both [the miners and the operators] are
lost to posterity." Jerry Bruce Thomas, "Coal Country:
The Rise of the Southern Smokeless Coal Industry and Its
Effect on Area Development, 1872-1910" (Ph.D. diss., University of North Carolina, 1971), 18-19. The vast number of
letters and reports from southern West Virginia mine workers contained in the NLT and UMWJ hopefully will correct
this mistaken assumption.

3 Tenth U.S. Census (1880), vol. 1, "Statistics of the Population of the United States," 852. Although there was no
racial breakdown by occupation in the 1880 census, which
included mines in Kanawha, Fayette, and Mason counties as
well as the Wheeling area in the northern part of the
state, secondary accounts indicate that very few of the
native born miners were black. Reports of black miners in
the Kanawha Valley appear in the NLT as early as September
1880. See the following NLT issues: September 11, 1880;
March 19, 1881; and June 4, 1881. Reports in the Engineer-
ing and Mining Journal (EMJ) throughout the early 1880s
note the links between the river miners around Charleston
and their Pennsylvania and Ohio counterparts in the river
trade. See the following EMJ reports: "Labor and Wages,"
January 8, 1887, 28; and "General Mining News -- Pennsylvania," February 9, 1889, 148.

4 On the Greenback movement, see NLT, June 5, 1880. An NLT
report of February 14, 1880, noted that Kanawha Valley
miners had forced local operators to open all company books
and records for inspection by committees of miners. On the
growth of the Knights of Labor in the Kanawha Valley, see
NLT, June 4 and October 8, 1881, April 28, 1882. Analysis
of the Knights of Labor Data Bank included in Jonathan
Garlock, "A Structural Analysis of the Knights of Labor"
(Ph.D. diss., University of Rochester, 1974), indicates that
by 1881, thirteen local assemblies existed in the Kanawha
Valley coal communities. Reports of black support of local
trade union organization and the Knights can be found in
NLT, June 4, October 22, and November 26, 1881.

[5] On the development and growth of the Norfolk and Western Railway a major study has been completed: Joseph T. Lambie, From Mine to Market: The History of Coal Transportation on the Norfolk and Western Railway (New York, 1954). On the town of Pocahontas, see: "Memoirs of Harriet E. Lathrop," Manuscript Room, University of Virginia Library, Charlottesville, Va.; American Manufacturer, August 8, 1884, 13; and Lambie, Mine to Market, 33-34. On N&W domination of the Flat Top-Pocahontas field, see Lambie, Mine to Market, 6-39.

[6] Lambie, Mine to Market, 39-41, 65, 70. The practice of loading three-ton coal cars for a flat rate of 75¢ was common in the Flat Top field in the 1880s and 1890s. Letter of April 25, 1895, from the Executive Committee of UMW District No. 25 to West Virginia Governor William MacCorkle, in MacCorkle Papers, West Virginia State Archives, Charleston. On the "slack dock" system and the high prices at the company store see NLT reports, December 13, 1884, August 15, December 19, 1885, and May 14, 1887. For a general discussion of the importance of these methods of exploitation on the development of the national miners' union, see Stephen Brier and Jon Amsden, "Coal Miners on Strike: The Transformation of Strike Demands and the Formation of the National Miners' Union," Journal of Interdisciplinary History (forthcoming, Spring 1977).

[7] Thomas, "Coal Country," 27, 83-90.

[8] The miners apparently broke the padlock and held the meeting. NLT reports, May 11, 1889, and August 2, 1890.

[9] Lambie, Mine to Market, 40.

[10] In late 1884, the NLT reported Hocking Valley, Ohio, miners working in Pocahontas and sending substantial sums of money to their brethren on strike in Ohio. A number of Pennsylvania mine workers came to Pocahontas during 1884 and 1885 for similar reasons. NLT reports, August 8 and 22, 1885. On the question of racial composition of the southern West Virginia work force, the only direct evidence for the 1885-1895 period would be the 1890 Census Manuscripts which were destroyed by fire. In their absence, the historian must rely on indirect evidence for racial breakdowns and patterns of migration. For example, reports in the NLT in late 1881 indicate that a Fayette County coal operator attempted to break a strike in his mine through the active recruitment of black workers from Richmond, Virginia. According to the NLT, labor agents flooded the Richmond black community with handbills. It is interesting to note that when the Richmond blacks arrived and discovered the strike in progress, they immediately returned home. NLT reports, November 26 and

December 3, 1881. Another indication of the source of black migration to southern West Virginia can be derived from an analysis of the mine workers killed in the famous 1883 Pocahontas mine explosion. The list of dead printed in the New York Times on March 14 indicated approximately fifty black miners and laborers (mostly recruited from the Lynchburg, Virginia, area), forty Hungarians, about fifty native whites (from "Pennsylvania and Virginia"), and ten Germans. The Times reported the following day (March 15) that "most of the killed were unmarried, the night force being mainly composed of the youngest and most vigorous men." Thomas, "Coal Country," 76, assumes that the eastern Virginia black migrants were farmers. The evidence above suggests a different interpretation. By the end of the decade of the 1890s, the Bluefield (Va.) Daily Telegraph (BDT) reported train loads of "colored laborers" being brought into Flat Top from eastern Virginia. BDT reports, June 27, November 7 and 22, 1899. Finally, the Immigration Commission Report on Immigrants in Industry, vol. 7, 145, concludes that "the expansion of mining in West Virginia in the 1890s was based on the migration of blacks, principally from Virginia."

11 Spero and Harris, The Black Worker, 22; Thomas, "Coal Country," 189.

12 This hypothesis will require further comparative research; nevertheless, it suggests a possible explanation for the deep commitment of southern West Virginia black miners after 1885 to the cause of unionism. See particularly Peter Rachleff, "Black, White and Gray: Working Class Self-Activity in Richmond, Va., 1865-1890" (M.A. thesis, University of Pittsburgh, 1976); Leon Fink, "Irrespective of Race or Party: The Knights of Labor in Richmond, Va., 1885-1886" (Unpublished paper, University of Rochester, 1975); and Howard Rabinowitz, "The Search for Social Control: Race Relations in the Urban South, 1865-1890" (Ph.D. diss., University of Chicago, 1973).

13 NLT, August 29, 1885.

14 On the organization of the Knights of Labor in the South, see Sidney Kessler, "The Organization of Negroes in the Knights of Labor," Journal of Negro History 37 (July 1952), 248-76; and Melton McLaurin, "Knights of Labor: Internal Dissensions of the Southern Order," in Essays in Southern Labor History (Westport, Conn., 1977). On the Knights of Labor assemblies in Pocahontas, see NLT reports, January 9, February 6, and October 2, 1886. On segregated facilities in Pocahontas, see American Manufacturer, August 8, 1884, 13; and "Memoirs of Harriet E. Lathrop."

[15] NLT, June 6, 1885, March 13 and April 10, 1886; Lambie,
Mine to Market, 91.

[16] NLT, October 2, 1886; and New York Freeman, November 26,
1886.

[17] A convention of Kanawha Valley miners elected four delegates and four alternates to attend the founding convention of the National Federation. NLT, July 11 and
August 8, 1885. On the growth of the National Federation,
see Andrew Roy, A History of the Coal Miners of the United
States (Columbus, Ohio, 1906), 244; and Chris Evans, The
History of the United Mine Workers of America (Indianapolis, 1918), vol. 1, 136-39.

[18] NLT, October 17, 1885, and April 10, 1886.

[19] The extent of the contract system in southern West Virginia mines and whether a racial hierarchy existed are unclear from the evidence. There is some indication that
blacks also functioned as contractors in certain pits.
Whether black contract miners hired only blacks or whether
whites hired whites as well as blacks is also unclear.
NLT reports, January 2, July 10, 24, and August 7, 1886;
March 31, 1888.

[20] NLT reports, May 21, June 4 and 25, 1887.

[21] On the general background of the merger of NTA 135 and the
National Federation to form the NPU, see Roy, History of
Coal Miners, 268-73; and Evans, History of the UMW,
vol. 1, 395-410.

[22] Moran migrated to West Virginia in the early 1880s from
Birmingham, Alabama, where he had played a central role in
the development of interracial political and trade union
institutions among that area's workers. Information on
Moran's Alabama background was generously given by Paul
Worthman, who is researching the working class movement in
Birmingham. References to Moran's work in support of the
Alabama Greenback movement and the organization of Bir-
mingham miners can be found in a series of letters from
Alabama workers to the NLT, reprinted in Labor History.
One of the correspondents, writing in 1879, described
Moran (who was living and working in Helena, Alabama) as
"a solid Greenbacker and a gentleman, and treats every
poor man alike when he can...." Also included in this
selection is an 1879 letter from Moran to the editor of
the NLT. Herbert G. Gutman, "Black Coal Miners and the
Greenback-Labor Party in Redeemer Alabama: 1878-1879,
The Letters of Warren D. Kelley, Willis Johnson Thomas,
'Dawson,' and Others," Labor History 10 (Summer 1969), 523,
530, 533-34. On Moran's role in the formation of the West

Virginia State Federation, see <u>NLT</u>, May 5, 1888.

23 <u>NLT</u>, April 20, 1889.

24 <u>NLT</u>, April 27, 1889.

25 <u>NLT</u>, July 20 and 27, November 30, December 28, 1889. It
should be noted that the founding of the UMW in 1890 did
not necessarily negate secret Knights of Labor organizations in southern West Virginia. Flat Top miners recognized that despite the growth of the UMW, they still
lacked the necessary power to sustain open trade unionism
on the Northern model. As a result of this fear of retaliation from local operators, the form of local organization adopted by Flat Top miners until the end of the 1890s
continued to be the secret Knights of Labor local assembly, affiliated with the national UMW. The continued allegiance of Flat Top miners to the Knights throughout the
1890s was not due solely to the defensibility of the
secret assembly, however. The Knights's inclusive ideology of organization was also particularly suited to the
heterogeneous character of the Flat Top-Pocahontas work
force. Thomas Burdette, a white Flat Top miner and union
stalwart, urged his fellow workers in 1891 to continue to
join the Knights of Labor. Describing the Knights as "our
good old order," Burdette concluded that the Knights "will
educate [Flat Top miners] in a way to love one another, so
that we all can come together in one mind and stand up in
the face of capital." UMW <u>Journal</u>, July 23, 1891.

26 <u>NLT</u>, April 12 and May 3, 1890.

27 <u>NLT</u>, May 17 and 24, 1890.

28 <u>NLT</u> reports, June 7, 14 and 21, July 12, August 16, Sep-
tember 6, October 4 and 11, 1890. Statistics for the
Freeman mines's work force came from the West Virginia
State Inspector of Mines, <u>Annual Reports for the First and
Second Districts For the Year Ended June 30, 1891</u>,
Charleston, 1892, 76. In March, in response to a wave of
organizing activity, the management of the Pocahontas
(Va.) mines was compelled to send an interpreter through
the pits to demand that the Hungarian miners patronize the
company store instead of independent Hungarian merchants
in the town. The Hungarians, whose employment four years
earlier had engendered a mass protest, were, in the words
of one miner, "beginning to see [that] organization is the
thing." <u>NLT</u>, March 22, 1890. The material importance of
the fight against the company store and the creation of
cooperatives can be gauged by a comparison of prices for
good purchased from company stores and independent merchants:

	Mercer and McDowell Co. Company Stores	Pocahontas, Va. Company Store	Outside Store
Flour, per bbl.	$8.50	$7.75	$5.75
Bacon, per lb.	.12 1/2	.10	.07
Sugar, per lb.	.12 1/2	.10	.08
Coffee, per lb.	.30	.28	.22

Source: NLT report, March 1, 1890.

29 NLT, October 4, November 8 and 15, 1890.

30 The election of other black master workmen is reported in
NLT, May 28, 1891. Davis's letter is in NLT, March 14,
1891. The importance of R. L. Davis's early role in the
UMW has been stressed by Herbert G. Gutman, "The Negro and
the United Mine Workers of America. The Career and Letter
of Richard L. Davis and Something of Their Meaning,"
J. Jacobson, ed., The Negro and the American Labor Movement (Garden City, N.Y., 1968), 49-127. Davis's attitude
toward white miners and the UMW's commitment to interracial organization has become something of an historical
cause célèbre in recent months. Disagreeing fundamentally
with Gutman's thesis (without ever making direct reference
to it), Philip Foner, in Black Workers and Organized Labor
(New York, 1975), 83, 95-96, has chosen to portray Davis
as extremely critical of white miners and the UMW because
of racist practices and ideology. Foner's view (and
Herbert Hill's, on whose unpublished manuscript Foner
bases his argument) is mistaken. Despite Davis's criticism of exclusionary policies of certain local miners'
unions and even some national leaders, he was fundamentally committed to coal miners' unionism as the vehicle
for black liberation. Davis's ideology of race and class
is illustrated in the discussion of the Raymond City, West
Virginia, strike.

31 After April 1891, with the founding of the UMW Journal,
the NLT no longer served as the official organ of United
States coal miners. On colored organizers in southern
West Virginia, see UMWJ, April 20 and May 21, 1891.

32 UMWJ, April 30, 1891. See also Moran's letter in UMWJ,
May 21, 1891, attacking miners who allowed racial or national differences to divide the cause. Whether Pocahontas white miners patronized the black-owned cooperatives
is unknown. Wilson's letter and the report of the black
cooperatives are in UMWJ, November 26, 1891.

[33] UMWJ reports, September 23, 1891.

[34] Ibid., October 22, 1891.

[35] Ibid., October 8, 1891.

[36] Ibid., October 15, 1891. A white striker at Raymond, responding to reports that black strikebreakers were supposedly preparing to take over the town by force, indicated that the whites were prepared to take up arms in self-defense: "Mr. Negro, we are ready for the place to be painted red." Ibid., November 5, 1891.

[37] Ibid., January 14 and 21, February 11, 1892.

[38] Ibid., March 3, 1892.

[39] Ibid., April 21 and 28, November 27, 1892.

[40] Letters from District 17 secretary-treasurer Henry Stephenson and UMW national organizer Phil Penna, UMW Journal, January 5 and 26, 1893.

[41] Ibid., October 27 and November 24, 1892.

[42] Ibid., January 26 and March 16, 1893. A letter in UMWJ, February 9, 1893, indicates that blacklisting was also pervasive in the New River field further north.

[43] Ibid., January 5 and November 3, 1893.

[44] Kenneth R. Bailey, "'Tell the Boys to Fall Into Line' United Mine Workers of America Strikes in West Virginia, January-June 1894," West Virginia History 32 (July 1971), 224-37.

Comment

A synopsis of the remarks by Herbert Gutman, City College
of New York.

Important methodological and historiographical questions
emerge from these two papers on the Knights of Labor in the
South -- questions that relate to working-class history generally and the writing of Southern working-class (both black
and white) history particularly. Who were the Southern workers? What sort of society did they live in? What is important and distinctive about the years between 1880 and 1890?
What is distinctively Southern about Southern labor history,
especially in the 1880s?

Brier's splendid study demonstrates convincingly that
(1) Southern blacks played a major role in the early development of unionism among the miners of West Virginia; (2) conventional assertions about white working-class racism over-
look the occasional dominance of class needs over racial
antagonism; and (3) a decade of experience distinguished the
coal miner of 1890 from his counterpart ten years earlier.
But Brier's paper evidences two serious shortcomings. The
author fails to describe adequately the structure of West
Virginia's new coal-mining industry and the social and economic conditions in which it developed. Nor does he properly
emphasize the full class experience of the miners themselves.
To understand their behavior, such as the decision for interracial trade unionism, Brier needs to explore the full dimensions of their pre-working-class and working-class experiences. Other difficulties in the analysis stem from the near
exclusive reliance on the National Labor Tribune. Although
the use of the Tribune in this instance supplies a welcome
corrective to its general neglect by labor historians, such
other sources as hostile local newspapers, court records, and
county histories might provide a more accurate perspective.

In his study of the Southern Knights of Labor, McLaurin properly emphasizes the dynamics of internal growth and decay as

a corrective to those labor historians who have attributed
the decline of trade unions solely to external forces.
Nevertheless, certain difficulties mar his list of internal
weaknesses. Who were the Southern Knights of Labor? Leaving
aside the black and white textile workers, what other workers
were drawn to the Knights? Furthermore, is McLaurin correct
in portraying a gap between Southern workers and their Northern leadership? The typical leader may have been alien to
the "South" but not to the Southern, urban, white, working-
class community, which was North European by birth or only a
generation removed.

Brier and McLaurin could profit from a somewhat different
perspective. The behavior of the Southern working class in
the 1880s must be examined as part of the process of "class
formation" and studied comparatively. Only then can historians distinguish between the distinctive and the common in
the Southern working class.

CHAPTER II

TEXTILES:
The Past and the Present

Organized labor's protracted struggle to organize Southern
textiles, the region's most important manufacturing industry,
mirrors the dismal past, ambiguous present, and hopeful future of much of the labor movement in the South. The following essays provide both an analysis of past failures and an
assessment of the current state of trade unionism in the textile industry. In the first essay, Dennis R. Nolan and
Donald E. Jonas examine textile unionism in the Piedmont during the first three decades of the twentieth century. Although not disputing the significance of such traditionally
identified obstacles to effective union organization as community and industry resistance, blacklisting, welfare capi-
talism, and the often depressed state of the industry, the
authors note that workers in other Southern industries, particularly coal, operate under similar conditions but still
have managed to organize effective unions. Textile unionism,
Nolan and Jonas argue, has failed to match this progress in
part because of its own shortcomings. The absence of long-
range planning, ill-timed and poorly conducted strikes, internal divisions, and the failure to build stable, permanent
unions have all qualified the textile union movement's potential for success. Ultimately, they conclude, textile unionism will not be able to solve the problems of the workers in
the industry until it first solves its own problems.

Bruce Raynor, an active participant in the frustrating efforts to organize Southern textiles, emphasizes the external
obstacles to effective trade unionism. Using J. P. Stevens
Corporation and Wellman Industries as case studies, Raynor
describes the "preventive labor relations" that have been
used to impede labor organization. Nevertheless, despite the
absence of substantial progress in the efforts to organize
textiles during the past quarter century, Raynor is optimistic about the future. The nature and character of the

textile labor force (traditionally cited as an important obstacle to effective organization) is changing significantly
with the introduction into the industry of large numbers of
black workers who do not possess the mill village psychology
and cannot be intimidated by management or community pressures. Moreover, the dramatic industrial growth of the South
during the past few decades will force the national labor
movement to devote more time and effort and a greater commitment of its resources to the organization of the Southern
labor force, including textiles.

Dennis R. Nolan is presently assistant professor of law at
the University of South Carolina, having previously engaged
in the private practice of labor law in Milwaukee, Wisconsin.
He holds an A.B. degree in Government from Georgetown University (1967), a J.D. from Harvard Law School (1970), and an
M.A. in History from the University of Wisconsin, Milwaukee
(1974). He has contributed to a number of professional
journals, including the Virginia Law Review, the New York
University Law Review, and the Political Science Reviewer.

Donald E. Jonas is a practicing attorney in Columbia, South
Carolina. He received a B.S. from North Carolina State University in 1973 and a J.D. from the University of South Carolina in 1975. Nolan and Jonas wish to thank Professors
Randall Bell and Patrick Hubbard of the University of South
Carolina School of Law for helpful comments during the preparation of their paper.

Bruce Raynor received the B.S. degree from the New York State
School of Industrial and Labor Relations at Cornell University. After serving in the Education Department of District
Council 37, American Federation of State, County, and Municipal Employees, Raynor was named director of the Education Department of the Textile Workers Union of America in 1973. He
held that position until the merger of the Textile Workers
Union and the Amalgamated Clothing Workers of America in June
1976. He was appointed associate director of education in
the merged union. Raynor directed the successful boycott
during the six-month strike at Oneita Knitting Mills in
Andrews, South Carolina, and assisted in the production of
"Contract, Contract," which was filmed in the aftermath of
the strike.

Textile Unionism in the Piedmont, 1901-1932
Dennis R. Nolan and Donald E. Jonas

Eventually every serious student of Southern labor grapples
with a most difficult question: Why has unionism made so few
inroads? In the case of the textile industry, the question
can be put more forcefully: Why have the textile unions
failed so completely to form stable local organizations and
to negotiate improvements in wages and working conditions?

Previous investigations have cited several factors hindering
textile unionism -- employer opposition, labor injunctions,
use of the militia or police on behalf of management, and
erratic market conditions -- but none has attempted to evaluate their relative importance.[1] With troubling similarity,
each work tends to blame textile unionism's failures on outside forces. In contrast, this paper explores several factors we feel have been underestimated in earlier studies,
namely, the problems workers and unions brought upon themselves. Rash and poorly planned strikes, internal feuds,
poor leadership, and the failure of interested groups to provide financial aid to those on the front lines were serious
enough to cause the failure of twentieth century organizing
drives even had the outside forces been much less hostile.
In saying this, it is not our intention to downgrade the importance of those outside forces but rather to indicate that
they do not provide a complete explanation.

This study is limited in time and place; it deals mainly with
the years from the formation of the United Textile Workers
(UTW) to the coming of the New Deal, though some background
material is required for a thorough understanding of that
period. The scope is also limited to one geographic area,
the Piedmont portions of Virginia, the Carolinas, Georgia,
and Alabama, which constitute the heartland of the Southern
textile industry.[2]

I

The Piedmont offered many advantages to the manufacturers,
who began the first campaign to industrialize the region,
among them a plentiful labor supply, an isolated market, and
the absence of the agricultural heritage which marked the
rest of the South.[3] Nevertheless, there was little industrialization of the region until an agricultural depression
after the Civil War freed capital for investment in textile
manufactures.[4] Almost simultaneously, community leaders re-
discovered William Gregg's prescription of industrialization
as a cure for the South's economic ills.[5] A new and more
successful cotton mill campaign swept the Piedmont as editors, industrialists, preachers, merchants, and bankers
staked out a new direction for the region and proclaimed the
birth of the "New South."[6]

On the whole, industrial development was financed locally,
frequently through the combination of community savings.[7]
The results of the campaign were phenomenal. From 1880 to
1890, spindlage in the Piedmont states doubled or tripled,
compared to the national average increase of 35 percent for
the same period. By the turn of the century, ownership of
the Southern industry was firmly established in local hands,
a pattern that continued into the 1920s.[8]

World War I brought an inflated demand for cotton goods,
which boosted production in both North and South. After the
war, the South gained an increased share of the textile market through its technological superiority, two-shift production, and cheap labor. As a result, the competitive pressure
of the South became a matter of great concern to Northern
manufacturers. Investment in Southern mills became increasingly attractive, and the South soon became the dominant textile region.[9]

The 1920s marked a new phase in the industrialization of the
Piedmont. Few new mills were built; but old mills were
greatly expanded and often sold to new owners, frequently
Northerners. The consequences of this development on employment were pervasive. Bigger and more efficient production
units and cutthroat competition demanded more efficient labor.
The demand for efficiency resulted in the "stretchout," as
operatives were required to handle more and more looms working at faster and faster rates. "Foreign" ownership meant
that the paternal aspects of employment were diminished. No
longer was the plant manager likely to be a local attorney or
preacher who might weigh human factors against the economic.
This "third cotton mill campaign" of the 1920s was everything
the second of the 1880s had not been. It was the result of
individual initiative rather than community spirit, and it
brought with it the Northern capital that had previously been
impossible to attract. Since the "audience" of the Southern

entrepreneur was now composed of profit-seeking investors,
his sales pitch emphasized the advantages of cheap labor, in
contrast with the previous campaign during which the entrepreneur sold his idea to the community on the basis of the
advantages to the labor force.[10]

These factors, the change in the Piedmont's conception of its
own labor, the drive for labor efficiency, and the new managers who were less restrained than their predecessors by
financial or social ties with the region, combined to shape
the pattern of labor relations in Southern textile manufacturing for decades. The mills tended to become even more
isolated, physically and socially, and this in turn heightened class prejudice. Workers in the mills became known as
"lintheads" and were often viewed with contempt. In the earlier days, if the mill worker was despised, "it was mainly
behind the arras"; but by 1920, there was no attempt to hide
such feelings.[11] These developments produced an explosive
situation which helps to explain the tinder-box nature of
textile labor disputes in the late 1920s.

The story of textile unionism in the first third of this century is largely the story of the United Textile Workers (UTW),
but the ultimate failure of that union is more understandable
in light of the failure of earlier organizing efforts. The
factors discussed in the preceding pages set the parameters
within which early textile unions operated. Most importantly, the community-based development of Piedmont mills
guaranteed solid community opposition to unions, which were
perceived as threats to the community itself. As a defensive
measure, early textile unions and later the AFL were forced
to adopt a "cooperationist" approach emphasizing their desire
to aid the industry rather than fight it.

The peculiar development of the textile industry provides
only a partial explanation for union difficulties; more important still were internal problems, and here, too, the
nineteenth-century experience is illuminating. There were
recurring fratricidal wars -- between socialists and nonsocialists and between skilled and unskilled workers -- and
an almost unbelievable tactical ineptness. Virtually every
textile strike in this period collapsed, marked by rash action, lack of solidarity, incompetent or nonexistent organizational efforts, and the failure to preserve a basis for
future action.[12]

Several unions played a significant role in textiles in the
nineteenth century, among them the Mule Spinners and the International Labor Union; but only two made much progress in
the Piedmont. The Knights of Labor and the International
Union of Textile Workers deserve particularly close attention.

Prior to the rise of the Knights, trade unionists showed no

interest in the unskilled textile workers. Under Master
Workman Terence Powderly, the Knights organized a large number of "mixed assemblies" composed of both skilled and unskilled workers. The mixed assemblies provided the first vehicle for the organization of unskilled textile workers and
became an effective method of appealing to the workers of the
newly industrialized South.[13] During the 1880s, the Knights
made a concerted attempt to organize the cotton mill workers
of the country beginning in the North in 1883 and in the
South about 1885. The success of this effort is difficult to
determine, but one scholar estimates that some 25,000 of the
nation's 200,000 textile workers joined the Knights.[14]

The Knights of Labor was troubled by an identity crisis
throughout its existence. It was in part a political organization, an ally of the agrarian populists and opponent of
the old Southern aristocracy; but it also drew strength from
industrial workers who viewed it simply as a labor movement.
Accordingly, the complexion of the organization varied
greatly from state to state. In North Carolina it emerged as
a major political force but engaged in little labor activity,
while in Georgia it acted more as a traditional labor organization; but even where most concerned with bread-and-butter
issues, the Knights had little success.[15] For example,
Augusta, Georgia, was the Knights' strongest textile center;
yet strikes there by the Knights were broken many times in
the 1870s and 1880s. Each defeat was marked by internal
bickering and lack of support from the national organization
or other labor groups.[16]

The second major predecessor to the UTW was the International
Union of Textile Workers (IUTW) which was organized by the
American Federation of Labor (AFL) in 1890 following the collapse of the Knights of Labor. The IUTW was soon torn by
disputes between craft and industrial unionists and between
socialists and nonsocialists. It tried to walk a middle path
on the former issue, but many of the strongest textile craft
organizations refused to cooperate. Those craft unions which
did join the IUTW exercised a great degree of influence.[17]
Daniel DeLeon's Socialist Trade and Labor Alliance (STLA)
fought with Gompers's AFL for control of the new union, almost bringing about a merger between the STLA and the IUTW in
the middle 1890s. Gompers managed to postpone action on the
subject at the 1896 IUTW convention, and thereafter he diverted the IUTW's attention by stepping up AFL organizational
efforts among Southern textile operatives. These internal
struggles and a lack of practical results so weakened the
IUTW that in 1897 an influx of Southerners under Prince W.
Greene of Georgia was able to seize control from the Northerners who had dominated the organization since its founding.
Greene was elected president and continued to hold high
office in the IUTW until its merger with the UTW in 1901.[18]

Unsuccessful strikes in the late 1890s forced the IUTW to
consider merging with Northern craft unions. Little came of
the merger efforts until the union had virtually destroyed
itself in a campaign for the ten-hour day in 1900 and 1901.
Strong IUTW locals were broken after bitter strikes in North
and South Carolina that were marked by the failure of the
national organization and the AFL to lend significant aid.
The union's most serious defeat came at Danville, Virginia.
The union had ample time to prepare for the strike; but by
striking, the local leadership departed from the cooperationist strategy suggested by Gompers and Greene. Accordingly,
neither the AFL nor the IUTW provided financial support to
the Danville strikers. Without funds to pay strike benefits
and with local leaders more concerned with politics than economics, the strike collapsed and the union was broken.

The IUTW had no choice but to merge with a craft organization, the American Federation of Textile Operatives, even if
that meant surrendering control of the national organization.
The new union was named the United Textile Workers of America (UTW). New England craft locals dominated the union's
first convention and chose Northerners to fill all offices;
yet even with this control, the craft unions refused to create a strong national organization. Local autonomy was retained, and per capita dues were set at only five cents per
quarter so that local treasuries could be kept strong. This
policy infuriated Gompers, who said that it made the UTW unable "to provide for raising sufficient funds for the successful propagation of organization or to carry out in full
its necessary duties." Nevertheless, the UTW was the only
hope for improving the textile labor situation, and Gompers
reluctantly gave the new union his blessing.[19]

Why did the IUTW fail so totally in the South? Employer opposition was clearly a major factor, but the textile union
movement in the nineteenth century could almost be said to
have defeated itself, and in this respect it presaged the
twentieth-century experience. The IUTW failed to exert
strong leadership. Lacking a sound financial base, it was
unable to carry through with its ambitious plans, and the AFL
denied it financial help at crucial times. And finally, the
union repeatedly engaged in strikes without adequate preparation, often reacting to spontaneous events rather than developing and implementing a feasible strategy.[20]

II

It should be remembered that the UTW was formed in a period
of desperation following the crushing defeat of the IUTW at
Danville. Its future in the South seemed no more promising
than its heritage; control by Northern craft locals and a
weak national organization indicated that organization in the
Piedmont would be of low priority.

Failure of the first major Southern strike of the UTW was
therefore not surprising. In March 1902, the Augusta Textile
Council threatened to strike unless wages were increased by
10 percent and focused their grievances on the King Mill, the
city's largest. Mill owners and the Augusta Cotton Manufacturers Association argued strenuously that financial conditions did not permit such an increase; the workers were not
convinced and struck on schedule.[21] The association responded by locking out all 7,000 textile workers in the city.

The King Mill employees had contacted the UTW for aid prior
to the strike, but the response was delayed by more pressing
problems in the Northeast. The UTW finally replied after the
strike had begun, saying that it would not formally authorize
the strike (to do so would commit it to supply strike benefits) but would support it in other ways. The union did levy
an assessment of five cents per member but contributed only a
total of $10,000.[22] The strikers were unable to exist with-
out substantial UTW support and began to drift back to work.
Some even sued the Augusta locals for breach of promise,
claiming that pledges of aid had not been kept.

Just as damaging to the union's cause were the activities of
other textile workers across the South Carolina border in the
Horse Creek Valley area who, on May 20, examined the King
Mill's books to determine whether the strike was justified.
The next day, the group announced at a mass rally that the
Augusta strikers had no just complaint and recommended a return to work. The Augusta mills reopened on May 22, and by
May 26, all were back in operation; the remaining strikers
were replaced with workers from South Carolina. On August 6,
the UTW Executive Council took the long overdue step of call-
ing off the strike.[23]

Although the defeat could have been predicted, its disastrous
consequences could not. Southern workers learned not to rely
on the UTW or, indeed, on any union. Employers became convinced that a firm stand could break a strike, and UTW leaders learned to avoid involvement in Southern disputes. The
UTW convention in 1902 in effect announced its abandonment of
the Piedmont by defeating a resolution authorizing a single
full-time organizer for that region. Perhaps unwittingly,
the 1903 convention completed that abandonment by adopting
more stringent financial policies and providing that locals
failing to pay would be expelled. Half of the locals thereby
expelled were located in the South, and the result of these
actions was inevitable. With only one exception, no Southern
delegate appeared at the UTW convention again until 1913; and
for over eight years after 1903, no UTW agent even toured the
Piedmont. A branch office was kept open in Charlotte, North
Carolina, but it carried on no significant activities. It is
notable that the history of the UTW written by its president,
Thomas McMahon, barely mentions the South before 1914 except

to complain that it was difficult to organize there. The AFL
also virtually ceased its efforts in Southern textiles. Its
total 1903 expenditure in the area was $443 for one organizer
in the field. That organizer's suggestion that an aggressive
campaign be initiated was rejected by the 1903 convention,
primarily because previous organizational efforts had proved
futile.[24]

For the next decade, the AFL and the UTW were torn by repeated battles between craft and industrial unionists. On
several occasions, most notably in Lawrence, Massachusetts
(1912), and Paterson, New Jersey (1913), the UTW actually
opposed textile strikes led by industrial unionists.[25] Only
a few years later, however, the craft unionists were unex-
pectedly instrumental in fostering Southern organization. In
1915, the UTW convention established a relatively high per
capita monthly tax on locals of twenty cents. UTW President
McMahon later wrote that this was "the turning point in the
history" of the union because the enlarged treasury allowed
greater organizational efforts. He might well have cited an
equally important factor, the withdrawal in protest of a number of the more conservative craft unions, for after their
departure, the UTW was less opposed to organizing the unskilled.[26] Southern supporters of the UTW benefited from one
other development, the increased demand for textiles during
World War I. As uninterrupted production became more important to mill management, union organizing became easier. Unfortunately, the UTW leadership had no strategy for taking
advantage of the economic situation and instead concentrated
on particular disputes as they arose. At the time, it seemed
as if these small successes were a prelude to greater
achievements; but the economy did not cooperate.[27]

By the fall of 1918, demand for textile products had dropped
drastically as the government canceled defense contracts. To
deal with rising unemployment, the Amalgamated Clothing Workers chose this inauspicious time to begin a campaign for an
eight-hour day and a forty-eight-hour week. The UTW joined
the campaign, proclaiming February 3, 1919, as the deadline
for the adoption of the new hours by mill managements. The
idea caught on in the South, fueled in part by wartime expectations but also by more complex sociological factors brought
by the changing nature of the textile industry.[28]

On the appointed day, a wave of strikes swept the Piedmont
and other areas as geographically diverse as Chattanooga,
Tennessee, and Sherman, Texas. The focal point was Columbus,
Georgia, where about 7,000 workers walked out. Disorder was
rampant, and the union had to withdraw its picket lines in
return for nonprosecution of strikers who had "cut up" a
strikebreaker. The mills made a minor but timely concession
on hours, which brought a temporary lull. In May, another
strike broke out in Columbus, this time over wages. Again, a

minor concession ended the strike, but only after one union
man was killed and several others wounded.[29]

Other strikes in the Piedmont were even less successful. In
Macon, Georgia, a strike involving 2,000 workers began in
August 1919, even after UTW officials warned that they did
not have sufficient funds to win the strike. The mills used
black strikebreakers, and the union was publicly discredited
when attacks on those strikebreakers resulted in the death of
one of them. Union leaders were jailed and the strike broken.
In the Horse Creek Valley area of South Carolina, a strike
for shorter hours resulted in a lockout and evictions from
company-owned housing. The strike was settled after the
union's strike funds were exhausted, with a slight reduction
in hours but without union recognition.[30]

The only positive results of the 1919 union effort were in
North Carolina. In February, several North Charlotte mills
eliminated the wartime bonus of 35 percent of wages and reduced the workweek to four days. The ensuing walkout lasted
four months and was finally settled on favorable terms:
union workers were reinstated without discrimination, although union recognition was withheld; the workweek was set
at fifty-five hours; the bonus was incorporated into wages;
and most astounding of all, workers were granted free rent
for the period of the strike. Similar settlements were
reached in East Charlotte and at least eleven other North
Carolina communities. The extent of the success in North
Carolina was apparent in the rise in UTW membership. By September 1919, forty-three new locals had been formed in North
Carolina, and as many as 30,000 operatives had joined the
union. The Raleigh News and Observer recognized the new
strength of organized labor, stating editorially that "the
Labor Federation is to be heard and recognized in North
Carolina, as in every other state."[31]

The effect of the Southern campaign on the parent union was
enormous. The UTW grew from 11,000 members in cotton mills
in 1914 to over 100,000 in 1920, of which some 40,000 to
50,000 were attributable to the South. Meanwhile, the nature
of the organization had changed toward a more industrial form.
In 1911, over 85 percent of UTW locals were organized on a
craft basis; but by 1920, more than half were on an industrial basis. More surprising still, the union could truth-
fully claim to have "won" over half of its strikes between
1914 and 1920. The UTW did not establish the eight-hour day
or forty-eight-hour week, but in many plants it did help to
reduce the hours to a relatively standard fifty-five per week.
A peak was reached by the beginning of 1920, when total textile union strength reached 110,000, or more than a quarter
of the 420,000 workers in the industry.[32]

The euphoria did not last. Even before the union savored its

victories, the results began to evaporate as industry entered
a period of severe economic decline. By the end of 1919, the
boom was over for the textile industry and its unions. A
year later, the slump had become a depression; and mill owners reacted by cutting wages as much as 30 to 50 percent,
fueling arguments for a major strike which the UTW tried to
postpone because of inadequate finances. The growing wage
disparity between North and South began to undercut Northern
standards, however, and forced UTW leaders to authorize a
strike in 1921. Again ill prepared, Southern locals got
ready for battle: on June 1, 1921, 9,000 workers in North
and South Carolina left their jobs. Under little competitive
pressure to remain open, mill owners patiently awaited the
inevitable collapse of the strike. By August, union strike
funds were exhausted, the industry depression had worsened,
and employer opposition had hardened. The workers were
forced to return to work for the same protested wages; the
previous years' successes were destroyed; and the union
quickly lost the bulk of its Southern membership.[33]

The North Carolina portion of the 1921 strike illustrates the
continuing harm done to the union cause by the craft/indus-
trial dispute. For many years the North Carolina State Federation of Labor was controlled by extremely conservative
craft union leaders primarily interested in protective legislation limiting access to the skilled trades. In the federation's 1921 presidential election, the textile workers were
primarily responsible for electing James F. Barrett, a vigorous trade union leader, rather than the craft unionists' candidate, a musician from Raleigh. Barrett in turn strongly
supported the textile strike of 1921. At a critical stage in
that strike, the defeated craft element released an anonymous
report from Raleigh implying that the craft unionists were
unsympathetic to the textile strikers. The report predicted
the annihilation of the textile union and conspicuously
failed to criticize the governor for sending troops; moreover,
it hinted that the craft unions would withdraw from the state
federation if the textile workers won their strike. It
seemed to the textile workers that the crafts were willing to
crush the strike even at the cost of wrecking the federation,
but the tactic seems to have worked: the strike was broken,
and the craft unionists regained control of the state federation at its 1922 convention.[34]

The Southern textile union movement was seriously wounded
after its 1921 defeat and the concurrent internecine disputes.
Small strikes occurred during the next few years in Charlotte,
Wilmington, and other towns; and some organizational attempts
were made by the AFL and the UTW,[35] but it was not until 1927
that union activity returned to the Piedmont on a large scale.
In August, of that year, a major strike occurred in Henderson,
North Carolina, over the failure of the Coopers, owners of
the Harriet Mill, to restore a 12.5 percent wage cut made in

1924.[36] As often happened, the strike began spontaneously,
and the union joined the activity shortly thereafter. On
August 13, a group of unionists headed by Alfred Hoffman of
the Hosiery Workers and T. A. Wilson of the State Federation
of Labor arrived and immediately began to sign up workers on
behalf of the UTW. Within a week, over 500 had signed application cards; but their efforts proved futile. On August 30,
management played its trump card and served eviction notices
on a number of strikers living in company houses. Without
Hoffman's approval or any formal authorization by the strikers, an ad hoc committee of workers agreed to resume work if
the eviction notices were canceled. On September 4, about
25 percent of the workers returned to work; and by September 10, the strike was over. Typically, the UTW made no effort to keep a local in town and abandoned the area.

The Henderson strike did have one positive effect on union
organization, in that it marked a new round of activity in
the South. During the strike, President Green of the AFL ex-
pressed his concern by writing an editorial in the American
Federationist on "Organization in North Carolina." The North
Carolina Federation of Labor sponsored the "Southern Summer
School for Women in Industry" at Burnsville in 1927, and
Hoffman of the Hosiery Workers set up the Piedmont Organizing
Council at Durham in 1928. The latter served as the stimulus
for a similar organization in Virginia, the Tidewater Labor
Conference.[37]

By April 1928, the interest of a number of North Carolina
unions led to a conference at AFL headquarters to discuss a
Piedmont campaign. The argument of the North Carolina leaders that worsening conditions in the textile industry would
afford great organizational opportunities was met with a
promise to assign an organizer if the federation "could find
one." President Green concluded by advising the delegation
that the AFL was willing to extend all possible assistance
short of financial help.[38]

Delegates from six Southern states met in Chattanooga during
October 1928 to continue discussion of an organizational campaign for the industrial workers, and the AFL convention the
next month in New Orleans adopted a resolution committing the
organization to call a conference of "organizations interested in organizing in the South and officers of state federations in the South in the near future to work out cooperation on problems in Southern campaigns." The AFL Executive
Council decided to hold this instruction "in abeyance until
the time was ripe to hold a conference." President Green informed the Executive Council in February 1929 that he had
made two speaking trips South to "help in developing a
healthy public opinion in support of cooperation and ...
cause a large number of influential men to look with a
greater degree of favor upon the A.F. of L."[39] Green's

statement reflects a difference of approach that seriously
handicapped Southern unions. While those unions viewed
strikes as the only effective weapon for protecting wages and
working conditions, Green seemed to believe that interruption
of production was an economic waste to be avoided at almost
any cost.

The year 1929 represented the peak of textile union activity
in the first third of the twentieth century, yet that activity came largely to naught. In light of the nineteenth- and
early twentieth-century experiences, an examination of the
year's three largest strikes -- Elizabethton, Gastonia, and
Marion -- reveals a thoughtless repetition of previous mis-
takes. Clearly, the textile unions had learned little from
the past. Poor planning, rash action, lack of financial support, internal feuds, and shortsighted settlements -- all
these doomed the 1929 strikes as they had earlier ones.

The first and largest of the 1929 strikes occurred outside
the Piedmont but is important because it set the pattern for
subsequent strikes within that area.[40] The German-owned
Bemberg-Glanzstaff Company operated two relatively new, efficient, and profitable rayon plants at Elizabethton, Tennessee.
A strike broke out in March over the twin evils of low wages
and the stretch-out, taking the UTW by surprise, perhaps because the local had been inactive for some time. After the
strike started, a new local with some 2,000 members was hast-
ily organized under the leadership of Paul Ayman, president
of the Tennessee Federation of Labor. The first Elizabethton
strike failed in confusion after a settlement was made, repu-
diated, reinstated, and ultimately ignored. Massive dis-
charges of union members and other violations of the settlement (including the kidnapping by local businessmen of
Hosiery Workers organizer Alfred Hoffman and AFL representative Edward McGrady) brought about a second strike that was
marked by massive defiance of a court injunction, dynamitings,
and agitation by members of the left-wing National Textile
Workers.[41]

With 5,000 workers to provide with relief, the Elizabethton
local was faced with enormous financial problems. The Emergency Committee for Strikers Relief collected thousands of
dollars, and the UTW itself spent heavily from its own meager
treasury, but the AFL maintained an indifferent attitude.
The federation did not even send out appeals for funds until
the second strike was well under way and the union was facing
a crisis. The AFL was more concerned with gaining the good
favor and assistance of the newly elected lieutenant governor
of New York, Herbert H. Lehman of the banking family that
financed the $14.5 million Elizabethton venture. Although
Lehman complied with an AFL request of May 1 that he urge the
Elizabethton management to deal with the strikers, his appeal
was rejected.

Without AFL financial support, the strike was bound to fail.
In a one-sided settlement worked out by Anna Weinstock, a
young Department of Labor mediator, the company agreed not to
discriminate against union members, "provided the employee's
activities were legitimate and were not carried on in the
plants." Much was made of an "impartial person" who would
act as final judge of discharge grievances. The fate of any
such dispute was preordained by the designation of E. T.
Willison, the mill's personnel manager, as the "impartial
person." Willison proceeded to blacklist hundreds of union
supporters and set up an "employees" shop organization which
took over the functions of the UTW but excluded union members.[42]

In the midst of the Elizabethton affair, one of the strangest
strikes in American history occurred in Gastonia, North Carolina.[43] The Loray Mill there was similar in some respects to
the sites of other textile strikes -- absentee ownership,
long hours, low wages, the stretch-out -- but differed in one
fundamental respect: it had been secretly organized by the
Communist-controlled National Textile Workers Union (NTW).
The NTW had carefully selected its target. "North Carolina
is the key to the South, Gaston County is the key to North
Carolina, and the Loray Mill is the key to Gaston County,"
said one spokesman. A small but determined group of NTW
organizers led by Fred Beal quickly built an underground
organization.[44]

From the outset of the strike, the Gastonia establishment focused upon Communism and the union's favorable stance toward
racial equality as the primary issues. The real issues were
painfully clear to the workers if not to management; some of
the worst conditions in the Carolinas prevailed at Gastonia.
A poorly maintained mill village, a series of wage cuts, and
a back-breaking stretch-out did more to bring about a strike
than did the NTW. More specifically, the unrest at Gastonia
was due largely to the actions of a previous mill superintendent who in late 1927 had reduced the work force from 3,500
to 2,200, implemented two wage cuts, and reduced costs by a
half-million dollars annually. Although this eventually resulted in some limited strike action and the superintendent's
replacement in November 1928, no positive action was taken to
resolve the situation or to improve conditions for remaining
workers.[45]

The 1929 strike began on April 1 following the discharge of
five union members. Four days later, Governor Gardner sent
in five companies of the state militia. This action was
taken at the request of mill owners after a striker and a
policeman engaged in a tug-of-war over a rope used to restrain strikers from the mill area. Local courts quickly issued sweeping injunctions against all union activity. When
these injunctions were violated, strikers were clubbed and

beaten in the streets and taken to jail en masse. Although
the strike was lost soon after it started, the NTW and its
leaders continued their activities for propaganda purposes
for several months.[46]

The opposition was as little concerned with the underlying
issues as the NTW. The local paper, the Gastonia Gazette,
joined with the business community, police, ministers, and
even the AFL in denouncing the strike. In the Gazette's
words, it hoped to save the community from the union of
"negro lovers, against America, free love, northern agitators,
Russian Reds." Even a Department of Labor mediator, Charles
Wood, declared that this "was not a strike but a revolt," and
that settlement was inconceivable until "the workers divorce
themselves from their communistic leaders."[47] The situation
became even more heated when articles about the strike from
the Communist Daily Worker were republished and "interpreted"
in the Gazette. Faced with this barrage, workers began to
abandon the NTW; and by April 15, the mill was back in full
operation. Mob violence took its toll on the remaining
strikers, and the Gazette urged more of the same. The union
struggled for another few weeks, until an outbreak of violence resulted in the death of Police Chief O. F. Aderholt
and the wounding of a striker and two policemen. A hundred
strikers were arrested, and all remaining NTW local support
evaporated. Bitter feelings continued throughout the summer;
and on September 13, an armed mob took revenge, forcing a
truck full of strikers off the road and shooting Ella May
Wiggins, mother of five and minstrel to the strikers. With
that, the strike ended.[48]

Gastonia, too, influenced union prospects in the Piedmont,
although far differently from Elizabethton. One very direct
effect was to end NTW activity in the South. In addition,
the strike added the specific fear of Communism to the undif-
ferentiated dislike of unions in the Piedmont. In its own
way, the NTW was just as foreign to the Southern textile
worker as the stretch-out or the craft feelings of the UTW.
In each case, outside forces simply used the textile worker
for their own purposes.

The third major strike, in Marion, North Carolina, contained
many of the same elements: absentee ownership, insensitive
management, and the stretch-out.[49] The Marion Manufacturing
Company ran a large mill in East Marion, with net assets of
well over $1 million. The company was financed primarily by
Baltimore capital; and its president, R. W. Baldwin, a Baltimore resident, spent only a few days each week in North Carolina. Although the mill workers were upset about low wages
(averaging $14 weekly) and long hours (sixty per week), the
immediate cause of the first strike at Marion was an inept
attempt by management to introduce the stretch-out. The number of looms attended by one person was increased as much as

100 percent without any increase in pay. The strike began
when the company officials bungled the introduction of the
stretch-out, ruining $40,000 worth of material. Management
then informed the workers that they would be required to work
an additional twenty minutes per day to make up for the loss.
The workers resisted and sent a delegation to Elizabethton
for help, returning with Alfred Hoffman of the Hosiery Workers.

On advice of UTW President McMahon, Hoffman attempted to
organize secretly and prevent a general strike; but when he
arrived in Marion on July 10, he found himself in the awkward
position of being unable either to prevent or to win a strike.
On July 11, twenty-two workers were fired for union activity.
In spite of Hoffman's warning that "there isn't a cent of
money for relief," the workers decided upon a showdown. A
protest committee was ridiculed by Baldwin when they demanded
reinstatement of the discharged workers and adjustment of
other grievances. After a brief consultation with Hoffman,
the entire work force of 650 walked out.[50]

Hoffman faced an impossible situation: he was already be-
sieged with requests for help from mills throughout North
Carolina and was a representative of the Hosiery Workers
organizing a UTW local as part of an AFL plan to organize the
South, but he received little help from any of the three
organizations. He was forced to wage a defensive battle;
thus, to keep relief costs down, he was forced to dissuade
other workers in Marion from joining the strike. Apparently
sensing the union's weakness, the management of a second mill
in Marion first fired 100 union members and then locked out
its entire work force in early August. The escalation continued when the UTW responded with an official strike order,
and the managers closed both mills.

The company obtained an injunction after some minor picket
line scuffles, and the militia was brought in briefly on
August 19. On August 28, a group of strikers removed the
furniture of a strikebreaker who had moved into the house of
an evicted striker and drove off deputy sheriffs with clubs
and stones. As a result of this incident, 148 strikers, including Hoffman, were arrested and charged with rebellion
against the State of North Carolina. The charge was later
reduced to rioting but resulted, on October 1, in conviction.
Hoffman was sentenced to pay a fine of $1,000, and serve
thirty days in jail. The three other defendants were sentenced to six months on the chain gang.

The militia was brought in again on September 1. Facing the
ever present shortage of funds, the injunction, pending legal
action against Hoffman, and the presence of the militia, the
union was forced to negotiate a settlement. A conference between management and representatives of the UTW, the North

Carolina Federation of Labor, and others resulted in a "gentlemen's agreement" ending the strike on September 11. The settlement granted the workers a fifty-five-hour week with a corresponding reduction in pay and a guarantee of nondiscrimination against workers for union activity.

It quickly became clear that mill owner Baldwin was not honoring the agreement; more than 100 union workers had been refused reinstatement. A second strike broke out in the early morning of October 2, and a large crowd remained to inform the day shift of the strike. Near dawn, Sheriff Oscar F. Adkins commanded the strikers to disperse and called for tear gas when they refused. A lame, sixty-eight-year-old striker named Jonas then attacked the sheriff with his cane; and the deputies opened fire, first shooting Jonas and then firing wildly into the crowd. Six strikers, including Jonas, were killed and eighteen wounded; one deputy was slightly injured.[51]

The New York Times reported that the "Marion massacre" outraged the responsible people and the press of the state, but Baldwin showed little remorse: "I read that the death of each soldier in the World War consumed more than five tons of lead. Here we have less than five pounds and these casualties. A good average, I call it."[52] Governor Gardner sent Judge W. F. Harding to conduct an inquiry. On October 3, Adkins and fourteen deputies were arrested for murder, but all were quickly released. With the strike still in effect, UTW Vice-President F. G. Gorman came to Marion to help settle the dispute. Baldwin remained adamant, announced his intention to recruit a nonunion work force, and immediately evicted strikers from company housing. The pastor of the East Marion Baptist Church delivered what some regarded as the decisive blow, notifying about 100 strikers of their removal from the church rolls. The totality of the union's failure was revealed by the acquittal of Sheriff Adkins and his deputies on December 22 so that, in the words of one juryman, "they could go home for Christmas." By then the Marion strike was a fading memory.[53] At least one organizer felt that the UTW could have built a stable organization at Marion with additional money and manpower; without either, the union collapsed with the strike, as it had in so many other towns.[54]

Many other strikes in 1929 followed the Elizabethton pattern, but several in the South Carolina Piedmont diverged from that pattern widely enough to deserve separate comment. The South Carolina strikes began in late March with a walkout of 800 employees at the Ware Shoals Manufacturing Company. Within three weeks, 8,000 workers at fifteen mills were affected.[55] The objective of the strikes was familiar: abolition of the stretch-out. These strikes were notable for their brevity, lack of violence, and rejection of outside organizers. The

only danger of violence came at Ware Shoals, where AFL organizers were threatened by nonunion strikers. On at least two
other occasions, UTW offers of assistance were rejected.
More notable still was the success of the strikes. At Ware
Shoals and Pelzer, the management agreed to abandon the
stretch-out; and before the end of April, all but four of the
Piedmont strikes were successfully concluded. The remaining
strikes were settled by May 19, with demands granted for adjustment of grievances by committee action, reemployment
without discrimination, and new wage scales to compensate for
increased work under the stretch-out.[56]

The South Carolina experience differed from that of other
states in a number of ways. First, most of the South Carolina mills were relatively small and locally owned, in contrast with the predominantly large and foreign-owned Tennessee and North Carolina operations. Mill managers did not reject worker delegations and modified or abandoned the
stretch-out rather than obstinately refusing to compensate.

Second, the workers themselves kept the issues and personal-
ities local and thus avoided such complicating factors as
"outside agitators" and ideology. As one contemporary observer concluded:

> the truth is that not one of these strikes could
> have been won if conventional strike tactics and
> union organizers had been used. The presence of
> an outside labor leader would have challenged that
> philosophy of class partnership which is the corner-
> stone of South Carolina life. For the time being
> the weakness of these leaderless strikes is their
> strength.[57]

Third, the South Carolina workers had a degree of political
influence denied to other Piedmont textile operatives. As
early as 1921, South Carolina limited factories to a fifty-
five-hour week, the only Southern state to do so. In 1929,
it was the only state to conduct a legislative investigation
of workers' grievances. That study was led by a former textile worker, Olin D. Johnson (later governor and United
States senator). The legislative report strongly favored the
workers and found that mill owners had provoked the strikes
by "putting more on the employees than they can do."[58] In
short, the South Carolina strikes were successful in part because the local business and political conditions were more
favorable to the workers, but also because the strikers did
not rely on ill-equipped outside forces to lead them.

The AFL's failure to take advantage of the 1929 wave of
Southern strikes brought it much criticism. A. J. Muste of
Brookwood Labor College was "puzzled and disappointed" by the
way the strikes had been conducted, for example, and Norman

Thomas wrote to President Green during the Marion strike
charging that the strike "has got little but kind words" from
the organized labor movement. Green defended the AFL by noting that over $19,000 had been raised for the South and stat-
ing that he had given "all the support I could through correspondence and assigned representatives."[59] In the late summer and early fall of 1929, textile unions and Southern state
federations of labor demanded that the AFL undertake a new
Southern campaign. Finally, after the "Marion massacre," the
AFL convention voted unanimous approval of a UTW resolution
authorizing the officers of the federation to seek voluntary
contributions and to call a conference of the international
unions to plan the campaign.[60] President Green issued an invitation to all 105 national unions to meet in Washington,
D.C., on November 14, 1929, to work out a policy for an organizational campaign. A sizable group responded to the invitation only to hear the usual excuses regarding the failure
of Southern organizing campaigns. The meeting soon digressed
into a discussion of organizing tactics; Southern delegates
advocated militancy and Northern officials argued for a
"quiet business-like procedure by which the union idea is
first sold to the boss in the office." It was subsequently
decided that William C. Birthright, Francis Gorman, and Paul
Smith would lead the Southern organizing campaign and would
open an office in Birmingham, Alabama. The immediate objectives of the campaign were to be the forty-eight-hour week,
higher wages, and the abolition of night work. The campaign
began with an organizational meeting in Charlotte, North
Carolina, in January 1930; about 229 delegates and organizers
from the AFL, national unions, and local craft unions attended.[61]

From the start, the Southern campaign was somewhat schizo-
phrenic. President Green spoke throughout the South trying
to sell his cooperationist approach, which was known as the
Pequot Plan. That plan envisioned that in return for wages
which were to be slightly higher than those of nonunion com-
petitors, the union would agree to deliver more efficient
production and to cooperate with management to reduce production costs, even at the price of a reduced work force. Under
the plan, no strike would be permitted until after two months
of conferences. If the workers went on strike before then,
the AFL pledged to help break the strike. Green also included a mild threat in his talks, warning his listeners that
"either we will speak for the Southern worker or the Communists will assume that function."[62] By contrast with Green's
approach, the UTW was conducting a traditional organizational
campaign, using strikes as well as persuasion. It supervised
its own affairs but took whatever help it could get from the
AFL. The UTW met with some success, particularly in Virginia
and the northern part of North Carolina and the more southern
areas of South Carolina, Georgia, and Alabama. But from
Elizabethton, Tennessee, through Gastonia, North Carolina, to

Greenville, South Carolina, there were few encouraging signs.

Considering the tremendous publicity given to the campaign, the results were minimal. The official report presented at the AFL convention in the fall of 1930 claimed that a total of 112 locals had been organized, of which thirty-one were in the textile industry. Because a voluntary contribution scheme had failed, the financially strapped UTW proposed that the AFL institute a special per capita tax to underwrite the campaign. The motion failed when the carpenters' delegate refused to give the unanimous consent required.

The differing organizational approaches of the UTW and the AFL reflected the continuing battles between craft and industrial unionists. The potential for conflict burst forth and led to defeat at the major strike of the 1930 campaign. Ironically, the defeat was at Danville, Virginia, where the IUTW had succumbed in 1901. As the earlier struggle had signaled the death of the IUTW and ushered in a decade without significant union activity, the 1930 battle strengthened the forces that would ultimately split the UTW and end union activity in the South until the New Deal.

The Riverside and Dan River Mills Company was, in 1930, one of the oldest and largest of the Southern textile firms, with 4,000 workers in a dozen plants. The company operated two facilities in the Danville area, one along the river in the heart of the town and another in the village of Schoolfield.[63] Unlike the scenes of the 1929 strikes, ownership and operation of the mills were in the hands of a local family, the Fitzgeralds. By Southern standards, the company was a model employer, and the Fitzgeralds were decidedly paternal in their concern for employees. Employees enjoyed higher wages and a shorter workweek than average and a welfare plan offering medical care, life insurance, social workers, and a YMCA. Since 1919, there had been an employee representation plan at Danville patterned after the United States Constitution.[64]

The dispute began in January 1930. Faced with a major drop in profits, President H. R. Fitzgerald instituted a moderate stretch-out and proposed a 10 percent wage cut to the company "legislature." The "senate" (composed of supervisors) accepted the wage cut, but industrial democracy broke down when the "house" (composed of representatives of the workers) rejected the proposal. Apparently shocked by this rejection, Fitzgerald abolished the representation plan, cut wages unilaterally, and eliminated overtime pay and pay for work stoppages due to lack of material.[65]

A local of the Loom Fixer's Association had existed at the plants since 1919. After the wage cut was announced, it sent a delegation to Richmond, where President Green was appearing

as part of his Southern speaking tour. Green in turn notified the UTW, which sent Frank Gorman to take charge. Assisted by Matilda Lindsay, a representative of the Women's
Trade Union League, Gorman immediately began to organize UTW
Local No. 1685. The union held its first public meeting on
February 9, and the response was overwhelming. By March 26,
the UTW local claimed 3,000 members. But Gorman did not want
to fight one of the better Southern employers. His purpose
was to organize, to set up the basis for future action, and
to test the reaction of the company. Anne McCormick, a correspondent for the New York Times, described the situation:
"The issue is joined between the old system at its best and
the workers trained under that system groping toward a new
system."[66]

The obvious difficulty with Gorman's approach was that unless
it could secure results, it would be no improvement over the
defunct industrial democracy. When the company began dis-
charging union workers, the situation turned into a tactical
standoff. The UTW drained its treasury to support the discharged workers while trying to restrain the other employees.
The company was experiencing a decrease in demand and was
therefore under no pressure to satisfy the union. Despite
increasing acts of discrimination, Gorman kept control for
several months. In March, Gorman had said that the local was
"facing its first real test as a no-strike union"; but by
August, the total of discharged unionists reached 2,500, and
Gorman had had enough. On September 9, he announced the end
of the no-strike pledge, stating "the time has come to move
against the enemy."[67]

On September 29, 4,000 workers walked out of the Danville
plants without the financial support of the UTW and against
the orders of the AFL, which still insisted on its cooperationist approach. Although the company immediately obtained
injunctions against mass picketing, the strike was entirely
peaceful. The strikers enjoyed wide support in the community;
and for many, it was like a holiday. Matilda Lindsay described the early days as "more like a picnic than a labor
war." As the days wore on, the weakness of the union's position became obvious. It cost about $1,000 daily to feed the
strikers and their families, and the UTW even stopped solic-
iting the local merchants since "Everybody is like we are --
broke." A local paper, the Bee, bitterly joked that even
"Old Man Hoar Frost" was an accomplice of the company. When
the temperature dropped to 28 degrees on October 22, "it was
a ruthless attack with little comfort in it for those men
loyal to union principles and doing post duty." Nor was comfort to be obtained from the AFL or Fitzgerald. The AFL convention in Boston rejected Green's appeal for a special levy
to finance the strike and settled instead for token voluntary
contributions. Fitzgerald repeatedly rejected offers of mediation, declaring flatly that "there is absolutely nothing

to mediate."[68]

With union funds scarce, the solidarity of the strikers began
to break; again, lack of support from fellow unionists doomed
a major strike. In self-defense, UTW supporters attempted to
shift the blame to the AFL. Norman Thomas, for example,
wrote that "frankly, we cannot acquit the A.F. of L. of blame
for not being prepared to meet this emergency which was bound
to arise in an organizing campaign."[69] As the union lines
broke, attacks on strikebreakers and other acts of violence
increased. An attempt to reopen the mill on November 24
brought mass picketing and further acts of violence, which
forced a reluctant Governor J. G. Pollard to order 900 state
militia to Schoolfield.

Renewed attempts by third parties to settle the strike were
rejected by Fitzgerald. Governor Pollard himself suggested
mediation but felt that unless both sides accepted his offer,
any action he could take would be considered "by one side or
the other, and perhaps both, as exhibiting partiality."[70]
President Green virtually surrendered in December when he
asked Fitzgerald to allow the workers to return without discrimination, but again there was no response. Green again
appealed to the Executive Council for its support; but that
body, apparently still miffed that the strike had been called
against its advice, refused to take any action. Green himself rejected the suggestion of the Southern Organizing Committee that another all-Southern conference be called, saying
that such an action would be "unwise and unnecessary" since
some "effective work" was being done in Georgia and South
Carolina through his cooperationist approach.[71]

By the new year, the strike was obviously beaten. The UTW
perhaps could have salvaged something by surrendering with
dignity and maintaining its organization; instead, Gorman
chose to save face. On January 28, 1931, he announced that
Fitzgerald had been honoring a "principle of labor" by "taking old employees back into the mills in considerable numbers
without raising the question of union membership," and that
the necessity of the strike therefore no longer existed. On
the following day Gorman left town.[72]

This was of course completely false. Indeed, Gorman's statement must have shocked Fitzgerald, who had thought he was
simply crushing a strike and suddenly found himself praised
for honoring "a principle of labor." Gorman's misleading
statement destroyed whatever credibility the union had, for
union members crowded around the gates the next morning only
to find that the company refused to take them back. Fitzgerald heatedly denied any nondiscrimination agreement, and
the press used his denial to ridicule the union for deceiving
the workers. Even the NTW attempted to capitalize on the
failure of the UTW, sending organizers to Danville who

promised to "expose the sell-out ... by the AFL Gorman outfit" and to collect information on "everything these fakers
did in selling us workers out."[73]

The Danville disaster and the worsening depression combined
to kill the Southern campaign. Danville cost the unions
$200,000 and drained their treasuries.[74] The strike was ex-
pensive for the company as well; but this, too, ultimately
hurt the workers, who found themselves unemployed. More important by far was the effect of the strike on other textile
workers. As Lorwin concluded:

> The workers asked why they should join a union that
> had shown itself incapable of supporting the promis-
> ing beginnings made by mill workers themselves. They
> had expected real aid from the AFL and attributed its
> failures to extend such aid to weakness and timidity.[75]

The Southern organizing campaign remained technically alive
until 1935, but there was little activity after Danville. A
series of North Carolina strikes in 1932 were primarily local
affairs, with little instigation or assistance from the UTW
or the AFL. The Birmingham office of the AFL closed that
year, though several presidents of state federations were retained as organizers. By early 1935, even these were dropped
from the payroll. The failure of the UTW was so widespread
that it took the powerful outside force of Roosevelt's New
Deal and a new organization, the Textile Workers Organizing
Committee, to rejuvenate the union movement in Piedmont textiles.

                              III

It is hard to avoid the conclusion that whatever the strength
of outside forces, the workers and their organizers were
often their own worst enemies. Time and again, burgeoning
union movements were crushed by poor preparation, lack of
strategy, internal divisions, inept leadership, and refusal
of those with a stake in the dispute (especially Northern
textile unions and the AFL) to support the striking workers.

That conclusion is reinforced when one looks at the other
reasons usually given for textile unionism's lack of success.
The textile industry suffers from the same erratic market
forces now as fifty years ago; but with that exception, the
other hindrances to unionization are less serious today. The
labor injunction barely exists, the federal government pro-
tects the right to organize, governors no longer dispatch the
militia to break strikes, and community opposition to unions
is no longer as strong as it once was. If those were the
primary deterrents to unionization before 1932, one would
have expected a drastic increase in union strength in the
Piedmont. Nothing of the sort has occurred, indicating that

the internal problems discussed above have not been cured and
that they remain sufficient to defeat attempts at organization.   To rephrase the argument, textile unionism will be unable to solve the problems of the Piedmont until it solves
its own.

Notes

[1] See, for example, F. Ray Marshall, Labor in the South
(Cambridge, Mass., 1967), 71-85, 101-33; Irving Bernstein,
The Lean Years: A History of the American Worker, 1920-
1933 (Baltimore, 1966), 1-43; Herbert J. Lahne, The Cotton
Mill Worker (New York, 1944), 175-239, and especially
240-60; and Glenn Gilman, Human Relations in the Industrial
Southeast: A Study of the Textile Industry (Chapel Hill,
1956), 288-317.

[2] The Piedmont is defined as "a plateau between the coastal
plain and the Appalachian mountains, including parts of
Virginia, North Carolina, South Carolina, Georgia and Ala-
bama." Random House Dictionary of the English Language
(New York, 1971). The Piedmont represents the heart of the
Southern textile industry today, as it did a century ago.
In 1860, the main Piedmont states (all except Virginia)
contained 60 percent of the total Southeastern spindlage.
This figure dropped briefly to 48 percent after the Civil
War but increased steadily thereafter to 88 percent in
1923. It is impossible to determine the distribution of
spindles between the Piedmont and Coastal Plain areas of
those states, but a relatively recent survey indicated that
95.2 percent of Georgia's spindles were located in its
Piedmont region. We estimate that figures for the other
states would not differ radically. See Gilman, Human Relations in the Industrial Southeast, 105. Gilman provides an
excellent background discussion of the Piedmont on pages 27
to 124. See also John K. Morland, Millways of Kent (Chapel
Hill, 1958), vii, 11.

[3] Ernest McPherson Lander, Jr., The Textile Industry in Ante-
bellum South Carolina (Baton Rouge, 1969), 13-28. See also
Gilman, Human Relations in the Industrial Southeast, 85-87;
and Rupert B. Vance, Human Geography of the South (Chapel

Hill, 1932), 42-46.

4 Harry M. Douty, "The North Carolina Industrial Worker, 1880-1930" (Ph.D. diss., University of North Carolina, 1936), 9; Richard W. Griffin, "Reconstruction of the North Carolina Textile Industry, 1865-1885," North Carolina Historical Review 41 (Winter 1964), 39-40; and Herbert Collins, "The Idea of the Cotton Textile Industry in the South, 1870-1900," North Carolina Historical Review, 34 (July 1957), 363.

5 Writing under the pseudonym South Carolina, Gregg published a series of articles entitled "Essays on Domestic Industry" in the Charleston Courier in 1844 describing the advantages of manufacturing and criticizing those who opposed it. The articles were quickly and widely reprinted across the South. Their effect was so great that one authority credits Gregg as being "almost wholly responsible" for the mills opened during that decade. Broadus Mitchell, The Rise of the Cotton Mills in the South (Baltimore, 1921), 42-43.

6 Gilman, Human Relations in the Industrial Southeast, 74; Marshall, Labor in the South, 12; and Collins, "The Idea of the Cotton Textile Industry," 358-70.

7 Certainly the profit motive was a factor in these public-spirited efforts, but a broader concern was a desire to salvage the decaying community and provide employment for the thousands of white farmers displaced by the Civil War and agricultural depression. W. J. Cash, The Mind of the South (New York, 1941), 178; Gilman, Human Relations in the Industrial Southeast, 81; and George Mitchell and Broadus Mitchell, The Industrial Revolution in the South (Baltimore, 1930), 30-33.

8 Local ownership was guaranteed by the success of the mills, which alleviated the chronic capital shortage of the region, and by the fact that Northern mills used surplus capital to expand existing mills rather than building new plants in the South. As late as 1922, a study concluded that 84 percent of Southern spindlage was owned or controlled by Southern capital. Lahne, The Cotton Mill Worker, 89.

9 Gilman, Human Relations in the Industrial Southeast, 107-109, 114; and Lahne, The Cotton Mill Worker, 90-91.

10 Gilman, Human Relations in the Industrial Southeast, 190-92.

11 Ibid., 194; Morland, Millways of Kent, ix, 174-77; and Liston Pope, Millhands and Preachers (New Haven, 1942), 67-69.

12 Cf. Melton A. McLaurin, Paternalism and Protest: Southern

Cotton Mill Workers and Organized Labor, 1875-1905 (Westport, Conn., 1971), pass.

[13] Norman J. Ware, The Labor Movement in the United States,
1860-1895: A Study in Democracy (Gloucester, Mass., 1959),
29, 157-59, 164.

[14] Robert R. R. Brooks, "The United Textile Workers of America" (Ph.D. diss., Yale University, 1935), 32. Although
there are no accurate figures on the number of cotton mill
workers who joined the Knights, there were at least 121
trade assemblies with membership from cotton mills. Of
these, twenty-two were in the South. Herbert J. Lahne,
"Labor in the Cotton Mills, 1865-1900" (M.A. thesis,
Columbia University, 1937), 166; Lahne, The Cotton Mill
Worker, 183.

[15] One North Carolina newspaper of the time charged that
"there can be little doubt that many who join the Knights
of Labor are activated by no special concern for working
men, but rather by a desire for personal gain. Some wish
the trade of the Knights of Labor and others seek votes."
Quoted in Harley E. Jolley, "The Labor Movement in North
Carolina, 1880-1922," North Carolina Historical Review 30
(July 1953), 359. On the same subject, see also Douty,
"The North Carolina Industrial Worker," 256; and Melton A.
McLaurin, "The Knights of Labor in North Carolina Politics," North Carolina Historical Review 49 (July 1972),
298. According to Professor McLaurin, author of a forthcoming book on the Knights in the South, Knights in the
coastal areas of Georgia actively engaged in political activity, although those in the Piedmont generally did not.
Interview with Professor McLaurin, April 2, 1976.

[16] See generally, William W. Whatley, "A History of the Textile Development of Augusta, Georgia, 1865 to 1883" (M.S.
thesis, University of South Carolina, 1964); and Merl E.
Reed, "The Augusta Textile Mills and the Strike of 1886,"
Labor History 14 (Spring 1973), 228.

[17] John Wesley Kennedy, "A History of the Textile Workers
Union of America, CIO" (Ph.D. diss., University of North
Carolina), 44; Lahne, The Cotton Mill Worker, 184.

[18] Samuel Gompers, Seventy Years of Life and Labor: An Auto-
biography (New York, 1967), vol. 1, 418-20; Mitchell, The
Rise of the Cotton Mills in the South, 172; and Lahne, The
Cotton Mill Worker, 185.

[19] Lahne, The Cotton Mill Worker, 187-88.

[20] Cf. McLaurin, Paternalism and Protest, 134-40, 150, and
176.

21 The owners contended that the firm had lost money in 1901
   and that the market was just beginning to improve. There
   seemed to be some truth to the claim. The Augusta Chronicle, never an extremely antilabor paper, warned the operatives that they were going into the strike with a false
   sense of security. McLaurin, Paternalism and Protest, 188.
   McLaurin's treatment of the 1902-1903 period on pages 188
   through 192 is a thorough one and is relied on here except
   where otherwise noted.

22 Lahne, The Cotton Mill Worker, 189-90; and Thomas F.
   McMahon, United Textile Workers of America (New York,
   1926), 24.

23 Brooks, "The United Textile Workers of America," 295; and
   George S. Mitchell, Textile Unionism in the South (Chapel
   Hill, 1929), 30.

24 Lahne, The Cotton Mill Worker, 190; McMahon, United Textile Workers of America, 24-25; Jolley, "The Labor Movement in North Carolina," 359; and McLaurin, Paternalism
   and Protest, 192.

25 See generally, James O. Morris, Conflict Within the AFL:
   A Study of Craft Versus Industrial Unionism, 1901-1938
   (Ithaca, 1958); Philip S. Foner, History of the Labor
   Movement in the United States (New York, 1965), vol. 4,
   198, 242, 306-66; and Brooks, "The United Textile Workers
   of America," 221-29.

26 McMahon, United Textile Workers of America, 25, 29; and
   Lahne, The Cotton Mill Worker, 195-203. The union had
   also been under pressure from the AFL for a number of
   years to renew its organizational efforts. See, for example, Convention Proceedings, UTWA, 1906, 11, 14-16, as
   cited by Brooks, "The United Textile Workers of America,"
   136.

27 On the impact of the war on labor generally, see Leo
   Wolman, Ebb and Flow in Trade Unionism (New York, 1936),
   21-24. UTW activities in the South during the war are
   discussed in Douty, "The North Carolina Industrial Worker,"
   280; Robert W. Dunn and J. Hardy, Labor and Textiles (New
   York, 1931), 185-86; Lahne, The Cotton Mill Worker, 200-
   204; Mitchell, Textile Unionism in the South, 33; and
   George Brown Tindall, The Emergence of the New South,
   1913-1945 (Baton Rouge, 1967), 332.

28 Tindall, The Emergence of the New South, 69-71, 333; and
   Mitchell, Textile Unionism in the South, 42-57.

29 Lahne, The Cotton Mill Worker, 204-205; and Brooks, "The
   United Textile Workers of America," 295-303, 305.

[30] Mitchell, Textile Unionism in the South, 39-41; and Dunn
and Hardy, Labor and Textiles, 186-88.

[31] The North Carolina strikes of 1919 are discussed in a number of works. See, for example, Douty, "The North Carolina Industrial Worker," 280-83; and Brooks, "The United
Textile Workers of America," 305. The estimate of 30,000
new members was made by a questionable source, textile
organizer Marvin Ritch, at the 1919 convention of the
State Federation of Labor. Mitchell, Textile Unionism in
the South, 33-47. The figure is given some credence by an
independent estimate that the two Carolinas had a combined
membership of some 45,000 in sixty-seven locals. Page,
Southern Cotton Mills and Labor, 73, as cited by Jolley,
"The Labor Movement in North Carolina," 369. The News and
Observer editorial appeared on August 12, 1919, as quoted
by Jolley, on page 371.

[32] Lahne, The Cotton Mill Worker, 203-204, 207; McMahon,
United Textile Workers of America, 40; and Brooks, "The
United Textile Workers of America," 53-54, 320.

[33] UTW membership dropped by three-quarters, from 80,000 in
1920 to 21,000 in 1921, as a result of the depression and
resultant strikes. Lahne, The Cotton Mill Worker, 207-209;
Douty, "The North Carolina Industrial Worker," 284-87.

[34] Douty, "The North Carolina Industrial Worker," 285-86.

[35] Ibid., 300. North Carolina unionists had made repeated
pleas to the AFL for an organizing campaign. AFL Executive Council Minutes, October 1925, 20; April 24-May 2,
1928, 87, as cited by Marshall, Labor in the South, 103.
The most serious organizing during the period was conducted by Alfred Hoffman of the American Federation of Full
Fashioned Hosiery Workers, a UTW affiliate. Although the
Hosiery Workers was primarily a Northern union, it was
concerned about the threat unorganized Southern mills presented to union standards. Taylor, The Full Fashioned
Hosiery Workers, 83, as cited by Douty, "The North Carolina Industrial Worker," 299.

[36] The discussion of the Henderson strike that follows is
drawn primarily from reports in the Raleigh News and Observer, August 11-September 10, 1927. See also Mitchell,
Textile Unionism in the South, 61-62; and Douty, "The
North Carolina Industrial Worker," 300-303.

[37] The American Federationist editorial appeared in September
1927. The Burnsville School invited distinguished academ-
ics such as Frank Porter Graham, later president of the
University of North Carolina, to lecture the students.
See, for example, Graham's letters to Katherine Grantham,

November 4, 1929, and to David Clark, editor of the bitterly antiunion Southern Textile Bulletin, December 7,
1929, in the Frank Porter Graham Papers, no. 1819, Southern Historical Collection, University of North Carolina.
See also Douty, "The North Carolina Industrial Worker,"
303-304. On the Piedmont Organizing Council and similar
efforts, see Marshall, Labor in the South, 102-103; and
Lahne, The Cotton Mill Worker, 216.

38 Marshall, Labor in the South, 104.

39 AFL Convention Proceedings, 1928, Resolution 18; and AFL
Executive Council Minutes, February 18-25, 1929, 45-46; as
cited by Marshall, Labor in the South, 104-105.

40 Except as otherwise noted, the discussion of the Eliza-
bethton strike is based on the following works: Irving
Bernstein, The Lean Years (Baltimore, 1966), 13-20; Brooks,
"The United Textile Workers of America," 313-14; Marshall,
Labor in the South, 105-107; and Duane McCracken, Strike
Injunctions in the New South (Chapel Hill, 1931), 94-113.

41 The Charlotte Observer provided thorough coverage of the
strike. Of particular interest are the articles of
April 5, 8, and 15, 1929.

42 Anna Weinstock recalls that the agreement did not protect
union activities "in the plants," which is more favorable
for the union that "at the plants," which is the way the
contract is usually quoted. We have not been able to lo-
cate the original document to resolve the discrepancy.
She also recalls that the settlement was unanimously approved at a meeting of the strikers and that Willison came
with high recommendations for fairness. Some months after
his appointment, he informed her that he wanted to go easier on the union members but that the company had given
him no choice. Interview with Ms. Weinstock, April 1,
1976. This view is given some support by AFL President
Green's enthusiastic claim that "we have succeeded in having a liberal man [Willison] installed as personnel manager." AFL Executive Council Minutes, August 8-20, 1929,
73, as quoted by Marshall, Labor in the South, 107.

43 Except where otherwise noted, the discussion of the Gastonia strike relies on Bernstein, The Lean Years, 20-28
and Lahne, The Cotton Mill Worker, 216-19.

44 Quoted in Robin Hood, "The Loray Mill Strike" (M.A. thesis,
University of North Carolina, 1932), 33-34. Fred Beal's
father provided a biographical sketch of his son after
Beal had been arrested in connection with the shooting of
the Gastonia police chief. International Labor Defense
press release, Charlotte, N.C., June or July, 1929, in the

Gastonia _Gazette_ Papers, no. 3867, Southern Historical Collection, University of North Carolina. See also the younger Beal's _Proletarian Journey_ (New York, 1937), pass.

45 Gilman, _Human Relations in the Industrial Southeast_, 184-85; and Tindall, _The Emergence of the New South_, 344.

46 _The Charlotte Observer_, April 2 and 3, 1929; and Bernstein, _The Lean Years_, 22.

47 _The Gazette_ is quoted in Tom Tippett, _When Southern Labor Stirs_ (New York, 1931), 83. The _Gazette_'s bias prompted a number of critical letters to the editor, most of which never reached print. See, for example, the letters of Fred Beal, April 13, 1929; W. C. Davis, April 15, 1929; and "Your Friend," July 2, 1929; in the Gastonia _Gazette_ Papers, no. 3867, Southern Historical Collection, University of North Carolina. Wood is quoted by Marshall, _Labor in the South_, 113.

48 _The Charlotte Observer_, June 8, 1929. It seems clear from the reports of non-Communist observers that whatever the motives of the NTW organizers, the strikers themselves were little concerned with ideology and were, to the contrary, highly patriotic. Thus Frank Graham describes Ella Wiggins: "One hundred per cent Americanism was somewhere deep in the heart of this mother who went riding in a truck toward what to her was the promise of a better day for her children." Letter to Nell Battle Lewis, September 23, 1929, Frank Porter Graham Papers, no. 1819, Southern Historical Collection, University of North Carolina.

49 Much of the data on the Marion mills is compiled in vol. 85, no. 47 of _Information Service_, Federal Council of Churches (December 28, 1929), which is cited by McCracken, _Strike Injunctions in the New South_, 79-93. Other major sources relied on in the following discussion are Bernstein, _The Lean Years_, 29-32; Lahne, _The Cotton Mill Worker_, 219-21; Brooks, "The United Textile Workers of America," 315-16; and Tippett, _When Southern Labor Stirs_, pass. (Tippett was a union organizer at Marion, and his book is therefore more partisan than scholarly on this subject.)

50 Bernstein, _The Lean Years_, 30.

51 _New York Times_, October 3 and 4, 1929.

52 Ibid., October 5, 1929. Baldwin was quoted in the _Asheville Citizen_, October 4, 1929, as cited by Samuel Yellen, _American Labor Struggles_ (New York, 1936), 319.

53 The classic discussion of the influence of religious

leaders on textile labor disputes is Pope's <u>Millhands and
Preachers</u>, especially 145-61. On the verdict of the
Adkins trial, see Yellen, <u>American Labor Struggles</u>, 320.

54 Tippett, <u>When Southern Labor Stirs</u>, 163-65.

55 <u>The Charlotte Observer</u>, April 1-20, 1929, pass.; U.S. Department of Labor, Bureau of Labor Statistics, Bulletin
651, "Strikes in the U.S. 1880-1936"; and Marshall, <u>Labor
in the South</u>, 119.

56 Marshall, <u>Labor in the South</u>, 119; <u>New York Times</u>,
August 22, 1929; Brooks, "The United Textile Workers of
America," 317; Tindall, <u>The Emergence of the New South</u>,
350; and Yellen, <u>American Labor Struggles</u>, 304.

57 Paul Blanshard, "One Hundred Per Cent Americans on Strike,"
<u>The Nation</u>, May 8, 1929, 554.

58 Bernstein, <u>The Lean Years</u>, 33.

59 A. J. Muste, "A.F.L.'s Biggest Task," <u>Labor Age</u> (October
1929); letter of Norman Thomas, August 14, 1929; and AFL
Executive Council Minutes, August 8-20, 1929, 73, and
October 6, 12, and 18, 1929, all cited by Marshall, <u>Labor
in the South</u>, 122.

60 The 1930 campaign up to Danville is treated in Bernstein,
<u>The Lean Years</u>, 33-36; Marshall, <u>Labor in the South</u>,
123-24; Lewis L. Lorwin, <u>The American Federation of Labor:
Histories, Policies, and Prospects</u> (Washington, D.C.,
1933), 253-56; and Tippett, <u>When Southern Labor Stirs</u>,
179-90. The following discussion is chiefly drawn from
those works.

61 <u>The Textile Worker</u>, 1929, 10, and 1930, 111, 138, 267, 647;
and Bernstein, <u>The Lean Years</u>, 35. The January meeting is
reported in the <u>American Federationist</u>, February, 1930,
145.

62 <u>The Textile Worker</u> records Green's progress monthly in
vols. 17 and 18. Wherever he went, he was feted by local
businessmen and politicians, but he seems to have had
little in the way of concrete results. See, for example,
the reports of his visits to Alabama and
Danville, 18, no. 1 (April 1930), 41-42, and 18, no. 3
(June 1930), 144-48. See also Dunn and Hardy, <u>Labor and
Textiles</u>, 190-96; and Brooks, "The United Textile Workers
of America," 147-58.

63 The discussion of the Danville Strike is drawn chiefly
from Robert S. Smith, <u>Mill on the Dan</u> (Durham, 1960),
pass.; Marshall, <u>Labor in the South</u>, 125-30; Bernstein,

The Lean Years, 36-40; and Lorwin, The American Federation of Labor, 254-56.

[64] The representation plan had been established after company President H. R. Fitzgerald became concerned with organizational activity in Southern textiles. The theory of industrial democracy, modeled on the United States Constitution, had been espoused by John Leitch in Man to Man: The Story of Industrial Democracy (New York, 1919). The book so impressed Fitzgerald that he bought 100 copies to distribute to employees and friends. Smith, Mill on the Dan, 263, 272-76; and The Textile Worker 18, no. 1 (April 1930), 31-33.

[65] The defection of the workers was a personal tragedy for President Fitzgerald. He was "drinking the hemlock," he told a New York Times correspondent. New York Times Magazine, June 15, 1930, as quoted by Smith, Mill on the Dan, 307.

[66] Gorman explained his strategy in his official report to the UTW, printed in The Textile Worker 18, no. 6 (September 1930), 345-55; New York Times Magazine, June 15, 1930, quoted by Smith, Mill on the Dan, 307.

[67] Smith, Mill on the Dan, 310.

[68] Both Ms. Lindsay and the Bee are quoted in Smith, Mill on the Dan, 313 and 319.

[69] "Appeal for funds on behalf of the Emergency Committee for Strikers' Relief," printed in The Textile Worker 18, no. 8 (November 1930), 490.

[70] Letter of Governor Pollard to Dr. S. C. Mitchell, November 28, 1930, Samuel Chiles Mitchell Papers, no. 1003, Southern Historical Collection, University of North Carolina. The Mitchell papers contain numerous other letters indicating attempts to help by such groups as the YWCA (letter from Eleanor Copenhaven to Dr. Mitchell, December 17, 1930) and the American Friends Service Committee (letters of Clarence E. Pickett and his secretary to Dr. Mitchell, December 18, 24, and 27, 1930).

[71] Smith, Mill on the Dan, 314; Marshall, Labor in the South, 129.

[72] The Textile Worker 18, no. 12 (March 1931), 733.

[73] After Fitzgerald's death in February of 1931, Gorman repeatedly claimed that the two men had indeed made an agreement through an intermediary and that the company broke it. The Textile Worker 19, no. 1 (April 1931), 8,

and 19, no. 3 (June 1931), 106. Apparently there had been an understanding between two intermediaries, a mining company official on behalf of the union and a brother-in-law of Fitzgerald, but not a meeting of the principals. Ibid., 19, no. 3 (June 1931), 105, and no. 4 (July 1931), 152-57.

[74] The Textile Worker 19, no. 6 (September 1931), 270. Gorman's estimate was $150,000. Ibid., 20, no. 6 (September 1932), 192.

[75] Quoted in Marshall, Labor in the South, 130.

Unionism in the Southern Textile Industry: An Overview

Bruce Raynor

Writing in 1949, Mary Heaton Vorse, a noted labor and muck-
raking journalist, commented upon major changes in the South,
including the great gains in unionization of the region's
basic industry -- textiles: "But with 120,000 textile workers in eight Southern states under union contract -- out of
450,000 organized all over the country -- there is a nucleus
whose importance cannot be ignored." Vorse used Danville,
Virginia, as "exhibit number one":

> The situation in Danville has altered so much since
> 1931, that anyone who was [involved in those turbu-
> lent days] and saw how isolated from the community
> the workers were [can hardly believe his eyes]. It
> was shocking to perceive. The Textile Workers Union
> headquarters is on the main street of the town....
> The new status of these ten thousand union members
> signifies an economic change which means as much to
> the city as to themselves.[1]

Mary Vorse pictured progress with hope and confidence in a
brighter future. But today in Danville, Virginia, a broken
union remains with less than 200 members (of 10,000 mill
workers) who maintain union headquarters as a last bastion of
hope. The wages at Dan River are less than those at many
nonunion Southern mills, and the union is even too weak to
handle grievances. Fear prevails in these mills and in the
community, where the "lintheads" are once again second-class
citizens, ungrateful to the "rich and wise men" who give them
jobs. They are among the South's 650,000 nonunion textile
workers no longer counted as part of the union nucleus which
today numbers only 50,000. What happened to the workers in
Danville between 1949 and 1975 was not unique; it happened in
differing degrees throughout the South.

Shortly after the publication of Vorse's article, the great
shutdown of the unionized New England textile industry accelerated. Hundreds of mills went out of business or moved
South to the land of cheap labor, tax relief, and no unions.
In response to the beginning of this mass exodus, the Textile
Workers Union of America (TWUA), an affiliate of the Congress
of Industrial Organizations, struck most of the unionized
mills to raise wages nearer to New England levels. Dan River
workers initiated their 1951 strike with a strong local union,
but it ended with a broken organization. The defeat showed
Danville workers who held the real power in the South; and it
effectively disheartened them, forcing them to conclude that
even a strong union was no match for Dan River. Despite several strikes since then, including an unsuccessful ten-week
strike in 1974 and strenuous efforts on the part of local
leaders and the union, the situation has only been aggravated.
Even more humiliating, the company arrogantly forced the
union to forgo a wage increase granted the nonunion industry.
Strikes in such other unionized Southern plants as those of
Fieldcrest, Erwin, and Cone produced similar results. Obviously, Mary Vorse's optimistic prediction was not fulfilled.
In the remainder of this paper, I would like to identify some
of the sources of past frustration in textile organizing, to
assess the current state of labor relations in the industry,
and to project future trends in textile unionism.

THE PAST: A HOSTILE ENVIRONMENT

Past failures in the organization of Southern textile workers
are the product of varied circumstances, but three factors
appear especially significant in determining the fate of textile unionism in the South during the last quarter century:
(1) the effective (if illegal) antiunion tactics employed by
mill owners, (2) a hostile political climate, and (3) the
nature of the Southern labor force.

PREVENTIVE LABOR RELATIONS

Two law firms, one located in Charlotte, North Carolina, and
the other in Atlanta, Georgia, have developed a technique of
"preventive labor relations" that serves as a model for the
Southern textile industry. Virtually all major chain corporations and many large, unorganized mills employ their services.
This uniformity of company strategy has produced a script all
too familiar to the TWUA. Two companies, J. P. Stevens Corporation, the second largest textile company in the world, and
Wellman Industries, have used this strategy with such zeal
that their activities provide a case study of the industry's
pattern throughout the South.

J. P. Stevens employs about 46,000 workers in eighty plants,

almost all located in the Southeast.[2] In 1963, TWUA and the
Industrial Union Department (IUD) of the AFL-CIO launched a
major drive against Stevens in an effort to score an organizing breakthrough in a large Southern chain. This goal was
viewed as the first step in breaking the industry's conspiracy against unions.

During the initial union organizing campaign, Stevens's supervisors threatened that "J. P. will close this plant if it
goes union."[3] In addition, they attempted to harass union
supporters to prevent them from talking to other workers.
They threatened workers with discharge if they signed a union
card or worked for TWUA. All are unfair labor practices
under the provisions of the National Labor Relations Act. As
a matter of course, the union filed charges against the company; sometimes as much as two years later, the charges were
upheld, and Stevens officials were forced to post notices
stating that they would discontinue their illegal activities.
But the damage already had been done to the organizing campaign, and a favorable National Labor Relations Board (NLRB)
decision twelve months later was meaningless. As a company-
sponsored blueprint for fighting unions states: "What must
be impressed upon every supervisor is that the penalty for
saying something may be the posting of a notice stating that
the company will not say it again, while the penalty for saying nothing could very well be unionization."[4]

Other tactics employed by Stevens include such devices as
posting on bulletin boards full-page reproductions of newspaper articles about the Zebra killings to whip up the racism
of white workers.* If the workers withstand this continuous
illegal pressure as the election date nears, the company es-
calates its activities. Company officials begin to selec-
tively fire the leading union supporters in direct violation
of the law. However, it normally takes two years before the
company has exhausted NLRB and court appeals and is forced to
reinstate discharged workers. Despite the large dollar figures in back pay settlements, the effect of this tactic has
been to make an election victory nearly impossible.

In the many union campaigns at Stevens plants, the company
has been forced to pay some $1.3 million in compensation to
workers who were discharged illegally.[5] In a speech on the
floor of Congress, Senator Birch Bayh outlined the situation
as follows:

> The struggle between Stevens and the unions has
> been long and ugly. Hundreds of workers have been
> fired for union activity and scores of charges of

---

* A series of random, racially motivated murders in the San
  Francisco area in which whites were the victims.

unfair labor practices have been filed with the
National Labor Relations Board. At each stage of the
administrative proceedings during the Board's investigation of the charges, after the administrative law
judges' consideration of the Board's review of the
judges' findings--the company has been found to have
committed repeated violations of the National Labor
Relations Act. In 14 different cases involving large
numbers of workers, the company has appealed the decisions of the administrative law judges, and each
time the National Labor Relations Board has found
J. P. Stevens guilty of illegal efforts to thwart
union organizing.

Then, after further appeals by the company, the decisions of the Board have been upheld eight times by
various U.S. courts of appeals and three times by the
U.S. Supreme Court. J. P. Stevens has paid under
court orders more than $1.25 million to workers
wronged by violations of their right to organize, but
has steadfastly refused to bargain with the Textile
Workers as required by law.

Both the second circuit and the fifth circuit have
found J. P. Stevens in contempt of court orders to
comply with the Labor Relations Act. Following the
fifth circuit's findings of contempt, the company
closed its plant in Statesboro, Ga., rather than deal
with the union.

Perhaps most symbolic of the lengths to which J. P.
Stevens has gone to obstruct the union effort was
the revelation that during a 1973 union campaign the
company had bugged the motel room of two organizers
in Wallace, S.C. In January 1975, J. P. Stevens paid
$50,000 to settle a suit brought by the Textile Work-
ers and the AFL-CIO because of the wiretapping.

The latest chapter in the fight is being played out
in Roanoke Rapids, N.C. In August 1974, the Textile
Workers won an election which established them as
the collective bargaining agent at the seven Roanoke
Rapids plants operated by J. P. Stevens. But in the
15 months since the election, the company has refused
to agree to any economic improvement sought by the
union, and once again the union has filed a charge
of refusal to bargain with the National Labor Relations
Board. The seemingly endless struggle goes on.[6]

Bayh observed in concluding his speech: "the endless
struggle between J. P. Stevens and the Textile Workers and
the IUD testifies to the fact that when big business chooses
to obstruct the process of unionization, the present law of

this country may be inadequate to compel business to the bargaining table."[7] Unfortunately, in regard to the J. P. Stevens Corporation, this is an understatement.

Another flash point in the textile industry's war against unionism is Wellman Industries, a synthetic fibers manufacturer located in South Carolina. This company employs about 1,000 workers, most of them black sharecroppers drawn from the large plantations in the Hemingway, South Carolina, area.[8]

The owner of this company is a dictatorial man named Jack Wellman who owns nearly everything in the area. This personal dominance has earned him the title of "Daddy Jack." In an early TWUA election campaign, after defeating the union through illegal tactics, Wellman carried out a mock funeral and buried TWUA at the front of his complex with great pomp, ceremony, and a casket. Despite such opposition, the workers began to organize in the early fall of 1971 with the assistance of TWUA. Initially, Jack "persuaded" the local motel to evict the organizers; and after a trailer was rented by the union, he forced the owner of the camp to expel the trailer. When the organizers refused to leave, a wire fence was erected around the trailer in full view of the highway, to intimidate the workers. Finally, the water supply to the trailer was cut off three days prior to the election.[9]

Among the new tactics Jack employed was a letter sent to each worker which stated, "The Textile Workers of America wants to give you a sound dose of tranquilizers and turn you into puppets.... This company has the legal right, -- if the strike is over wages, hours or working conditions to replace permanently every single person that goes out on strike with no obligation to take them back."[10]

The day a union supporter was illegally fired, the plant safety board stated, "Don't Let the Next Fire Be Yours." Jack also employed the Hemingway First Baptist Church and the local school to assist in getting all citizens to a community meeting where the subject was the evils of union organizing. He went so far as to provide each student from kindergarten to high school with a notice for their parents emphasizing the importance of attending the meeting. Workers were told that if TWUA won the election, the Wellman workers would be denied credit from local merchants. Also, the Hemingway radio station refused to sell TWUA time spots, in violation of FCC regulations.[11]

The company won the election by twenty-two votes. But the NLRB set the election aside for "repeated and flagrant" violations of the law. Subsequently, the majority of the workers voted for TWUA in the rerun election, and the union was certified as the collective bargaining agent. For the next four

years, Wellman used the Labor Board and court procedures to
avoid bargaining with the union. When these delays were exhausted, company representatives, under the compulsion of a
court order, finally met with TWUA leaders, and contract negotiations are currently in progress.

TEXTILE WORKERS AND SOUTHERN POLITICS

Southern politics constitutes another important element in
the hostile environment in which textile unionism traditionally has existed. Politics in the South has long been dominated by conservative Dixie Democrats. Through disenfran-
chisement of the black population and control of the poor
white vote, they managed to retain nearly complete control
over elections in this region. Poll taxes, Ku Klux Klan activities, literacy tests, and other tools of political manip-
ulation were used to this end.[12]

The textile industry is able to exert tremendous political
muscle in this region. Unlike the politically weak garment
industries located in large, diverse urban areas, it wields a
powerful influence in national politics. Politically, the industry totally dominates the Carolinas and exerts a major influence in Alabama, Georgia, Virginia, and Tennessee. In
North Carolina alone there are 264,600 textile workers, with
130,488 more in South Carolina.[13] One out of seven workers
in North Carolina and one out of six in South Carolina is employed in the textile industry.

In nearly every presidential cabinet over the past decade
there has been a direct representative of the industry. Former secretary of commerce and current head United States
trade negotiator, Frederick Dent, a textile manufacturer, and
President Ford's former presidential campaign chairman, "Bo"
Calloway, are but recent examples. In the 1950s, Robert
Stevens of J. P. Stevens served as Eisenhower's secretary of
the army. Senator Sam Ervin of North Carolina was retained
by Roger Milliken of Deering Milliken in a case against TWUA
in the Supreme Court. This arrogant show of power and influence is rare for more sophisticated Northern industries but a
traditional hallmark of Southern textile employers.

One young union member employed at a fiber glass plant in the
unorganized textile town of Anderson, South Carolina, said of
Senator Strom Thurmond, "He'll get elected forever because
those damn textile workers will never stop voting for him no
matter what he does."[14] This frustrated sentiment expresses
the reality of Southern politics. Textile workers have been
traditionally counted on to vote the Dixiecrat ticket in per-
centages large enough to make all opposition meaningless.
Interestingly enough, this has usually been done with little
statewide campaigning. A combination of blind allegiance to

the Democratic Party and the work of local political machines
has proven sufficient to guarantee victory. Most of the organizations which participate in politics in other parts of the
country do not exist in the South. Unions are too weak to
have much influence, and many candidates who receive labor
support do not want it publicized. This unchallenged role
has made the industry even more powerful than its size and
prestige warrants.

The Harriet and Henderson Cotton Mill strike in Henderson,
North Carolina, which lasted from 1958 to 1960, provides an
example of how mill owners used their political influence to
defeat organized labor. These mills for fourteen years had
had a strong union which negotiated contracts with the company on a regular basis. The company, however, decided to
break the union and announced that the new contract would
have to omit the clause giving the union the right to arbitrate grievances. Despite a reluctance during this period to
be backed into unwanted strikes, the union was forced to
order a walkout to protect its ability to represent workers
effectively on a day-to-day basis. The company controlled
the local government and had a great deal of influence in the
statehouse. Company-provoked violence, National Guard troops
breaking picket lines, and the mobilization of the town
against the union followed. Nevertheless, these tactics
failed to break the ranks of the more than 1,000 strikers.
With the "neutrality" of the governor, the company framed
TWUA's Southern vice-president and seven strike leaders for
conspiring to dynamite company property. Despite appeals to
the Supreme Court, these eight men were sentenced to terms of
imprisonment from between two to ten years. The strike was
broken, and the union disappeared from Henderson, North Carolina.[15]

THE TEXTILE LABOR FORCE

Industry opposition to labor organization and the antiunion
activities of state and local officials go far in explaining
organized labor's failure in Southern textiles; however,
there are more subtle but equally crucial reasons which per-
tain largely to the South. Southern mills recruited whites
from declining small farms and introduced them to factory
life. They created mill villages cut off from the external
world. The mill owner was the benevolent "father" who provided spiritually and economically for "his" workers.[16]
These companies sold mill houses to the workers in the 1940s
and 1950s but retained the basic social structure of the mill
village. YMCAs for all aggregations, churches, schools, sometimes hospitals, and a job were all provided by mill owners,
who are still called "Charlie" (Cannon) and "Daddy Jack"
(Wellman).[17]

Historically the textile mills, particularly in the South,
have provided a means for small farmers to enter industrial
society. This process of integration into the fabric of life
in towns and work in factories was done somewhat differently
in the South. Here, total communities were provided by the
employer, complete with religion, some education, houses,
stores, and a job. Many studies on mill village life go into
depth on the means used to create competent factory workers.[18] For our purposes, an example will suffice. In a
study commissioned by the Cotton Manufacturer's Association
in 1948, William Hays Simpson states:

> Before coming to the mill the employees in general
> were improvident laborers or unsuccessful small farm-
> ers who had not developed a sense of pride in their
> homes. A neat or tidy village could only be had by
> the direct action of the company or through the man-
> agement's active influence. Today in certain mills,
> rules regarding neatness have been promulgated; others
> give flower seed and shrubery free and offer prizes to
> encourage the beautification of yards.... While cotton
> mill communities contain some of the cleanest homes in
> the South, they also have many dirty ones, much to the
> despair of the owners. There is no uniformity in this
> matter, but efforts are extended by various organized
> groups within the mill villages to eliminate the ten-
> dencies toward untidiness where they do exist.[19]

The private lives of the workers were completely dominated
and molded by the mill owners. These executives saw themselves as public benefactors fulfilling a mission toward "less
fortunate souls." In this process they destroyed mountain
traditions and the culture of the yeoman farmers and formed a
new person -- the textile worker.

This great human transformation did not stop when the men,
women, and children entered the mills. Here, they were subject to the whims of the lowliest "bossman" or "overseer."
(Both terms are still in use today.) Most of the jobs were
relatively simple and could be learned in a short period of
time. More than anything else, they required continued attention. "This constant state of alertness to breaks and
stops creates a high degree of stress for the textile worker
and contributes to his highly emotional response."[20] This
may be partially responsible for the long history of short,
violent protests by textile workers resulting in equally short
and unsuccessful strikes. This problem persists today with
displays of outrage which quickly subside without the ability
for further organizational development. The reason such traditional labor issues as wages or working conditions do not
create a sustained response from textile workers lies in the
worker's self-image.

The Southern textile worker sees himself as outside America's
dream of success. He does not expect to do better than work
in a mill. This is true despite the fact that most Southern
workers readily avow that a textile mill is a demeaning place
to work. He does not consider himself capable of rising
above his poor circumstances and accepts the safety of the
status quo.

> For the most part, he is content to remain within the
> culture which presents him with few decisions to make
> and creates few problems to meet. Dissatisfaction,
> where it does arise, is quickly repressed by the pre-
> vailing feeling that new desires and standards are not
> for the textile worker. In recent years, employers
> have reinforced this attitude by reiterating the theme
> that their employees cannot and should not expect the
> wage and benefit standards found in other industries.[21]

They may hope for their children but have little ambition
themselves. Though they can be outraged by such injustices
committed by bosses as increasing workloads or firing a popular worker for no reason, this is short-lived and seldom results in a long-term effort on the part of the employees.
They retain their faith in the mill owner's intentions and
accept the bleak future that inevitably lies ahead for textile workers. Today's Southern textile employee, as in old
mill villages, is a second-class citizen. He often returns
from work covered with lint (whence comes the derogatory nick-
name linthead) and makes barely enough to survive. Like his
parents, he owes money to small credit agencies which flour-
ish in all mill communities. This also ties him to the status quo through fear of losing a job and having a home taken
for debts; home ownership remains a symbol of adulthood in
the South. All these characteristics have stifled the progress of textile unionism for the past hundred years. In the
last decade, this pattern has begun to change among the
younger and better educated. It is now not uncommon for high
school graduates to work in mills. In addition, the expanding influence of the media, especially television, has in-
truded. Younger workers and blacks have reacted differently
to the traditional tenets of the industry -- hard work, low
pay, and passivity.

One of the most significant developments influencing the textile labor force in recent years has been the growing influx
of black workers. Minority participation in this industry
has steadily increased from less than 1 percent in 1964 to
13.1 percent in 1971 and 17.9 percent in the first quarter of
1975.[22] This trend is expected to continue to increase due
to the availability of unemployed blacks in the Southern textile centers. The Southern black percentage is estimated to
be 25 percent, and many plants in the Carolinas are predominantly black.

Thus far, this development has helped union organizing. Most of the major organizing victories in the past five years have depended heavily on overwhelming black support in combination with a minority of the white votes. At the present time, a large percentage of black workers is nearly enough to qualify a particular mill as an organizing target. Black workers do not have the mill village psychology with its "faith" in the goodwill of the employer. As a black textile worker at Field- crest Mills in Columbus, Georgia, states, "We know that the bossman's not going to do anything for us -- the white folks thinks he's their friend. Black people know that's wrong."23

Since many blacks are coming off the land as former small farmers or sharecroppers, they are not bound by the mill tra- ditions. Most families are first or second generation tex- tile mill hands seeking a better future. The promise of the civil rights movement seems to have reached deep into many of the small towns and rural communities with the prospect of a brighter future. A union often is viewed as one proven means of getting that improvement. This is especially true of younger blacks who have not even heard of the past history of broken, defeated unions.

They believe in unity and conceive of a union as a means to fight against their oppression. In this response, they are normally frustrated by the caution and slowness of their white co-workers. Many union organizing campaigns have col- lapsed despite the active support of 95 percent of the blacks because of a failure to reach the white workers.

Another important difference between the older white textile workers and the blacks is the attitude toward the immediate supervisor or "bossman." Black workers view this individual as no more than an equal and often as an inferior; conse- quently, they feel no loyalty toward foremen and have very little trust in them. When a company unleashes its antiunion campaign, the traditional influence of line supervisors is almost nonexistent to the black workers. They know where the company representatives "are coming from" and, therefore, view their appeals as laughable. The white workers respond in an opposite fashion, putting much faith in the appeals for "solving all your problems without bringing in an outsider" and "give us another chance."

A coalescence of all these responses occurred in 1973 during a strike for union recognition against Oneita Knitting Mills in Andrews and Lane, South Carolina. In the late 1940s, Oneita Knitting Mills closed its unionized plants in Utica, New York, to head for the delta region of South Carolina. Initially they hired only white workers and grew as a non- union concern during the boom period in the Southern industry. In the early 1960s, the International Ladies' Garment Workers' Union organized the plant and struck for union recognition.

At the time of the strike, the company employed two blacks in
a total work force of some 700 people. The strike lasted
eight months and was led by the local chapter of the Ku Klux
Klan. Seeing the Civil Rights Act on the horizon, Oneita began to hire black sharecroppers as strikebreakers which enabled the company to operate the plant and defeat the strike.
When the workers returned to work, they did so without any
written contract and no union. Over the next eight years,
the company hired blacks to replace white workers who retired
or quit. In 1971 the workers again began a union organizing
campaign with the assistance of TWUA. At the same time,
within fifty miles three other textile plants with a majority
of black workers were in the process of organizing. All four
groups of workers voted for a union in a close run of NLRB
supervised elections. Many whites who had been leaders of
the earlier union drive did not support the TWUA effort and
in some cases worked against the organizing campaign. The
new leadership was mostly black and reflected the 75 percent
black majority among the nearly 1,000 workers. Of the total
group, approximately 85 percent were women, which changed
very little from a decade earlier.

After fifteen months of fruitless negotiations, the workers
grew impatient, and a strike vote was taken. Union leaders
were very reluctant to pursue such a tactic since no major
union recognition strike had been won in the textile industry
in that area for many years. The earlier defeat and a high
proportion of sharecroppers in the surrounding towns also
were factors militating against calling a strike. However,
after an overwhelming vote to strike, nearly 90 percent of
the workers stayed at the plant gates on January 7, 1973.

As expected, the company mobilized the state, county, and
local law enforcement agencies to intimidate the strikers and
to protect scabs entering or leaving the plant. Also, the
local community exerted pressure against the strikers through
credit agencies and other economic means. Many long-standing
debts were called in and the normal accommodations denied.
Southern textile workers are some of the most debt ridden
people in America, their few luxuries attained through long-
term installment purchases. Cars, furniture, appliances,
groceries, homes, insurance, medical care, and even clothes
are bought on credit and repaid over a long period of time.
Therefore, this brand of pressure is one of the most effective in "disciplining" striking textile workers into returning to work.

While most of the strikers remained on the picket lines for
the six months' duration of the strike, the company was able
to hire many new workers. Over the years between 1963 and
1973, much of the white population had either taken better
jobs or moved away; hence, the only available supply of
strikebreakers were the hundreds of poor black sharecroppers

living in the surrounding areas. Oneita was able to hire
many of these people to cross the picket lines and to work in
the plant. Often, family members of striking union members
crossed the union lines. The only explanation for this unusual phenomenon is that there is no tradition of "the picket
line" as found in the coal fields or auto towns; crossing a
union line because someone needs the money is acceptable.
Very little real hostility was evident between family members
who were on opposite sides of the struggle. Hostility was
reserved for the strikebreakers who were unknown and thought
of as outsiders. Due to the multiracial makeup of both the
strikers and scabs, the racial issue played no major role
during the six-month shutdown.

However, the company was unable to convert these farm workers
into efficient factory hands in a short period of time.
There was much discussion among union supporters of the poor
work being done by the strikebreakers in comparison to the
usual employees. This lack of productivity was further complicated by a failure of the strikebreakers to adapt to the
attendance requirements of factory life. Absenteeism became
a major problem for Oneita even though the company successfully continued to hire new workers. These problems were aggravated by a national boycott undertaken by TWUA, with the
cooperation of the AFL-CIO. These forces brought about a
union victory in July, complete with a respectable contract
and a substantial wage increase.

The inability of the company to force the experienced workers
back into the plant was a very unusual occurrence. Black
strikers seemed more willing to stay together and wait out
the company. They held Oneita in contempt and had absolutely
no loyalty to the company; many turned the struggle into an
exciting, vibrant affair, complete with original songs and
several mass marches. Unity became the theme of this strike
and resulted in success which has established the Oneita
local union as one of the strongest in the entire South.[24]

THE PRESENT: THE NEW AND THE OLD

The current status of Southern textile unionism is an uneven
blend of optimistic signs mixed with very slow real progress.
Textile workers still receive wages $1.38 below average hourly
earnings for all manufacturing workers.[25] Working conditions
and work loads are among the most oppressive in all American
industry. However, the underlying social status of unions in
this industry is much more complex and significant than these
figures indicate. Several case studies provide a fairly accurate portrait of the state of textile unionism in the South
at the present time.

NEWBERRY, SOUTH CAROLINA

This textile town has two unions in local mills, the United
Textile Workers of America and the TWUA. Both locals are in
plants owned by the Kendall Company, a national chain controlled by the Colgate-Palmolive Corporation. This conglom-
erate operates twenty-seven textile factories with 7,400 production workers.

The TWUA local union in Newberry is one of the oldest operating unions in the South. It successfully survived the 1934
general strike and has constructed a fine union hall. Traditionally, this was a white local union; few blacks are employed by Kendall. In past strikes, the local gave food and
financial assistance to black strikers while barring them
from membership. Beginning in 1966, Kendall hired black
workers, who by now constitute 50 percent of the mill hands.
Kendall was one of the last textile companies to "capitulate"
to the 1964 Civil Rights Act. Many of the older black workers who had desired union membership for years joined the
local in 1964 when admittance first became possible. However,
the younger blacks entering the plant viewed the union as a
white institution which did not want or deserve their support.
The local's membership gradually dropped to its current level
of slightly more than half the 450 workers employed. Consequently, its strength has eroded to a point of an inability
to solve many grievances or negotiate contracts beyond the
industry-wide pattern.

In a recent labor education institute, a discussion of this
racial split among workers revealed several underlying attitudes and conceptions that are very informative. Pinkney
Moses, a black mill hand who has worked at Kendall since 1948,
expressed a feeling that the younger blacks "don't feel welcome in the union hall." A long-time union leader named
Mattie Lee Mays referred to the 1951 Southern strike when "we
gave you all food and money even though you weren't in the
union." "But you wouldn't let me in Mrs. Mays -- don't you
remember me askin' all those times to sign a card?" Moses responded. Mattie Lee replied, "But Moses you know that's the
way things were down here then, now we want the colored in
and they won't join, I mean except for a few of the good ones
like you. What do these young ones have to kick about, they
weren't even around then, nobody ever kept them out of the
union."[26] Moses had no answer to Mattie Lee Mays's last
statement, and the discussion ended with a resolve to sign up
the young blacks. These sentiments reveal the absence of any
clear understanding among the older whites or blacks as to
why young black workers resent the union. Therefore, the
older white workers view the local as their own property and
do not feel they need to change anything to accommodate the
younger blacks except allow them to obtain membership. They
view the blacks' reluctance as ignorance about unionism.

Moreover, despite the weakness of the union, as long as it remains they feel no pressing need to change anything or sign
up the blacks. They have accepted as enough the modest improvements won over a long period of time and have very limited ideas toward change.[27]

CONE MILLS

TWUA represents about 5,000 workers at eight plants of the
giant Cone Mills Corporation. These factories are all large
units and are located in and around the Greensboro, North
Carolina, area. Since the defeat of the union in the 1951
strikes, the locals at Cone have been very weak. Despite a
number of attempts to build the membership strength for
strikes, this situation has remained unchanged. Several
times over the years the company has attempted to decertify
TWUA by getting a majority of the workers to vote against the
union. This has been against the background of less than 10
percent union membership among the 5,000 workers.

In every case, the workers have voted by a clear majority for
TWUA representation! This occurred despite the weakness of
the union in handling local problems or raising wages. Over
the last ten years, the composition of the work force has
changed greatly to number about 20 percent black. This has
resulted in more grievances and departmental disputes but no
greater strength for the union. Blacks probably see the need
but lack the will. The workers desire union representation
but are unwilling to participate or support the local. At
this point, the company has come to accept a weak union and
has given up trying to decertify TWUA despite the low membership figures.

The local leadership is comprised of very dedicated older
union stalwarts who are veterans of many battles against Cone.
They have learned to live with the weakness of the union and
are even prepared for one more showdown. However, while they
have accepted the company's attitude, local leaders are understandably very critical of the great bulk of the workers.
Long-time local President Duffy Burke at the White Oak Mill
commented: "These people are funny down here, they bitch all
the time but won't stick together to do anything about it."[28]
Duffy's explanation appears accurate but is superficial.

Presently, Cone workers are primarily young and have not been
asked to unite for a struggle against the company. Everyone
involved, from supervisors to local union leaders, has been
convinced that Cone cannot be beaten but that the union does
have a place, one of weakness but of assured continuing existence. The younger workers view the union as either unwilling or unable to do anything to help them. Their reality is
one of low wages and poor working conditions, and they see
little hope of changing anything.[29]

CANTON COTTON MILLS

Canton Cotton Mills dominates the mill town of Canton, Georgia, in the northern part of that state and employs nearly 1,000 workers. This old denim mill was organized in the early 1960s in a spontaneous campaign carried on by the workers in the two plants. In the early years, the local union constructed a "TWUA Community Center" as their union hall.

Over the past ten years, membership has increased gradually to its present level of 90 percent. The workers are largely white with a sizable minority of blacks. These two groups get along well, and blacks are represented in the leadership of the local. The local union carries on many recreational activities centered around religion and publishes a very successful union newsletter. Social gatherings are unknown due to racial fears, but there appears to be mutual cooperation and even respect. The local has fought one strike successfully, which has established a relatively powerful position in relation to the company in collective bargaining.

One of the main reasons for the strength of this local is that it was initially organized as an integrated union. While racial antagonism is not absent, the local is accepted in both the white and black communities. Vigorous internal politics keep the local leadership vibrant and innovative, contributing to the continued membership growth. Many grievances are won by the local, which helps convince new workers to join and even participate.

The relative newness of this local is possibly the greatest single factor in its success as an organization. Another is that there are virtually no other employers in or around Canton; and therefore, most local residents work there at some time during their lives. Many younger workers are high school graduates who are not satisfied with work in a cotton mill but have decided to remain in the Canton area. These workers choose the location despite the job and, while they are there, try to improve the situation. Their influence has been decisive in keeping the union vibrant and militant. Isolation has resulted in helping to increase the strength of the union rather than weaken it, as one might expect. Another important factor is that when the plants were organized, they were the only manufacturing facilities owned by this company and therefore mediated against a prolonged battle with the union.[30]

THE FUTURE: A DARK YESTERDAY BUT A BRIGHTER TOMORROW

The broad scope of this paper encompasses a bleak history and a mixed present for America's textile workers. The overwhelming odds stacked against these citizens often seem

insurmountable. Organized labor is filled with former TWUA
staff members working for other unions. Frustration, decreas-
ing economic resources, and defeat have taken their toll on
once spirited union leaders who have chosen to work within
more secure perimeters. Former textile staffers are found in
government agencies, legal work, politics, and often back in
the mills. Hundreds of prounion textile workers have suffered disruptive moves, loss of jobs, social excommunication,
and severe personal stress after the many defeats in strikes
and organizing campaigns.

This dismal picture, however, has begun to show signs of hope
for the workers in their efforts to better themselves. Despite all the unfavorable circumstances mentioned about organizing, TWUA currently is receiving three or four times more
requests from workers for unionization than can be accommo-
dated with the present staff. In a recent leaflet blitz at
the nonunion mills to raise industry wages, a worker responded to the organizer, "I've been workin' here for nineteen years and the union's never tried to get in, but when
you're set -- let me know -- I'm ready." Similarly, there
are literally thousands of textile workers who have been
through past campaigns, worked in former unionized mills, or
just believe in trade unionism. These men and women identify
themselves immediately to the union organizer and are willing
to put their jobs on the line at any time. This core of
Southern textile unionists includes thousands who work in
nearly every mill in the region. They represent a very real
hope for future organizing activity.

The second group which on occasion has ignited the die-hard
unionists is the blacks entering the industry. Most see the
union as a vehicle to better themselves and their communities
and remain deaf to company propaganda. These people are beginning to supply the needed numbers to the veteran union
sympathizers in order to turn the tide.

Another major portent of a happier future is the influx of
both blacks and whites returning from the North to the South.
They have experienced successful unions in auto, steel, and
other industries and return to the textile industry with much
higher expectations. Increasingly, individuals of Southern
background with Northern experience are becoming leaders of
organizing campaigns and even local unions. Along with this
trend is the movement of diverse industries into the textile
belt. Electronics, auto, rubber, and steel plants are being
built in the long-time textile centers of the South. The resulting competition for workers increases wages and improves
working conditions and also creates higher wage expectations
and better treatment among the workers who have remained in
the mills. They compare the offerings of the nonunion textile industry to the new companies and are brought abruptly
into the twentieth century.

A final factor involved in the outlook for a brighter future
is the state of the American labor movement. With the note-
worthy exception of the public employee and service unions,
nearly every labor organization in this country is declining
in membership. Much of this decline is because union membership is concentrated in the deteriorating Northern and Mid-
western manufacturing centers. In Power Shift, Kirkpatrick
Sales documents the vast shift in population and industry
from the Northeast and Midwest to the Southern rim of the
United States. Most new plants and plant expansions are occurring in this portion of the country, and unions in most industries are weakest there. The dramatic increase in the
portion of the total market controlled by nonunion construction firms is highlighted by the weakness of Southern building trades unions. Steelworkers, chemical workers, and the
building trades are only the beginning of a long list of
labor unions which have recently suffered major setbacks in
the South. This situation has forced organized labor to take
a closer look at the region and the laws governing union organizing. A growing interest in "breaking the South" and re-
forming the National Labor Relations Act is becoming evident
among all unions. Both these goals are of crucial importance
to Southern textile workers who desire to organize.

All these factors lead one to the conclusion that the future
will be brighter for Southern textile workers. As a Stevens
worker said to a disheartened union organizer after an election defeat, "Don't worry, we gonna get there somehow."[31]

Notes

[1] Mary Heaton Vorse, "The South Has Changed," Harper's Magazine (July 1949), 28.

[2] Moody's Investors Service Inc., Moody's Industrial Manual, vol. 2 (New York, 1975), 3364. (This figure is accurate as of October 31, 1974.)

[3] Verbal testimony of Roanoke Rapids Workers at NLRB Hearings, Winston-Salem, N.C., 1974.

[4] Richard S. Brese and Robert B. Pearlman, "The Union Election -- It's You and Him -- or Them Period," Textile Industries Magazine (November 1973), 48.

[5] The Nation (October 25, 1975), 392-94.

[6] U.S., Congress, Senate, Debate on S 19763 to amend the National Labor Relations Act, Congressional Record, 94th Cong., 1st sess. (1975), 121, 68.

[7] Ibid.

[8] Michael Pollack, "Union Busting in the South," Textile Labor 32 (March 1971), 3.

[9] Ibid., 4.

[10] Ibid., 3.

[11] Ibid., 4, 5.

[12] North Carolina Department of Labor in cooperation with the U.S. Bureau of Labor Statistics (October 1975), 2; and South Carolina Employment Security Commission (October 29,

1975), 2.

[13] Ibid.

[14] Conversation with author, Anderson, South Carolina, April 1974.

[15] Textile Workers Union of America, Almost Unbelievable (New York, 1961), 14-18.

[16] Harry Boyte, "The Textile Industry: Keel of Southern Industrialization," Radical America 6 (March and April 1972), 11.

[17] Solomon Barkin, "The Personality Profile of Southern Textile Workers," Labor Law Journal 11 (June 1960), 8.

[18] Herbert J. Lahne, The Cotton Mill Worker (New York, 1944); Liston Pope, Millhands and Preachers (New Haven, 1942); Jennings J. Rhyne, Some Southern Cotton Mill Workers and Their Villages (Chapel Hill, 1930); and William Hays Simpson, Southern Textile Communities (Charlotte, 1948). This latter work was financed by the Cotton Manufacturers' Association and is an apology for the industry. However, it contains much useful information on mill village life.

[19] Simpson, Southern Textile Communities, 28.

[20] Barkin, "Southern Textile Workers," 5.

[21] Ibid., 9.

[22] Telephone conversation with Robert Ray of the U.S. Bureau of Labor Statistics, May 9, 1975.

[23] Statement of local union officer in Columbus, Georgia, November 1975.

[24] The author's personal involvement in this strike provides the information in this passage.

[25] U.S., Department of Labor, Bureau of Labor Statistics, Employment and Earnings 22 (October 1975). The general manufacturing average was $4.73, and the textile average was $3.37.

[26] Conversation with the author, Newberry, South Carolina, March 1975.

[27] The author's personal experiences and discussions with many union staff members are responsible for the information contained in this section.

28 Conversation with the author, Greensboro, North Carolina, February 1975.

29 Author's experience.

30 Ibid.

31 Conversation with the author, Wallace, North Carolina, May 1975.

CHAPTER III

COAL:
Industrial Warfare
in West Virginia

The West Virginia coal fields witnessed some of labor's finest achievements and also its darkest defeats. Although outside interests and capital were heavily involved in the ownership of West Virginia mines, both of the following writers agree that the mine workers and their unions represented an indigenous movement unaffected by alien ideology from either the Left or the Right. In his paper on Frank Keeney, David A. Corbin, writing from a New Left perspective, attempts to show from West Virginia coal miners' experiences that workers often organized from the "bottom up"; that they had other concerns besides wages, hours, and working conditions; and that the roots for the "Miners for Democracy" movement go deeply into the workers' past tradition. The model for Corbin's conclusions is the career of Frank Keeney, whose leadership followed a rugged independence typical of his West Virginia origins. However, Corbin and Daniel P. Jordan, the second essayist, disagree over the extent of Keeney's involvement with the sixty-mile march on Logan County in 1921.

Jordan's account of the "Mingo War" between 1919 and 1922 highlights a series of events long neglected by historians, although this protracted struggle between West Virginia miners and the coal operators received extensive national attention and press coverage at the time. While dealing with the details of the "war" itself, the author also provides a rigorous analysis of the events and the participants. Like so many of labor's struggles during this period, the balance of power was heavily weighted against the miners because of, among other reasons, the unity of the operators as opposed to a "fractured organization" within labor, the role of governments and courts, and the operators' tactics. Jordan agrees with Corbin that West Virginia miners, at least during the Mingo War, were not primarily interested in "bread and butter" gains. The basic issues, he argues, were union recornition and the right to belong to a union.

In these two accounts, both authors find local uniqueness in
this labor struggle as well as similarities with labor movements elsewhere during the period. For Jordan, there is almost an established West Virginia tradition based on geography and culture. The existence of mountains, trees and cover,
partisanship, and guns helped breed violence and conceal its
perpetrators. This ethos spilled over into relations between
coal operators and unions once the lines of combat were drawn.
Whether these traits portrayed by Jordan contributed to the
spirit of revolt which Corbin finds in the miners' movement
is not clear. Nevertheless, the two essays provide new material and judgments on the role of the miners in American labor history.

Daniel P. Jordan, a Phi Beta Kappan and former Thomas Jefferson Fellow at the University of Virginia, received the Ph.D.
from that institution in 1970 and is acting chairman of the
Department of History at Virginia Commonwealth University.
He is the author of over thirty articles, essays, and reviews
in various scholarly journals and founded the Richmond Oral
History Association and the Richmond American History Seminar.

David A. Corbin's academic career so far has been devoted to
the study of various aspects of West Virginia political and
labor history. He has undergraduate and M.A. degrees from
Marshall University and is currently teaching and completing
a Ph.D. in American labor history at the University of Maryland.

The Mingo War: Labor Violence in the Southern West Virginia Coal Fields, 1919-1922
Daniel P. Jordan

PRELUDE, 1919

Nestled amid the Appalachian mountains in the extreme south-western part of West Virginia, the counties of Logan and Mingo have attracted little national attention.[1] Two exceptions were Mingo's notoriety as home ground of the Hatfield-McCoy feud in the late nineteenth century and the later Mingo War -- the generic name for a bitter, bloody struggle to unionize the rich but inchoate bituminous coal fields of southern West Virginia between 1919 and 1922. The war's storm center was in Mingo and Logan, citadels of nonunion strength; but it spilled into adjoining counties and into Kentucky as well.

Even in a period of prominent national industrial disorders, the Mingo War was headline news.[2] In some ways it was a microcosm of the era's labor history; in other ways it was sui generis. In either case, it was significant for the scope, variety, and duration of its violence and for the vital conflict it represented between national coal operators and the United Mine Workers of America (UMW), a conflict with ramifications for the union movement in general.

To understand the Mingo War's origins and importance, one must examine two aspects of the bituminous industry in 1919: (1) the status of the industry's unionization in the country at large and (2) the critical value -- to operators and organized labor alike -- of the nonunion fields in Mingo and Logan counties.

The UMW was organized in 1890 with about 20,000 members of a total 255,244 mine workers.[3] The conditions of World War I lifted it to unprecedented strength; and by November 1918, it had 409,844 paid-up members out of a total of 762,426 miners.[4]

The immediate future, however, was foreboding. Within the
house of labor itself, the UMW was being undermined on both
the Left and the Right -- by Communist agitators and remnants
of the Industrial Workers of the World, and by the conservative American Federation of Labor (AFL) under Samuel Gompers.[5]
In addition, the Armistice brought external threats to the
UMW's war gains. Peace in Europe foreshadowed an end to the
federal government's protective policy, to wage and price
controls, and to the coal operators' forced tolerance of the
union. It also meant renewal of antilabor tactics, the return of job-competing soldiers, and a projected rise in the
cost of living in the face of static or declining wages.

Perhaps most menacing of all, the Armistice curbed what had
been an unequaled domestic and foreign demand for American
coal. This sudden cutback was especially untimely for the
miners since by late 1918, the bituminous reserve among key
industries was already a healthy 63 million tons.[6] The
Armistice also laid bare a serious new threat to the UMW.
The great demands of the war period had neutralized the competitive advantages of the fast-developing nonunion fields.
But after 1918, the UMW was forced to meet this challenge directly or face disastrous consequences.

Several flourishing nonunion fields lay in the southern half
of West Virginia, "the El Dorado of the Soft Coal Industry."[7]
First exploited in the 1890s, they enjoyed many natural advantages over older, union fields, not the least of which was
superior and easily accessible coal. In addition, nonunion
operators there could cut wages according to market fluctua-
tions and retain a competitive edge over those wage-bound by
UMW contracts. Finally, nonunion fields could cripple any
national strike by continued production. Thus from beyond
the state, union miners and union operators alike shared a
serious economic stake in bringing the UMW to southern West
Virginia.

At this time -- with union strength at its peak, but with
enormous problems on the horizon -- John L. Lewis emerged as
chieftain of the UMW. Beginning as a miner in Iowa, Lewis
quickly moved up the union hierarchy. At the annual convention in 1919, he became acting president, replacing an ineffectual and incapacitated incumbent and vowing "no backward
step." Under Lewis's leadership, the convention announced a
heady list of demands, including a six-hour day, a five-day
week, and a 60 percent wage increase. It also laid plans for
a national strike to begin November 1, 1919, and moved to implement a long-time Lewis goal -- an all-out assault on the
nonunion fields.[8]

To accomplish the latter, Lewis could count on an aroused
membership, a full war chest, and a degree of competent sub-
ordinate leadership. District 17 of the UMW, which covered

most of West Virginia, was headed by Frank Keeney, a lifelong
miner, veteran of many labor battles, native of the state,
and an adroit leader. His associates exhibited mixed capaci-
ties.[9]

Although active in West Virginia since the 1890s, the UMW had
met with little success until the violent strikes of 1912 and
1913 brought a large sector of northern and central fields
into the union fold. Wartime conditions, including a labor
shortage, led to further gains.[10] By 1919, the UMW claimed
54,000 members among 91,000 West Virginia miners. Of 37,000
nonunion workers, over a third worked in Mingo and Logan.[11]

Settled in the colonial era, the region of Logan and Mingo
long had had a static population of mountaineers. Isolated
from the outside world, these people were much devoted to a
subsistence way of life in which "gun toting" and "moonshin-
ing" were common. A dramatic change occurred in the late
nineteenth century. Railroad lines were built into the area
so outside investors could tap "the greatest storehouse of
high-rank coal in the United States, if not in the world."[12]

Often representing absentee owners, local operators parlayed
the field's natural advantages into fantastic production
totals.[13] Logan went from less than 500 tons in 1900 to 11
million in 1920; Mingo from 1900 to 1920 saw its production
soar from half a million to 3 million tons in the same period.
By 1920, West Virginia ranked second only to Pennsylvania in
production of bituminous coal. Logan, Mingo, and the neigh-
boring nonunion counties of McDowell and Mercer produced
38.21 percent of the state's total. From 1912 to 1922, the
nonunion fields of West Virginia produced from 7 to 10 percent of _all_ national tonnage.[14]

The bituminous industry put Mingo and Logan on the map.
Williamson, county seat of the former, immodestly proclaimed
itself, "The Heart of the Billion Dollar Coal Field."[15] A
Logan circuit judge once told a pair of visiting United
States senators: "Coal, gentlemen, is king here. It is our
existence. Take from us our coal and we have nothing left.
We shall return to the days of the bobcats and wilderness."[16]

Coal operators in Logan and Mingo were determined to preserve
their competitive superiority over the union fields and early
adopted measures to prevent organization of their mines.
Perhaps their most potent weapon was virtually absolute control over their employees. This circumstance allowed for
great abuse of authority, but it evolved quite naturally from
the prevailing doctrines of industrial statesmanship and the
feudalistic, paternalistic, company-camp system which had
contributed to the rapid development of the bituminous industry in a previously isolated area. In opening the West Virginia back country, the operators acquired large tracts of

land on which they constructed the rudimentary accouterments
of civilization for their employees and their families.[17]
The workers were largely native Americans, many being mountaineers turned miners, and many others being Southern black
migrants.[18]

In these circumstances, the miner became bound to the will of
the operator, was helpless in the face of company power, and
was vulnerable to pressure in every facet of his life.[19]
Most of the Logan-Mingo operators were benevolent despots.
Despite certain grievances, the miners' working and living
conditions compared favorably to those in older, organized
fields.[20] Altruism aside, this was the case in part because
of the newness of company facilities and in part because the
employers recognized that reasonably content miners were un-
likely converts to unionism.[21]

But the power of property rights and such venerable tactics
as "yellow dog" contracts and a liberal resort to court injunctions did not exhaust the traditional means of assuring a
nonunion purity.[22] The employers also relied heavily on the
"mine guard" or "private army" system.[23] This system had
several variations, all effective. In one form, the operators hired Baldwin-Felts private detectives. Two of their
well-known specialities were evicting union-sympathizing or
union-joining workers and their families from company houses,
and serving as undercover agents in the mines or within the
union and reporting names and union activities to the operators.[24]

Another variation, especially popular in Logan County, was
the "special deputy" system. Logan coal managers, for example, paid the county over $108,147 in 1920 and 1921 for the
express purpose of hiring additional antiunion deputy sheriffs and justices of the peace.[25] Don Chafin, the most famous Logan sheriff in this era, admitted under oath in 1921
that after a decade of holding various county offices, his
official salary was only $3,500. His personal worth, however,
was about $350,000 and included many coal holdings. In 1921,
Chafin became a partner in a coal company and eventually acquired an estate exceeding a million dollars.[26] Generous
private contributions from the operators enabled him to maintain a public-payroll army of up to forty-six active deputies
(many of whom were simultaneously drawing company checks) and
about 500 inactive ones who retained both badges and authority.[27] According to Chafin, this system "was the only method
by which the law and order could be maintained in Logan
County."[28]

An essential ingredient of law enforcement in Logan was keeping union organizers out of the county. Chafin's name was
synonymous in UMW circles with the worst forms of intimidation and violence in union busting. Rumors of atrocities

frequently drifted from Logan, and enough well-documented incidents exist to establish the brutal efficiency of Chafin's
operation.[29]

Thus by the fall of 1919, the lines were clearly drawn. Both
the UMW and the Logan-Mingo operators perceived that the
stakes were fabulously high. The result was four years of
bloody industrial warfare in southern West Virginia.

A CHRONICLE OF VIOLENCE, 1919-1922

The Mingo chain of violence developed in three broad and
roughly chronological stages. Each was triggered by its own
unique set of circumstances, but the root cause was the labor
crisis provoked by the UMW's invasion of the nonunion counties. The stages were: (1) the first march on Logan, September 1919; (2) the union push in Mingo, spring 1920 to
October 1922; and (3) the second march on Logan, August and
September 1921, and its aftermath, 1921 and 1922. In se-
quence, they represent a turbulent, lawless progression from
labor's desperate hope to its total defeat.

THE FIRST MARCH ON LOGAN

On September 4, 1919, hundreds of irate union miners throughout central West Virginia journeyed to the mouth of Lens
Creek near Marmet, a few miles from Charleston in a remote
area of Kanawha County.[30] The leaderless assembly, which
quickly grew to several thousand persons, was a response to
the forceful repulsion of UMW organizers from Mingo and Logan
counties and to a rash of atrocity stories emanating from
there. According to rumor, miners and even their wives and
children were being beaten and killed. Whatever the union
men's intentions, the common ground was a proposed armed
march to Logan, about thirty-five miles distant.

UMW District 17 President Frank Keeney hurried from across
the state to Lens Creek in response to a wire from Governor
John J. Cornwell. Three times Keeney tried to disperse the
miners; finally, the governor was sent for. In a gesture of
rash courage, Cornwell drove without protection to the hostile zone, arriving about 10 p.m., September 5. Camp fires
scattered throughout the ten-acre creek bottom revealed about
5,000 men with rifles. Many were Army veterans in uniform
with gas masks and other equipment.

The governor mounted the back of a torchlit truck and reminded the workers of state law against such armed assem-
blages, of their responsibilities to the UMW and to their employers, of his readiness to call for federal troops, and of
his willingness to investigate the Logan reports. Although

the governor's address and Keeney's pleading persuaded many
miners to disperse, hundreds remained; and by the evening of
September 6, about 1,500 men had moved to Danville, within
ten miles of Logan. In the meantime, Keeney had rushed three
investigators with credentials from Cornwell to the Logan
area, and the governor had arranged for use of United States
soldiers. Acting as Cornwell's special representative,
Keeney went to Danville, where he learned of the impending
call for troops. He also discovered from the union delegation in Logan that the rumors of brutality had been greatly
exaggerated and that no deaths had occurred. Keeney relayed
the news to the marchers, who agreed to return home on special trains.

Despite the potential for violence inherent in the assembling
of thousands of aroused, armed miners, no incidents occurred.
As promised, Cornwell soon sponsored an investigation. Its
results confirmed the harsh antiunion tactics of Sheriff
Chafin and the Logan operators. Of future significance was
the emotional charge of the march and the attention it focused on Logan. In addition, for the miners it revealed the
ease and effectiveness of the assembly-march pattern of protest. For both the governor and the operators, it demonstrated the expedient nature of a call for federal troops and
the impact of this threat on the workers.

THE UNION PUSH IN MINGO

By the spring of 1920, considerable union sentiment had developed among Mingo miners.[31] Besides long-standing grievances, many miners were disturbed by their failure to share
in the liberal pay increase awarded union areas by the U.S.
Coal Commission in early 1920 and by a local wage reduction.
Sentiment soon became agitation; and after calling a temporary strike in Mingo, dissident employees contacted Keeney in
Charleston. The UMW granted a charter and dispatched organizers. On May 6, in Matewan, two union officials addressed
a crowd of about 3,000 persons. By mid-month, several thousand workers had enrolled in twenty-two locals.[32]

Some operators, mostly of small mines, signed UMW contracts.[33]
The vast majority, however, responded by firing union members
and evicting them from company houses.[34] For the latter task,
Baldwin-Felts detectives were imported in early May. This
led to the first major outburst of violence in Mingo County.
Twelve Baldwin-Felts agents, headed by two of the Felts
brothers themselves, had spent the day of May 19 evicting
families near Matewan. The detectives then gathered on the
town's main street at the depot for the 4 p.m. train to Bluefield, their headquarters. In the meantime, Albert and Lee
Felts confronted two local officials sympathetic to the miners -- Mayor Cabell Testerman and his very tough chief of

police, the diminutive Albert Sidney "Two-Gun Sid" Hatfield.
The latter was a fast-draw marksman. A heated argument developed before a growing and armed crowd over the evictions
and other matters, perhaps including a bribe attempt by the
Feltses. The Felts brothers presented a warrant for Hatfield's arrest; the mayor and his chief branded it a fake.
Tensions mounted. One of the Feltses drew his gun and fired
a shot, which was probably aimed at Hatfield but which mortally wounded Testerman. A spray of bullets from all directions followed. Hatfield blazed away with both guns.

In less than a minute, seven of the detectives (including
both Feltses), two miners, Mayor Testerman, and a teen-age
bystander had been killed. Hatfield later said he would
"take credit for all seven" of the dead agents. He added,
however, that their bullets had shot a hat off his head and a
gun from one of his hands, that "It was my life or theirs,"
and that he had done "no more than [what] any other red
bloodied American would have done in my place."[35] "The Matewan Massacre" made Sid Hatfield a folk hero among the miners.
It and the sensational trial which followed intensified the
UMW's organizational effort as well as the operators' resistance.[36] As reporter Arthur Gleason prophesied on May 29,
"This section of the State is now a powder mine, ripe for
blowing up."[37]

In the meantime, companies continued to fire, evict, and
lock out union miners and to refuse to deal with their representatives. In late June, the miners called a meeting in
Williamson attended by approximately 4,000. Demands for a
worker's status equal to that of the state's northern fields
were prepared for presentation to the operators. The latter
refused categorically to recognize the existence of the union
in Mingo, much less receive its communications. On July 1, a
strike order was issued designed "to keep intact the ranks"
of the discharged miners, who then numbered about 2,700.[38]

The lockout-strike officially continued for twenty-eight
months -- until late October 1922, when the UMW acknowledged
defeat.[39] This period, especially the first half, was marked
by sporadic and brutal guerrilla warfare. It was also a war
of attrition in which the operators never lost their enormous
initial advantage. As measured on the critical barometer of
tonnage production, the miners were beaten as early as December 1920, when the prestrike level was restored.[40]

The degree of lawlessness during the strike earned the county
the apt sobriquet of "Bloody Mingo." The climate of the
strike zone is suggested in some representative extracts from
the New York Times coverage of, for example, 1920 alone:
"Four Shot, One Dying" (July 5); "Deputy Sheriff Ambushed"
(July 14); "Mine Attacked, Two Wounded, 1,000 Shots"
(July 23); "Three-hour Battle, Six Killed" (August 21); "Mine

Dynamited" (October 17); "Two Dead in Pistol Fight" (November 18); "Striker Murdered Aboard Train" (November 23); "Train Ambushed" (November 30); "Miners' Camp Shot-up" (December 7); "Miner Badly Beaten" (December 10); "Strikers' Tent Colony Fired On" (December 12); "Operator's Home Burned" (December 16); and "Mines Fired On" (December 23). The summer months of 1921 were equally violent.[41]

Other indicators reveal the broad dimensions of lawlessness within the strike zone. Harry Olmstead, official spokesman for the operators, filed before the Kenyon Committee of the United States Senate a chronological listing (July 1920 to July 1921) of 125 "disturbances, assaults, killings, explosions, burnings and so forth," as well as a lengthy, separate list of men killed (May 1920 to July 1921) and the circumstances of each demise.[42] Frank Keeney estimated a death total at over 100 by July 1921. A West Virginia newspaper counted forty killings in Mingo in July and August 1920 alone.[43]

Such massive disorder provoked, of course, enormous local, state, and national efforts to restore the peace. West Virginia governors declared martial law -- complete with serious restrictions on the miners -- on three separate occasions (Cornwell in November 1920, and Ephraim F. Morgan in May and again in June 1921).[44] Twice before, after local officials and then the state constabulary and militia had proven helpless, United States infantrymen were called in. About 450 troops served from August 29 to November 3, 1920; and another 500 were there from November 28, 1920, to January 16, 1921.[45] On the latter occasion, Governor Cornwell declared Mingo County "in a state of insurrection" and turned it over to the commanding general of the Fifth U.S. Army Corps![46]

Outbreaks in May 1921 led to renewed appeals for federal soldiers. President Harding, however, exercised more restraint than had Wilson. After a careful investigation, he refused to dispatch troops because West Virginia had not "exhausted all its own resources" and because the U.S. Army was not a national police force. As a result, Mingo was again placed under martial law. This time it was occupied by the state constabulary, aided by an authorized "vigilance committee" of over 500 local citizens, virtually all of whom shared an antiunion stake.[47]

Perhaps outstanding in its inhumanity was the plight of several thousand evicted strikers and their families in the UMW-sponsored tent colonies in the area. Hundreds lived the entire twenty-eight months separated only by canvas from wind and rain in every season and snow and freezing temperatures in the winters. On subsistence rations, often with dirt floors and lacking sanitation facilities (much less schools and hospitals), frequently harassed by state or local police, these embattled miners and their wives and children were living testimony to the American system manqué.[48]

THE SECOND MARCH ON LOGAN AND AFTERMATH

The single most inflammatory episode in the Mingo War's chronicle of violence was the second march on Logan.[49] Its origins, like those of the first, remain controversial.[50] Important clues, however, are found in a variety of events in July and August 1921 which frustrated and aroused union workers throughout central West Virginia.

On July 14, a United States Senate committee under William Kenyon of Iowa began its investigation of the state's industrial disorders. Its broadly publicized hearings reopened past wounds and kindled false hopes for a future settlement.[51] In the meantime, a series of well-advertised disturbances and UMW setbacks in Mingo County during the summer months reached a climax on August 1 when Sid Hatfield was fatally shot by Baldwin-Felts agents on the courthouse steps in Welch.[52] There was agitation for a mass meeting; and a week later, between 700 and 1,000 miners assembled in Charleston. They drafted, for presentation to Governor Ephraim F. Morgan, a seven-point demand for resolution of the bituminous war.[53] Morgan temporized and eventually turned a deaf ear. Shortly afterward, the state supreme court announced a pair of decisions unfavorable to the union. One upheld martial law in Mingo; the other sustained the imprisonment of a group of miners and UMW officials in Williamson. The operators closed a series of mines, idling workers. Finally, a spate of fresh atrocity stories emerged from the strike zone.

Against this background, armed miners began to gather at Marmet on August 20. Rumors predicted either a protest rally in the state capital or a march through Logan to Mingo, some sixty miles distant. As for the latter, Frank Keeney announced, "I wash my hands of the whole affair."[54] On August 21, Sheriff Dan Chafin declared that "no armed mob" would be allowed to cross the Logan County line and that he was preparing to meet the "invasion."[55]

A few days later at Marmet an estimated 5,000 miners were addressed by the ninety-one-year-old legendary labor agitator, Mrs. Mary Harris "Mother" Jones.[56] Despite her traditional role as insurrectionist par excellence, she urged the workers to disperse and capped her speech with a telegram from President Harding promising action on behalf of the UMW. Unfortunately for her, the telegram was immediately exposed as bogus, and the march to Logan began.[57] There was some confusion as to motive and much doubt as to who was in charge. Most of the miners were on foot, but others went by car or horseback.

Some even commandeered freight trains, one of them styled
"the Smith & Wesson Special."[58] With hundreds of World War I
veterans (many in partial uniform) among them, as well as
nurses, chaplains, commissary wagons, and the like, the
marchers presented a comic-army image.

Meanwhile, in response to alarming calls from a panic-
stricken Governor Morgan, the War Department had dispatched a
battle-tested troubleshooter, Brigadier General Henry Bandholtz, who promptly took charge of the mushrooming crisis.
Arriving in Charleston in the early morning hours of
August 26, he immediately conferred with Governor Morgan, who
confessed his inability to deal with the situation, then with
UMW officers Keeney and Mooney, whom Bandholtz warned he
would hold "responsible for the acts committed by the law-
breaking members of their organization" if they did not stop
the march. Also warning that federal troops would be employed if necessary, at 5:30 a.m., he dispatched Keeney and
Mooney by taxi, armed with a personal ultimatum, to intercept
the march. That afternoon, Keeney and Mooney telephoned from
Madison in Boone County to say that the miners, having held a
mass meeting, had agreed to disperse.[59]

The following day, Bandholtz met with many of the marchers
himself. He reported to Harding that troops were unnecessary.
Morgan issued an "all quiet" statement and confirmed it in a
letter to the president. At this point the disorders would
probably have ended -- except for two unfortunate developments.[60] First, there was an unaccountable delay in providing transportation home for the marchers. Second, on the
night of August 28, the state police staged an incredibly
ill-timed raid against a group of miners near Sharples in
Boone County.[61] Two deaths and several injuries resulted.
This "Sharples Massacre" triggered a renewal of the march,
now uncontrollable; and within hours thousands of irate,
armed miners were advancing along a broad front toward the
Boone-Logan border.

On August 30, with a major battle imminent, Harding commanded
an "orderly dispersal" by noon, September 1.[62] UMW leaders
from John L. Lewis down endorsed the president's proclamation,
which was printed and plane-dropped over the area.

Despite these appeals, hostilities erupted on August 31. The
next three days saw almost continuous firing on a twenty- to
thirty-mile front between an estimated 5,000 to 7,000 miners
and about 1,200 to 3,000 Logan defenders, initially commanded
by Sheriff Chafin. Both sides received reinforcements from
throughout the state, and Chafin's forces used airplanes to
reconnoiter and to drop homemade bombs on the attackers.[63]
The severest fighting occurred at the gateway to Logan County
in the "Battle of Blair Mountain." On-the-spot coverage was
provided by a host of reporters, many of whom were well-known

World War I correspondents.

Late in the afternoon of September 1, after the president's deadline had passed unheeded, Bandholtz cabled for aid. Earlier the same day, the secretary of war had sent the Eighty-eighth Light Bombing Squadron under Brigadier General Billy Mitchell.[64] On September 2, the secretary dispatched 2,100 troops, including a chemical warfare unit and eight trench mortars -- all under Bandholtz's command.[65] The awesome federal force appeared in the area on September 3 and was genuinely welcomed by all concerned (though for different reasons). The firing immediately ceased. Hundreds of miners surrendered and were peacefully disarmed and allowed to return home. After almost a week's fighting, an uncertain peace came to Logan. An estimated million rounds had been fired. Miraculously, the confirmed dead numbered only four.[66]

The action quickly shifted from the battlefield to the courtroom.[67] Coal operators parlayed the armed march into a series of blanket indictments against UMW miners and their officials, including Keeney and Mooney. A Boone County grand jury indicted 302 persons. Its counterpart in Logan delivered over 900 charges of either murder, "pistol toting," or insurrection. Meanwhile, upper-level union officers were also being arrested for their alleged roles in earlier disorders in Mingo.

The indictments brought trials which lasted for years. The most significant ones, however, were held, on a change of venue, in the Jefferson County circuit court during the spring of 1922. Involved were almost 600 miners and UMW officials charged with murder and treason, both carrying a maximum death penalty. They were tried in the same red brick, Charles Town courthouse where John Brown had been tried for treason in 1859.

Aided by counsel furnished by the coal operators, the prosecution chose to test its treason case against William Blizzard, twenty-eight, president of a UMW subdistrict and alleged commander of the march.[68] Because of the conspiratorial nature of the charge, the trial had important implications for not only the state and national UMW but for the labor movement in general and attracted the presence of John L. Lewis himself. A sensational affair lasting over a month, it ended with Blizzard's acquittal.[69] Subsequent trials focused on rank-and-file marchers and resulted in two murder convictions and one for treason. Although the vast majority of charges were eventually dismissed, Keeney, Blizzard, and other officials were still tied up in court as late as the summer of 1923.[70] The final case was heard in 1924.

OVERVIEW AND CONCLUSION

Merely to chronicle the Mingo War, a valuable approach in
many ways, nevertheless tends to destroy or obscure overarch-
ing themes, continuing currents of motive, and other larger
patterns often unrevealed in specific incidents. An overview
of the Mingo conflict must include an analysis of the major
adversaries -- in terms of each's particular institutional
framework, view of the issues, strategy, tactics, and weapons -- and of the war's effects and significance.

The principal antagonists were of course the coal operators
of Mingo and Logan counties and the UMW, both of whom had
supporters throughout the state and beyond. To bolster their
defense against the union and for other reasons, the coal operators had earlier organized themselves on a field-wide basis. During the Mingo War, the Williamson Operators' Association established a special committee to break the strike.
It was headed by Harry Olmstead, an aggressive, authoritative, articulate spokesman and leader. Member operators were
assessed contributions to a joint campaign fund and were expected to implement policy decisions. Olmstead's committee
provided legal counsel, publicity, Baldwin-Felts reports, and
statistical information.[71] Despite massive holdings in the
area by outside titans such as U.S. Steel, policy seems to
have been determined locally.[72] And it was administered with
unitary dispatch and efficiency.

The union effort, conversely, suffered from fractured organization. The UMW had thirty-five locals within the strike
zone and several subdistricts in the state at large, headed
by District 17 -- and each component retained constitutional
prerogatives for independent action. Also involved were the
West Virginia Federation of Labor and the international UMW,
both in turn members of the AFL. The various levels and
types of partly autonomous, partly dependent unions created
problems which were compounded by personality differences
among the leadership. It all combined to splinter both decision making and its implementation in the UMW effort.[73] On
the positive side, Keeney and his immediate associates were
generally capable leaders and did receive generous, if dis-
jointed, support from many quarters.[74]

From first to last, the fundamental issue in the Mingo War
was unionization or "the right to belong to a labor union."[75]
Many miners and the UMW itself considered that right to be
beyond debate in modern industrial America and one which provided workers both self-protection and a means of achieving
tangible benefits. The operators, however, also claimed
their rights, among them, the "constitutional [ones] to run
[their] business according to [their] own notions."[76] These
included the property-vested freedom to hire or fire an individual worker and to recognize or not recognize his

organizations.[77] Although both antagonists often cast their
positions in loftier rhetoric, the basic conflict of rights
remained: "It is either one or the other," said an operator,
"union or nonunion -- that is the primary question."[78]

Many specific issues were contained within the broader matter
of unionization. The UMW took the initiative in defining
these concrete points of contention. Of first magnitude was
a complaint against the mine guard system.[79] It was also
against "the essential characteristic of a coal-mining civilization ... the extent to which the employer, the company,
controls things."[80] Other charges were raised by individual
workers against almost every aspect of the nonunion fields:
the monopolistic company store, the miners' insecurity of
residence, wages (scale, frequency of payment, and method of
computation), and work hours and conditions.[81] In the minds
of many employees, correction of these grievances, real or
imagined, constituted the tangible benefits of unionization.

The operators responded in two ways to the UMW's charges.
First, as a defensive parry, they denied their validity and
sought to establish the benefits inherent for workers in the
unorganized Mingo and Logan fields.[82] Second, they took the
offensive by seeking to deprecate the UMW before the employees and the public at large.[83]

The mine war developed on two fronts, one internal, one external, with an occasional overlapping. Internally, it focused within the strike zone itself and consisted of, for example, the maintenance of tent colonies by the UMW and the
importation of strikebreakers by the operators. The external
front was conducted beyond Mingo and Logan counties and involved the antagonists and some third interest, for example,
the West Virginia governor or the federal executive, judicial,
or legislative branches. The operators sought to prevent
unionization of their workers. In Mingo, this meant breaking
the strike; in Logan, preserving the status quo. The UMW
concentrated on winning in Mingo and thereby establishing a
base for organizing Logan.

To implement their essentially defensive strategy, the operators devised two general tactics. First, on both internal
and external fronts, they sought to discredit the union.
Second, they sought to destroy the union; externally through
court proceedings, internally by continuing coal production
in the face of the union bid and by maintaining incessant
pressure on all vestiges of the UMW in the area.

In their attempt to discredit the union, the operators' bill
of particulars was long -- but hardly novel. In their view,
the UMW, past and present, stood guilty of: irresponsibly
breaking contracts; defying constituted authority; illegally
conspiring with union operators to invade the nonunion fields;

having a socialistic constitution and radical leadership and
goals; desiring to monopolize all coal production in America
in order to put the nation at its mercy; destroying the good
relations between employer and worker; wanting to establish a
Soviet system; plotting terror, subversion, and violence;
tending, when successful in gaining a union mine, "to decrease production, lower efficiency, and destroy initiative";[84] intimidating strikebreakers and nonunion workers;
being "the most tyrannical of all labor unions";[85] being more
interested in power than in the workers' welfare; ignoring
the fact that the workers did not want a union; and wanting
to take over and operate mines with no compensation to the
owners.[86]

The operators circulated these indictments with monotonous
repetition by every means of communication at their command,
including the services of famed evangelist Billy Sunday.[87]
He was brought into southern West Virginia in a plush railroad car and promptly roasted union "radicals" -- to the tune
of:

> I cannot believe God had anything to do with the cre-
> ation of these human buzzards. I'd rather be in hell
> with Cleopatra, John Wilkes Booth and Charles Guiteau
> than to live on earth with such human lice.
>
> The radicals would turn the milk of human kindness
> into limburger cheese and give a polecat convulsions.
>
> [Having removed his coat and tie, he "rolled up his
> sleeves and flung open his shirt" and stated:] If I
> were the Lord for about 15 minutes I'd smack the
> bunch so hard that there would be nothing left for
> the devil to levy on but a bunch of whiskers and a
> bad smell.[88]

While trying to smear irreparably the public image of the UMW,
the association sought simultaneously to limit the union's
operational effectivensss. Court orders served this purpose
admirably. Dozens of crippling indictments were brought
against the UMW in southern West Virginia. Two pertinent decisions by higher federal courts were Hitchman Coal Co. v.
Mitchell (S.C., 1917), which upheld the individual "yellow
dog" contract,[89] and International Organizations, etc. v. Red
Jacket C.C.C. & C. (C.C.A., 4th, 1927 -- but filed in September 1920), which sustained lower court injunctions against
the union's officers for having "combined and conspired to
interfere with the production and shipment of coal by the
nonunion operators of the West Virginia mines" in violation
of the Sherman Act.[90]

State and lower federal courts during the period variously
enjoined the UMW: either to halt or severely limit its

organizing activities in Mingo, Logan, and adjoining nonunion
counties; to neither mention the strike in progress nor approach strikebreakers in the adjoining Kentucky field; to
terminate its nationwide "check-off" system; and to abandon
the Mingo tent colonies and to cease its relief program for
strikers there.[91] In sharp contrast to the operators' legal
success, the union was conspicuously unsuccessful in its own
resort to the courts for relief from intimidation of its organizers and eviction of its members.[92]

A corollary of suppression by injunction was suppression by
indictment -- as secured by the operators against miners and
union officials in the wake of the Mingo and Logan disorders.
There were few convictions; but such trials served to discredit the UMW, incapacitate its leadership, and drain its
treasury.

The operators complemented their efforts to destroy the union
in the courts by an aggressive campaign within the strike
zone itself. Even before the trouble began, they enjoyed a
position of immense strength in their power over company-camp
workers, in the mine guard system, and in their efficient
organization by field-wide associations. To that solid base
were added other weapons of war. To maintain coal production,
several hundred strikebreakers were imported. Much pressure
was applied on the strikers themselves (excluding those who
had been blacklisted) to encourage their return on a nonunion
basis.[93] Ten weeks after the strike began, the Williamson
Association announced increased wages.[94] At different times
it also published amnesty offers, current payrolls (attractive to a worker subsisting on UMW strike rations), tonnage
figures, and frequent statements announcing the strike's ter-
mination.[95] The employers also spent large sums protecting
their men and property. In Mingo they led the appeals for
law enforcement -- by whatever agency was required.[96]

The operators also waged an internal campaign against the UMW.
They were able to parlay various martial law conditions into
suppression of the union.[97] The evidence also suggests oper-
ator-financed intimidation and brutalization of organizers
and union men in Mingo and bribe-motivated action against the
unions by public officials and company functionaries.[98] The
Chafin treatment in Logan was notorious.[99] Finally, UMW tent
colonies were harassed in a variety of legal ways, including
police raids, "sanitation" investigations, and disputes over
title to their land.[100]

Meanwhile, UMW tactics went through two phases. The first,
in the spring and summer of 1920, consisted of such standard
methods of invading a nonunion area as dispatching professional organizers, holding miners' meetings, forming locals,
providing for those discharged or evicted for union membership, and petitioning the operators for union recognition.

Adjusting to continued employer intransigence, the UMW
launched a second tactical phase. It began roughly in late
summer of 1920 and lasted until defeat was acknowledged in
1922. During that period, the union conducted: (1) internally, a holding operation to keep the strike alive; and
(2) externally, defensive measures against the operators'
court war and a vital offensive effort to secure the intervention of a powerful "third interest" which would compel --
by law or force of public opinion or prestige -- the companies to negotiate with (and thus to recognize) the union.

The task of maintaining a strike in the area was enormously
difficult. At best, the union could claim to have sustained
several thousand discharged workers for a twenty-eight-month
period, no small feat but unfortunately irrelevant in light
of continued production.[101] More aggressive efforts also
fell short. In the early weeks, union committees met strikebreakers arriving on trains, tried to persuade them to leave,
and provided transportation home for those who did.[102] Picketing proved ineffectual. Finally, although neither authorized nor condoned by UMW officials, the strikers themselves
committed many acts of violence against the operators, their
men, and property.[103] Even this disreputable approach failed
to seriously affect production.

The union's best hope was intervention by a third party
powerful enough to force negotiations. Every channel was exhausted to secure that end. The campaign was waged by UMW
officials from the local level through Lewis himself; within
the house of labor by individual locals and their national
unions, as well as by the AFL; and finally, by friends of
labor, in groups like the American Civil Liberties Union and
by individuals like Rabbi Stephen Wise and attorneys Frank
Walsh and Samuel Untermeyer.

Targets for this massive pressure included elected officials
in West Virginia, United States senators and congressmen, and
the president and his cabinet. The message was delivered
variously -- in personal and public letters, conventions,
elections, press releases, private conferences, mass meetings,
and even violent outbursts such as the two Logan marches.[104]

This tactic seemed successful in two instances, but both were
hollow victories. The first was a West Virginia investigation authorized by Governor Cornwell following the first
Logan march. It exposed conditions hostile to labor but
brought no remedial legislation. The second was the Kenyon
Hearings in 1921. Again of value for its disclosures, it resulted in no concrete gains.[105] The union's frustrations
were symbolized in the way the hearings closed. In a surprise move on the last day of testimony, UMW counsel Frank
Walsh entered a dramatic plea for mediation by the committee
itself. Operator attorney Colonel Z. T. Vinson responded:

> The committee knows our attitude. We will not have
> anything whatever to do, under any circumstances with
> the United Mine Workers of America or their represen-
> tatives.... We have no settlement to make and no con-
> ference, nothing but a controversy with a lot of out-
> siders. We stand absolutely on our rights.[106]

The statement indicates a view completely impervious to external pressures of the sort engendered by the union. It focuses on the basic issue and suggests the puny impact of the
UMW attempt to prompt intervention by a powerful third party.

Another failure of the UMW in the Mingo War was its previously noted inability to halt coal production in the strike
zone. Both failures, of course, were the result of not one
but many circumstances adverse to the union. Some of these
conditions -- such as the operators' massive initial advantages and the UMW's internal weaknesses -- have been discussed, but others deserve comment.

The position of the employers was immensely strengthened during the Mingo War by at least six developments, most of them
external. First, there was an exuberant demand for coal
triggered by the national strike of 1919 and lasting until
late 1920, but recurring during the strike of 1922. This
meant enormous profits for the nonunion fields and gave the
consumer public a vital stake in their continued operation.[107]
Second, the employers benefited from a national postwar sentiment which was indifferent or unfriendly to the union movement and which, in the wake of the turbulence of 1919 and the
Red Scare, became hostile to it. This climate in turn was
reflected in the federal government's cool attitude toward
organized labor. Third, the operators shared in antiunion
gains made on other fronts, for example, in the "open shop"
movement in the steel industry and court injunctions in
others.[108] Fourth, they were secure in the postwar reality;
there was "no legal way ... to compel arbitration" or union
recognition.[109] Fifth, they were able to concentrate their
efforts on a single target -- the UMW in West Virginia. The
union, conversely, suffered from the inherent division of resources of a multifront campaign across the country. It
launched, for example, two major national strikes (1919 and
1922) during the period.[110] Finally, the operators wisely
capitalized on the mountaineer-miner's provincialism, his
hostility to outside forces, and his individualism -- all of
which worked against the union push.[111]

For the international UMW, the loss in Mingo was a major ca-
lamity. The defeat marked the beginning of a decline in membership and influence not reversed until the 1930s.[112] In
West Virginia, it was just short of a deathblow. The financial costs alone bankrupted District 17 and led to the resig-
nation of its leaders and loss of its autonomy in 1924.

This -- and the continued, unrestrained competition of the
triumphant southern fields -- forced most of the state's
mines to revert to a nonunion status. Membership cascaded
from over 40,000 in 1921 to a low of several hundred in 1932.
This in turn meant a loss of dues-paying members for the West
Virginia State Federation, which had also felt financial
strains from its support of the UMW during the Mingo War.[113]

Ironically, the victorious operators soon paid severely for
their smashing defeat of the UMW. Heady with success and
spurred by soaring prices in the early 1920s, the coal companies vastly overexpanded. When the markets dipped, there
was "no union minimum wage to prevent the operators from bidding for coal contracts by underselling ... each other."[114]
Thus there occurred a pre-1929 depression in the West Virginia coal fields.

The Mingo War is in many ways representative of the turbulent
industrial disorders which plagued the nation after World
War I. In southern West Virginia, as in the country at large,
an aggressive labor force, fortified by war gains but feeling
a post-Armistice insecurity, launched a major offensive, with
unprecedented demands. The response of the coal operators
likewise fits a broader pattern. Similarities with management elsewhere exist in strategic goals, tactics, and ultimate success. Other typical aspects were Mingo's violence,
the governmental response it provoked, and the impact of defeat on the various unions.[115]

While part of a larger picture, the Mingo War also had distinctive qualities -- both in what happened and in what
failed to happen. It was set apart from many other labor
disorders by having unionization itself as the fundamental
issue and not wages, working conditions, or hours.[116]

Although violence was typical of postwar industrial disorders,
the degree, variety, and duration of Mingo's stand out in
twentieth-century America. Its exceptional character merits
examination. Several explanations are possible.[117]

One explanation was the long-standing mountaineer tradition
of using direct force as the ultimate arbiter. It was "gun-
toting country" despite severe state laws restricting the use
of weapons.[118] A newcomer to the union leadership later recalled, "Carrying a gun quickly became automatic, like putting on a tie or lacing one's shoes."[119]

A second explanation, and a corollary to the first, was the
mountaineer's belief that he was somehow if not above the law,
at least the personal embodiment of it. This deep-rooted
tradition is itself explained in part by the late arrival of
concepts to the contrary in the long inaccessible region.
The gun statute was but one of many sections of the state

code which was a mere dead letter in Mingo.[120] Said the en-
gineer who built the railroad line into Matewan: "The problem is how the authorities can be taught to enforce the
law."[121]

A third was the lack of any neutral center, any moderate middle position on the union question. The degree of partisanship mounted as the disorders continued until, for example,
even local ministers reached for guns and joined the Williamson vigilance committee in 1921. "The only ... sin," Malcolm
Ross observed, "is to be lukewarm for the cause."[122]

A fourth was terrain -- scarcely unimportant, given the other
conditions. The mountainous, heavily wooded area no doubt
had much to do with the ambush, hit-and-run, sniper-type violence which helped name "Bloody Mingo."[123] Finally, the war
illustrates what might be called the dynamic quality of lawlessness or a domino theory of violence. Given the environment, it is understandable how one incident provoked others.
The concept of attack and retribution, etc., etc., was endorsed by legal, historical, and sociological conditions --
and encouraged by those of geography. As in the Logan
marches, events and emotions often moved quickly beyond the
control of responsible leadership.

The Mingo conflict is also distinctive among contemporary labor disorders for what failed to happen. The postwar era was
among the nation's worst in race relations. The color line
had been rigidly drawn, the Ku Klux Klan had reemerged, and
several bloody riots had occurred. The frequent use of
Negroes as strikebreakers inevitably provoked violence. The
Mingo War, however, was an interracial affair, unmarked by
the racially inspired lawlessness common to many other industrial disturbances.

In 1920, about 18 percent of West Virginia's miners were
Negroes. Their portion of the total population in Mingo and
Logan was 8.3 and 11.6 percent respectively.[124] Blacks had
joined the UMW in the state since the 1890s, and two sat on
the District 17 executive committee in 1920. They were active on both sides in every phase of the Mingo War. Hundreds
participated in the two marches on Logan. They lived beside
white families in the Mingo tent colonies. With other strikers, they were often arrested, jailed, and tried indiscrimi-
nately. On the employers' side, scores of them never left
their jobs, and scores were brought in as strikebreakers.
The Mingo War was neither conducted along racial lines nor
marked by racial violence; and as such, for the times, it was
certainly atypical.[125]

Mingo also failed to experience either any substantial Red
Scare hysteria or known activity by alien radicals. Despite
the operators' occasional attempts to label the UMW as being

socialistic and revolutionary and to warn against foreign
hordes and ideologies, the Mingo War was throughout a back-
yard American affair.[126]

On the union side, the conflict was almost completely home
grown. Keeney and his associates were natives of the state
virtually to a man and had even added their voices to the national antiradical chorus.[127] On a larger perspective, statistics for 1920 reveal that 93.4 percent of Logan's and 97.3
percent of Mingo's population was native born.[128] In addition, there is no evidence of serious radical or alien agitation in southern West Virginia during the Mingo War -- a minority claim among major labor disturbances of that era.[129]

The Mingo conflict, 1919 to 1922, was thus a war within a
war -- both representative and unique -- and deserving of
more attention than it has received from scholars of labor
history and of the era.

Notes

[1] There is no comprehensive, scholarly account of the Mingo
War in print. Among the unpublished theses and disserta-
tions which include it within a larger context are Charles
P. Anson, "A History of the Labor Movement in West Virginia" (Ph.D. diss., University of North Carolina, 1940);
and John M. Barb, "Strikes in the Southern West Virginia
Coal Field, 1919-1922" (M.A. thesis, West Virginia University, 1949). The present study draws heavily from five
primary sources. First is the William Jett Lauck Collection, Alderman Library, University of Virginia, cited hereafter as Lauck MSS. A consultant economist, Lauck was involved in the Mingo War and wrote several articles about it.
He served as counsel for the United Mine Workers of America
during the Kenyon (United States Senate) Committee Hearings
in 1921. The Lauck Collection includes scrapbooks of contemporary newspaper clippings on Mingo, bound volumes of
testimony, briefs, and the like, presented during the Kenyon Hearings; and several boxes of miscellaneous papers,
pamphlets, press releases, broadsides, and articles, as
well as correspondence concerning Lauck's investigation of
the Mingo War. The second major source is the Kenyon Committee's published hearings and reports: U.S., Senate,
Committee on Education and Labor, West Virginia Coal Fields,
Hearings, 3 vols. (Washington, D.C., 1921-1922), hereafter
cited as Kenyon Hearings. Third are the valuable, eyewitness accounts of Albert F. Hindrichs, The United Mine Workers of America and the Non-Union Coal Fields (New York,
1923), which has much pertinent material on West Virginia,
where the author, then a Columbia University economist, re-
searched in 1921; and Winthrop D. Lane, Civil War in West
Virginia: A Story of the Industrial Conflict in the Coal
Mines (New York, 1921), a strongly prolabor survey by a
New York Evening Post reporter. Fourth are the recollections -- published long after the fact and not always with

accuracy on details -- of participants in the conflict.
Chief among these would be Fred Mooney, Struggle in the
Coal Fields: The Autobiography of Fred Mooney, Secretary-
Treasurer, District 17, United Mine Workers of America, ed.
J. W. Hess (Morgantown, W. Va., 1967); and John L. Spivak,
A Man in His Time (New York, 1967), both of which are good
for the UMW side of the conflict; Howard B. Lee, Bloodlet-
ting in Appalachia (Morgantown, W. Va., 1969), written by
the state's attorney general between 1925 and 1931; and,
for the operators' position, Walter R. Thurmond, The Logan
Coal Field of West Virginia: A Brief History (Morgantown,
W. Va., 1964). Finally, contemporary magazines and newspapers contain hundreds of news and feature stories on the
Mingo War; especially helpful is the New York Times, 1919-
1923. Of less value were several local histories, including three overlapping and sharply antiunion accounts by
coal company official George T. Swain, Facts about the Two
Armed Marches on Logan (Charleston, W. Va., 1962), History
of Logan County, West Virginia (Kingsport, Tenn., 1927),
and The Incomparable Don Chafin (Charleston, W. Va., 1962).
On Dark and Bloody Ground: An Oral History of the U.M.W.A.
in Central Appalachia 1920-1935 (privately printed, 1973)
is a fine collection of reminiscences prepared as a National Endowment for the Humanities Youth Grant project under the direction of Anne Lawrence, but its use is limited
by a failure to get legal releases from the persons interviewed. A recent overview with some suggestive insights
but with thin documentation is Hoyt N. Wheeler, "Mountaineer Mine Wars: An Analysis of the West Virginia Mine Wars
of 1912-1913 and 1920-1921," Business History Review 50
(Spring 1976), 69-91.

2 For newspaper attention to the Mingo War, see "Mingo Scrapbooks," Lauck MSS; several items in the clippings file of
the West Virginia State Department of Archives and History,
Charleston; and the following press surveys reported in The
Literary Digest: "The Battle of Tug River," 69 (May 28,
1921), 16; "The Blame for West Virginia's War," 70 (September 10, 1921), 16; and "Treason and Reason," 73 (June 17,
1922), 14-15.

3 Leo Wolman, Growth of American Trade Unions, 1880-1923 (New
York, 1924), Table I, 110-11.

4 Figures on paid members in November 1918 are from Hindrichs,
UMWA and the Non-Union Coal Fields, Table 20, 179. The
figure for total miners in 1918 is from U.S. Geological
Survey, "Coal in 1919-1921," Mineral Resources of the
United States, 1921 - Part II: Nonmetals (Washington,
1924), 497.

5 On the threat from the Left: David J. McDonald and Edward
A. Lynch, Coal and Unionism: A History of the American

Coal Miners' Unions (Indianapolis, 1939), 139, 143; and
Philip Taft, Organized Labor in American History (New York,
1964), chap. 30, pass. On the restraining influence of
Gompers, see the revealing comment of John L. Lewis, in
Saul Alinsky, John L. Lewis: An Unauthorized Biography
(New York, 1949), 28.

[6] Hindrichs, UMWA and the Non-Union Coal Fields, 173.

[7] Lane, Civil War in West Virginia, 43.

[8] The convention and Lewis's vigorous program for 1919, including the national strike, are covered in Alinsky, Lewis,
26-35; Selig Perlman and Philip Taft, Labor Movements,
1896-1932, vol. 4 of History of Labor in the United States,
by John R. Commons et al. (New York, 1935), chap. 36; and
Arthur E. Suffern, The Coal Miners' Struggle for Industrial Status (New York, 1926), 99.

[9] For biographical data on Keeney, see Kenyon Hearings,
vol. 1, 103; Lane, Civil War in West Virginia, 85-88; and
Spivak, Man in His Time, 63; as well as Edmund Wilson's
later, laudatory estimate of his leadership ability, in
"Frank Keeney's Coal Diggers," New Republic 67 (July 8,
1931), 195-99, and (July 15, 1931), 229-31. For Fred
Mooney, Harold Houston, and other Keeney associates, see
Kenyon Hearings, vol. 1, 15; and Lane, Civil War in West
Virginia, chap. 13. Mooney's candid and often unflatter-
ing appraisals of the District 17 leadership are found in
his Struggle in the Coal Fields, 53.

[10] Charles Ambler and Festus P. Summers, West Virginia: The
Mountain State (Englewood Cliffs, N.J., 1958), 445-51;
Anson, "History of the Labor Movement," 113-24, 219-23;
Kyle McCormick, The New Kanawha River and the Mine War of
West Virginia (Charleston, W. Va., 1959), 130-50; Perlman
and Taft, Labor Movements, 326-35; and U.S., Department of
Labor, Annual Report, 1919 (Washington, D.C., 1920), 1043.

[11] Lucy Lee Fisher, "John J. Cornwell, Governor of West Virginia, 1917-1921, Part II," West Virginia History 24 (July
1963), 377; and Arthur Gleason, "Private Ownership of Public Officials," Nation 110 (May 29, 1920), 724-25.

[12] The quote is from the reprint pamphlet of the Janu-
ary 23-25, 1921, Baltimore Sun, which was published as
W. Jett Lauck and John W. Owens, The Investigation by the
Baltimore Sun of the Mingo County[,] West Virginia Coal
Strike (Baltimore, 1921?), 5, a copy of which is in Lauck
MSS, Box 4742-92. For Mingo's early history and growth as
a coal field, see Phil Conley, History of the West Vir-
ginia Coal Industry (Charleston, W. Va., 1960), chap. 13;
Kenyon Hearings, vol. 1, 7; Lauck and Owens, Investigation

by the Baltimore Sun, 4-5; and State of West Virginia Geological Survey Commission, Geographical Survey: Logan and
Mingo (Wheeling, 1914), 6-10, and pass. Both Mingo and
Logan are covered in the account by a long-time operator
in the area, Walter R. Thurmond, in his previously cited
Logan Coal, especially chaps. 1-4. Population figures for
1920 were 41,006 for Logan and 26,364 for Mingo, according
to U.S., Bureau of the Census, Fourteenth Census of the
United States Taken in the Year 1920 (13 vols., Washington,
1921-1923), vol. III, 1107. In 1910, Logan's population
was only 14,476 and Mingo's 19,431 (ibid.), while the combined population in 1890 was a mere 11,101 (Swain, Logan
County, 157).

13 For a detailed analysis revealing a massive intercorporate
relationship, see the charts and pamphlet prepared by
Lauck, or at his request, in Box 4742-91, Lauck MSS. For
additional comments about the gigantic holdings in the
area by U.S. Steel and the Norfolk and Western Railroad,
see Lane, Civil War in West Virginia, 119-21; for a defensive treatment of the absentee owner question by an operator, see Thurmond, Logan Coal, 40-42.

14 James H. Thompson, Significant Trends in the West Virginia
Coal Industry, 1900-1957 (Morgantown, W. Va., 1958), 7, 9.
See also U.S., Bureau of the Census, Fourteenth Census,
vol. 11, 234; and Waldo E. Fisher and Anne Bezanson, Wage
Rates and Working Time in the Bituminous Coal Industry,
1912-1922 (Philadelphia, 1932), 33.

15 Malcolm Ross, Machine Age in the Hills (New York, 1933),
143.

16 Quoted in Winthrop D. Lane, "The Senators Tour West Virginia," The Survey 47 (October 1, 1921), 24.

17 The literature, pro and con, on company towns is volumi-
nous. Harshly critical are Arthur Gleason, "Company-owned
Americans," Nation 110 (June 12, 1920), 794-95; Dale
Fetherling, Mother Jones, The Miners' Angel (Carbondale,
Ill., 1974), 182-83; Lane, Civil War in West Virginia, especially 16-17 and chaps. 2 and 4; and Spivak, Man in His
Time, 60-61; and, for a sample of the UMW charges before
the Kenyon Committee, see Kenyon Hearings, vol. 2, 654-56.
More balanced are Hindrichs, UMWA and the Non-Union Fields,
chap. 5; and Lauck and Owens, Investigation by the Baltimore Sun, pass. For a favorable view, see American Constitutional Association, Life in a West Virginia Coal
Field (Charleston, W. Va., 1923), pass.; Lane, Civil War
in West Virginia, chap. 3; Logan Coal Operators' Association, "A Few Facts and Figures in Regard to Logan District" (n.d., n.p.) in Box 4742-92, Lauck MSS. For operators' testimony before the Kenyon Committee, see Kenyon

Hearings, vol. 2, 869-70, 907-908, 913, 918-21, 935-36;
New York Times, May 29, 1921; and Thurmond, Logan Coal, 56,
64-65.

[18] According to the 1920 census (vol. 3, 1105, 1108), Logan's
population was 81.8 percent native white and Mingo's 89,
against West Virginia's overall 89.9. Pertinent subdivi-
sions are: for Logan, a total population of 41,006, with
33,559 native whites, 2,710 foreign born whites, and 2,191
Negroes. See also, Kenyon Hearings, vol. 1, 7; and
Sterling D. Spero and Abram L. Harris, The Black Worker:
The Negro and the Labor Movement (New York, 1931), 216-21.
The subject of "The Negro and the Labor Supply" in the
state's coal industry is covered in Anson, "History of the
Labor Movement," 65-69.

[19] The operator's inherent power in a company-housing system
is one of many examples. Almost all miners lived in company houses and thus, in effect, were subject to sudden
eviction. Many housing contracts gave the company authority to remove "improper or suspicious persons" from the
premises and held the lessees responsible for preventing
such persons from being there in the first place.
Hindrichs, UMWA and the Non-Union Coal Fields, 63-64. One
operator said the advantage of company housing was "to
have men concentrated so as to have proper supervision
over them, to better control them in times of labor agitation and threatened strikes." Quoted in Hindrichs, UMWA
and the Non-Union Coal Fields, 63.

[20] This is the conclusion of Hindrichs, who made the most
thorough, scholarly, and dispassionate investigation of
the subject. Hindrichs, UMWA and the Non-Union Coal
Fields, 9. Even the stoutly prounion Gleason and Lane
concur. Gleason, "Company-owned Americans," 795; and
Lane, Civil War in West Virginia, 92. Conditions in the
state's mining camps, union and nonunion, while much improved over previous decades (and this improvement "attributable solely to the growing strength of the miner's
organization," Hindrichs, 81), were much deprived by national standards. For a tale of horrors that is comprehensive and heavy with both statistical and pictorial evidence, see U.S., Children's Bureau, The Welfare of Children in Bituminous Coal Mining Communities in West Virginia (Washington, D.C., 1923).

[21] Hindrichs, UMWA and the Non-Union Coal Fields, 59, chap. 5,
pass.; and Lane, Civil War in West Virginia, 35.

[22] Lane, Civil War in West Virginia, chaps. 9, 10.

[23] On the "mine guard" system in general, see Gleason, "Private Ownership of Public Officials," 724-25; Lane, Civil

War in West Virginia, chaps. 7-8; Lauck and Owens, Investigation by the Baltimore Sun, 10, 17-18; John W. Owens,
"Gunmen in West Virginia," The New Republic 22 (September 21, 1921), 90-92; and Arthur Warner, "Fighting Unionism with Martial Law," The Nation 113 (October 12, 1921),
395-96 -- all of which are hostile to it. The system
dated back several decades in West Virginia; see Lane,
above, 92; Carolyn Karr, "A Political Biography of Henry
Hatfield," West Virginia History 28 (January 1967), 141;
and Neil Shaw Penn, "Henry Hatfield and Reform Politics:
A Study of West Virginia Politics from 1908 to 1917" (Ph.D.
diss., Emory University, 1973), 333-34. It was a key issue in the state's violent strikes of 1912 and 1913; see
Anson, "History of the Labor Movement," 220-21; and it was
declared illegal by a West Virginia law (1913) which,
characteristically, lacked a punitive clause. Kenyon
Hearings, vol. 1, 543. Democratic Governor John J. Cornwell, 1917-1921, who was elected with some labor votes,
soundly condemned the mine guard system but claimed he
lacked authority to combat it and had little impact on it.
John J. Cornwell to William Green, n.p., September 4, 1920,
cited in Fisher, "Cornwell," 55; and Mooney, Struggle in
the Coal Fields, 59-60, 66. It was also denounced in the
report of a legislative investigating committee (1919), in
the West Virginia State Republican Platform of 1920.
Lauck and Owens, above, 10, 17-18; and Kenyon Hearings,
vol. 2, 945. It was not abolished, however, by effective
statute until the 1930s. Ambler and Summers, West Virginia, 462; Evelyn L. K. Harris and Frank J. Krebs, From
Humble Beginnings: West Virginia State Federation of Labor, 1903-1957 (Charleston, W. Va., 1960), 151; McCormick,
New Kanawha River, 134; and Mooney, Struggle in the Coal
Fields, 128-92. As one prominent operator put it, the
practice, even before being outlawed, had become "unnecessary" due to "the development of good roads and the resulting ability of the State Police to get to the mines
quickly." W. P. Tams, Jr., Smokeless Fields of West Virginia (Morgantown, W. Va., 1963), 60. The operators, when
forced to admit that it existed, defended the "mine guard"
system as a legitimate means of protecting what they considered to be the inalienable rights of property. See,
for example, the revealing testimony of William H.
Coolidge, Kenyon Hearings, vol. 2, 916-17. The system no
doubt was regarded as cheaper than the equally efficient
alternative of paying deputies from public taxes which
also would have risked reevaluation of the operators' fan-
tastically underassessed property. Kenyon Hearings,
vol. 2, 914-15, and vol. 3, 1055-56; and Hindrichs, UMWA
and the Non-Union Fields, 75.

24 For a general sketch of the agency and its general manager,
Thomas L. Felts, see McCormick, New Kanawha River, 170-71.
Felts's testimony before the Kenyon Committee is recorded

in Kenyon Hearings, vol. 2, 881-905. Other pertinent testimony is found in Kenyon Hearings, vol. 1, 85-88, 177,
210-15, 392; and in the New York Times, January 28, 1921.
See also, for the undercover aspect of the Baldwin-Felts
agency, Kenyon Hearings, vol. 1, 355-92; Winthrop D. Lane,
"The Labor Spy in West Virginia," The Survey 47 (October 22, 1921), 110-12; Lane, Civil War in West Virginia,
79; and McCormick, above, 165-66. See also Edward Levinson, I Break Strikes! (New York, 1935), 17, 26, 151-57,
209-10; Mooney, Struggle in the Coal Fields, 72-77; and
Spivak, Man in His Time, 59-60, 91-93. Levinson awarded
"The blue ribbon for wanton killings ... to the Baldwin-
Felts organization" (p. 151).

25 Kenyon Hearings, vol. 2, 867-68, 1020; vol. 3, 7-8.
Chafin's deputies and their salaries, November 7, 1921,
are recorded in ibid., 601.

26 Chafin was one of the principal figures in the Mingo War
and perhaps the most controversial. College educated,
from a politically powerful local family, an astute busi-
nessman and Democratic chieftain, he was greatly admired
by the Logan operators and, at the same time, was the bete
noire of the unions and later spent time in a federal pen-
itentiary. Local historian George T. Swain elevates him
to sainthood in the pamphlet The Incomparable Don Chafin,
cited earlier, while coal magnate Walter R. Thurmond gives
a laudatory sketch in his Logan Coal, 86-87. Chafin in
the flesh was far different than Chafin in reputation.
One reporter covering the treason trials in 1922 expected
the sheriff to be crude and rustic. Instead he found "a
youngish-looking, well groomed, perfectly composed man of
athletic build, rather good-looking ... [who appears] more
like a star halfback that has become a stockbroker than
the typical county sheriff." Baltimore Sun, May 16, 1922,
clipping in Box 424, Lauck MSS. His local power seemed
limitless. Dale Fetherling recounts the story: "a for-
eigner who sought the right to vote after obtaining his
citizenship papers appeared before the Logan County board
of registrars to establish his qualifications. He was
asked to name the president of the United States. Without
hesitation, he replied, 'Meester Don Chafin.'" Mother
Jones, 181. Additional biographical detail is found in
Lee, Bloodletting, chaps. 12 and 16; and McCormick, New
Kanawha River, 163-65. Chafin's financial status was revealed in Kenyon Hearings, vol. 3, 1064, 1074-77.

27 Gleason, "Private Ownership of Public Officials," 724;
Harris and Krebs, From Humble Beginnings, 151; Kenyon
Hearings, vol. 3, 1055, 1073; and McCormick, New Kanawha
River, 164. The UMW had at least one deputy sheriff on
its payroll for a few months in 1920; and although it was
never proven, the operators charged former Mingo Sheriff

George T. Blankenship with having been subsidized by the
union. Kenyon Hearings, vol. 1, 173, 200-201; and Lane,
Civil War in West Virginia, 104.

28 Quoted in the Allentown, Pennsylvania, Chronicle and News,
October 29, 1921, a clipping in Box 424, Lauck MSS.

29 There are many well-established examples of Chafin's antiunion tactics. For example, in something of a comic mix-
up, an "organizer" for the Knights of Pythias arrived in
Logan to conduct an initiation but was "taken out of town
in a car, beaten, and thrown along the roadside" before
the deputies realized the unfortunate man was not the kind
of "organizer" they were paid to take care of. Gleason,
"Private Ownership of Public Officials," 725; and
McCormick, New Kanawha River, 156. Another well-known incident occurred on October 15, 1919, when fifty-one UMW
officials and organizers entrained in Charleston for Logan.
En route, armed guards boarded the train; and it was noted
that it was also being followed by an engine with two ca-
booses filled with additional armed men. The organizers
were told "Don't let your feet touch dirt in Logan
County" -- a warning the union officials obeyed to the
letter. See Gleason, above, 924; McCormick, above, 156;
and Lane, Civil War in West Virginia, 62-63. Other samples of the "Logan treatment" are noted in Gleason, above,
724-25; McAlister Coleman, Men and Coal (New York, 1943),
91; and Mooney, Struggle in the Coal Fields, 63-64, 97,
120-21. There appears to have been no doubt about the purpose of the special deputies. The admiring local historian of Logan County noted a few years after the Mingo War,
"It became the duty of Don Chafin to keep organizers out.
They have never yet organized Logan." Swain, Logan, 271.
West Virginia Attorney General E. T. England, a resident
of Logan and former state senator from that county, said,
in 1921, that the company-paid deputies served "to keep
out organizations." Kenyon Hearings, vol. 1, 543; see
also, vol. 1, 551, and vol. 2, 719-21. State Superintendent of Public Safety Colonel Jackson Arnold told United
States Senators William S. Kenyon and Samuel M. Shortridge,
in September 1921, that if the law were administered im-
partially, the organizers would inevitably unionize the
nonunion counties. Ibid., vol. 1, 551. Chafin, for his
part, told reporter McAlister Coleman at the time that he
was battling "commonism" in Logan County. Coleman, Men
and Coal, 91.

30 Except as otherwise indicated in the notes, this reconstruction of the first march is based on: John J. Cornwell's memoirs, A Mountain Trail to the Schoolroom, the
Editor's Chair, the Lawyer's Office, and the Governorship
of West Virginia (Philadelphia, 1939), 57-59; Fisher,
"Cornwell," 377-80; Kenney's and Mooney's accounts, as

recorded in Kenyon Hearings, vol. 1, 169-70, and in
Struggle in the Coal Fields, 63-67; the secondary accounts
of Ambler and Summers, West Virginia, 454; Barb, "Strikes,"
chap. 4; and McCormick, New Kanawha River, 144-46, 156;
and the reportage of Lane, Civil War in West Virginia,
105-109, and "West Virginia--The Civil War and Its Coal
Fields," The Survey 47 (October 29, 1921), 180, and the
New York Times, September 6-9, 1919. Minor discrepancies
appear. The "spontaneous" nature of the Marmet gathering
is questioned by a prolabor contemporary, John L. Spivak,
who suggests surreptitious planning by the UMW. Man in
His Time, 69. The official investigation, promised by
Cornwell, led to a sixty-nine-page Report and Digest of
Evidence Taken by Commission Appointed by the Governor of
West Virginia in Connection with the Logan County Situation (Charleston, W. Va., 1919), a partisan document hostile to the union.

31 In addition to the basic sources annotated in note 1, for
briefer overviews see: Ambler and Summers (the historian's view), West Virginia, 454-60; Coleman (an insider's
view), Men and Coal, 99-103; Fisher (a governor's view),
"Cornwell," 380-83; John A. Fitch (a liberal's view),
"West Virginia," The Survey 45 (March 12, 1921), 850-52;
Harris and Krebs (the union's view), From Humble Beginnings, 149-63; Rand School of Social Science (a date-by-
date view), American Labor Year Book (New York, n.d.),
196-200; Bennett Milton Rich (a presidential view), The
Presidents and Civil Disorder (Washington, D.C., 1941),
158-61; Anna Rochester (a Communist's view), Labor and
Coal (New York, 1931), 196-98; and Ross (another insider's
view), Machine Age in the Hills, 139-54.

32 For the origins and context of the UMW push, see AFL Proceedings, 1921, 195; Alinsky, Lewis, 28-42; Ambler and
Summers, West Virginia, 454; Gleason, "Private Ownership
of Public Officials," 724; Harris and Krebs, From Humble
Beginnings, 152-53; Lauck and Owens, Investigation by the
Baltimore Sun, 13-18; Mooney, Struggle in the Coal Fields,
71-72; Suffern, Coal Miners' Struggle, 101-104; Perlman
and Taft, Labor Movements, 475-80; and especially the testimony before the Kenyon Hearings presenting both the UMW
account (vol. 1, 5, 15-16, 74, 80-81, 103-104; and vol. 2,
103-104) and the operators' version (vol. 2, 8-9); the New
York Times, May 20, 1920; and the revealing article by a
former employer-engineer in Mingo in the New York Times,
September 5, 1921.

33 Of the twenty-two (of several score) operators initially
signing UMW contracts, only three were classified "large."
Kenyon Hearings, vol. 1, 124-30.

34 Much was made of the inhumanity of the eviction process

(not to say of its questionable legality). Veteran reporter McAlister Coleman wrote that he had seen much labor
violence across the nation but that the brutality of the
Mingo evictions was "unique in the recent history of industrial conflicts ... [and that they] were planned in
cold blood and carried out in a sadistic manner, with the
women and children of the miners as their innocent victims." Coleman, Men and Coal, 101. See also Mooney,
Struggle in the Coal Fields, 71-72.

35 The quotes are from the Washington Times, January 29, 1921,
a clipping in Box 426, Lauck MSS.

36 Of the feuding Hatfields and a former miner, Sid was
twenty-seven years old, with a "slight build ... and a
most ingratiating smile." Ibid., December 12, 1920. He
"never drank nor smoked" and paid "$250 a year to keep a
Presbyterian preacher in Matewan." Ibid. The Baldin-
Felts' revenge was not to be denied. In the course of a
series of trials following the massacre, Sid Hatfield and
an associate appeared in Welch, West Virginia, on August 1,
1921. Walking unarmed up the courthouse steps, they were
met by a group of Baldwin-Felts men who fired seventeen
bullets into Sid and thirteen into his colleague. On the
"Matewan Massacre," the resulting trials and Welch shooting, and the principal, Sid Hatfield, see Barb, "Strikes,"
59-64; Dale Fetherling, "Massacre at Matewan," The Appalachian South 1 (Fall and Winter 1966), 10-12; Lane, Civil
War in West Virginia, chap. 11, pass.; Lee, Bloodletting,
52-72; Levinson, I Break Strikes, 209-10; McCormick, New
Kanawha River, 150-53; Mooney, Struggle in the Coal Fields,
72-77, 87-88; New York Times, May 20 and 21, 1920,
March 20 and 21, May 23 and 24, and December 5, 1921; Ross,
Machine Age in the Hills, 144-45; Nancy Sue Smith, History
of Logan and Mingo Counties (n.p., n.d.), chap. 24; Spivak,
Man in His Time, 88-93; and the extensive collection of
press clippings, in Boxes 426 and 427, Lauck MSS. Details
vary.

37 Gleason, "Private Ownership of Public Officials," 724, 725.

38 Quote is from Lauck and Owens, Investigation by the Baltimore Sun, 7. Developments from late May through July 1
are covered in the Kenyon testimony cited in note 30 as
well as vol. 1, 6-11; plus the New York Times, May 21, 23,
and 29, and July 1 and 2, 1920. While the evicted miner
figure on July 1 was about 2,700, the total union miners
were an estimated 6,000 throughout the strike zone, which,
although focused on Mingo, also included portions of
McDowell and Mercer counties as well as part of Pike
County, Kentucky, across the Tug River from Mingo. See
Ambler and Summers, West Virginia, 455; and Kenyon Hearings, vol. 1, 5-6, 11, 15.

[39] New York Times, October 27, 1922. The UMW simultaneously announced plans to move the remaining 1,000 Mingo strikers and their families to union fields.

[40] See charts on pages 23 to 25 in "Statement of Harry Olmstead, July 14, 1921," in Box 4792-93, Lauck MSS; as well as Kenyon Hearings, vol. 1, 236-41; and New York Times, December 6, 1921.

[41] These contrived headlines apply, respectively, to the following: New York Times, July 6, 15, and 24; August 22; October 18; November 19; and December 1, 5, 8, 11, 13, 17, and 24, 1920.

[42] Kenyon Hearings, vol. 1, 264.

[43] Respectively: Kenyon Hearings, vol. 1, 268-69, 170-71; and Morgantown Post, November 28, 1920, as cited in Harris and Krebs, From Humble Beginnings, 153.

[44] The proclamations are recorded in Kenyon Hearings, vol. 1, 272-77. See also Elizabeth Cometti and Festus P. Summers, eds., The Thirty-fifth State: A Documentary History of West Virginia (Morgantown, W. Va., 1966), 541-44. For an example of the severe restrictions which martial law carried for the strikers, see New York Times, November 30, 1920. As one law enforcement agent asserted in 1921: "The big advantage of this martial law is that if there's an agitator around you can just stick him in jail and keep him there." Quoted in Hindrichs, UMWA and the Non-Union Coal Fields, 153. One use of this "big advantage" occurred on July 8, 1921, when D. S. Robb (a national UMW officer in charge of its Mingo relief program) and eleven other officials were arrested in Williamson while planning the distribution of food, clothing, and supplies to strikers and their families in the tent colonies. The charge was "unlawful assemblage." Robb and his associates were jailed and refused release either on bail or writ of habeas corpus. Robb and four others, in fact, were not released until they had agreed to leave the state immediately and never return. New York Times, July 9, 10, and 16; May 22, 24, and 27; and June 15, 1921. For a dispassionate analysis of the legal implications of martial law in the Mingo War, see Robert S. Rankin, When Civil Law Fails: Martial Law and Its Legal Basis in the United States (Durham, N.C., 1939), 126-36.

[45] Edward Berman, Labor Disputes and the President of the United States (New York, 1924), 209.

[46] New York Times, November 30, 1920.

[47] On Harding's prudent course, see Berman, Labor Disputes,

210-11; and Rich, Presidents and Civil Disorder, 158-61,
the quote being from the latter, p. 160. For the Williamson "Vigilance Committee," see Hindrichs, UMWA and the
Non-Union Coal Fields, 152-53; and Kenyon Hearings, vol. 1,
230-36, 342-46.

48 For a comprehensive, firsthand report, see New York Times,
December 6 and 7, 1920. See also Coleman, Men and Coal,
100; Kenyon Hearings, vol. 1, 166-68, 318-20, 340; Lauck
and Owens, Investigation by the Baltimore Sun, 3; Mooney,
Struggle in the Coal Fields, 77-78; and the press clippings -- stories, with photographs -- in Box 426, Lauck
MSS. The Red Cross refused aid since the miners' plight
was not due to "An Act of God." Alinsky, Lewis, 39.

49 Except as otherwise indicated in the notes, this reconstruction is based on the following: Anson, "History of
the Labor Movement," 232-36; Ambler and Summers, West Virginia, 454-60; Barb, "Strikes," 100-109; the previously
cited Literary Digest press survey entitled "The Blame for
West Virginia's War"; Coleman, Men and Coal, 103-104; the
official union position in Harris and Krebs, From Humble
Beginnings, 153-55; Kenyon Hearings, vol. 1, 545-46,
vol. 2, 874-76, 966-98, 1032-35, and vol. 3, 1057-63; the
photographic essay of Lane, "Civil War," 177-83; Lee,
Bloodletting, chap. 13; McCormick, New Kanawha River,
154-75; Mooney, Struggle in the Coal Fields, 89-100; New
York Times, almost daily from August 20 through Septem-
ber 20, 1921; the strongly prolabor, eyewitness report of
Arthur Shields, "The Battle of Logan County," The Liber-
ator 4 (October 1921), 16-20, which is in Box 4742-93,
Lauck MSS; Spivak, Man in His Time, 102-104; Spero and
Harris, Black Worker, 368-69; the prooperator account in
Swain, Logan County, 161-79, The Incomparable Don Chafin,
and Logan; and finally, coverage from the federal level as
recounted in Berman, Labor Disputes, 211-13; and Rich,
Presidents and Civil Disorder, 161-67. As in the case of
the first march and the Matewan Massacre, some factual
discrepancies occur among these sources; as a rule, recollections written years later (such as Lee's, Mooney's, and
Spivak's) are less reliable on details than are firsthand
reports in the press.

50 For various interpretations, see especially, Lane, "Civil
War," 182; and Mooney, Struggle in the Coal Fields, 89-90;
but also New York Times, May 9, 1922; and Kenyon Hearings,
vol. 1, 545-46.

51 The Kenyon Hearings were held sporadically until October 27, 1921, and included an informal investigation in
West Virginia by Senators Kenyon and Samuel M. Shortridge
of California. See Lane, "Senators Tour West Virginia."
Extensive press clippings on the senators' tour of West

Virginia and on the committee's hearings in Washington are
found in Boxes 424 and 426 of the Lauck MSS. The committee's final reports are found in Kenyon Hearings, vol. 3,
3-30. Kenyon's recommendation of a federal labor code and
board is noted in Robert H. Zieger, Republicans and Labor,
1919-1929 (Lexington, 1969), 217.

52 New York Times, August 2-4, and 7, 1921.

53 Harris and Krebs, From Humble Beginnings, 155. See also
New York Times, August 8, 1921; and Kenyon Hearings,
vol. 1, 545-46. The conciliatory role of the UMW leaders
is described in Mooney, Struggle in the Coal Fields, 89.

54 Quoted in New York Times, August 21, 1921.

55 Quoted in New York Times, August 22, 1921.

56 A survey of her long career in labor agitation with samples of her vitriolic language is Fetherling, Mother Jones;
see also Judith Elaine Mikeal, "Mother Mary Jones: The
Labor Movement's Impious Joan of Arc" (M.A. thesis, University of North Carolina, 1965), the appendix of which
contains several inflammatory speeches delivered by
Mrs. Jones in West Virginia; and the sketch by Joseph
Leeds, "The Miners Called Her Mother," Masses and Main-
stream 3 (March 1950), 38-50. Her speeches were so abu-
sive and incendiary that the Williamson Operators' Association "hired a stenographer to take down her words and
printed them -- as being self-condemnatory -- above their
own chaste comment: 'Good citizens of Mingo will repudi-
ate any such utterances.'" Ross, Machine Age in the Hills,
148. Her personality and activities in the Mingo War era
are also described in Mooney, Struggle in the Coal Fields,
58, 68-69, 89-91; and Spivak, Man in His Time, 70 ff.

57 Her motives in the bogus telegram incident remain a mys-
tery. Mikeal states "the inside story ... will probably
never be known" but gives some possible explanations.
"Mother Mary Jones," 88. See also Fetherling, Mother
Jones, 186, 189-90; and McCormick, New Kanawha River, 169.

58 Ambler and Summers, West Virginia, 456.

59 New York Times, August 27, 28, and 30, 1921; Kenyon Hearings, vol. 3, 1032-33.

60 A view shared by Bandholtz, New York Times, September 3,
1921.

61 Mooney, Struggle in the Coal Fields, 95.

62 New York Times, August 30, 1921. The president also

threatened the use of federal troops if the proclamation
was not obeyed.

63 The comic-tragic air war proved ineffective, though not
for a lack of intent to inflict bodily harm. One Logan
authority admitted in court having used "improvised bombs
filled with explosives and gas." Baltimore Sun, May 18,
1922, Box 424, Lauck MSS. The charge was made that the
bombs also included acid and grenades. New York Globe,
May 5, 1922, Box 424, Lauck MSS. One of the bombs was
displayed during the treason trial. The contents were a
bizarre mix of deadly missiles and junk. Baltimore Sun,
May 10, 1922, Box 424, Lauck MSS. For various aspects of
this unique domestic air war, see: Ambler and Summers,
West Virginia, 457; the photographic (including pictures
of Mitchell's squadron and of a homemade bomb) essay of
Lane, "Civil War," 178, 182-83; Maurer Maurer and Calvin
F. Senning, "Billy Mitchell, the Air Service, and the
Mingo War," West Virginia History 30 (October 1968), pass.;
Mooney, Struggle in the Coal Fields, 97; and Rich, Presi-
dents and Civil Disorder, 165; as well as New York Times,
August 27, September 2-4, and 15, 1921, and May 4, 16,
and 17, 1922.

64 Several U.S. Air Service planes were already in the area
for reconnaissance missions, and General Mitchell had made
an earlier trip to West Virginia himself. The Eighty-
eighth Squadron's armament included machine guns and 150-
pound nonpoisonous tear and nauseous gas bombs. Although
causing quite a stir locally, the aerial contingent
dropped no bombs, served chiefly in reconnaissance roles,
and used tear gas only in a demonstration for the press.
Eight of the approximately twenty planes crashed or crash-
landed with four fatalities before their return to Langley
Field, Virginia. See Maurer and Senning, "Billy Mitchell,"
pass.; and the extensive citations in note 63. Mitchell's
personal solution to the miners' march was simple. As he
told a reporter: "Gas ... we wouldn't try to kill these
people at first. We'd drop tear gas all over the place.
If they refused to disperse then we'd open up with artil-
lery preparation and everything." Quoted in Maurer and
Senning, "Billy Mitchell," 343.

65 Rich, Presidents and Civil Disorder, 164-65.

66 Mooney, Struggle in the Coal Fields, 98.

67 The post-march trials are covered in Ambler and Summers,
West Virginia, 457-59; Lane, "Civil War," 183; Lee, Bloodletting, chaps. 14 and 15; McCormick, New Kanawha River,
14-15; and Swain, Logan County, 176-79, The Incomparable
Don Chafin, and Logan; as well as New York Times, September 18 and 24, and October 15, 1921, January 14, 15, and

April-June, pass., 1922. An extract from the Logan County
grand jury's "Indictment for Treason, February 4, 1922,"
is reproduced in Cometti and Summers, The Thirty-fifth
State, 547-49. The treason charge is ably analyzed and
put in historical perspective in James G. Randall's "The
Miners and the Law of Treason," North American Review 216
(September 1922), 312-22. Critical of the way the law was
used against the miners is Richard D. Lunt, "The Struggle
Against the Law to Organize the Coal Fields of West Virginia," paper presented at the Southern Labor History Conference, Atlanta, Ga., April 1976.

68 A convenient summary of the prosecution case as well as
that of the defense is found in New York Times, May 18,
1922. The State's ready resort to treason charges aroused
much press comment. Editorialized the New York Times on
May 30, 1922 (p. 12): "in West Virginia indictments for
treason seem to be thrown about as carelessly as if they
were indictments for the larceny of a chicken."

69 At one point, the rival attorneys seemed on the verge of a
fist fight if not a shoot-out. Washington Herald, May 2,
1922, Box 424, Lauck MSS.

70 New York Times, April 15, June 21, July 27, and August 11,
1923; Mooney, Struggle in the Coal Fields, chap. 10, pass.

71 Lane, Civil War in West Virginia, 79; Ross, Machine Age in
the Hills, 145; Kenyon Hearings, vol. 1, 12, 177, 210-15,
263-64, 292, vol. 2, 881-82, 893, 896.

72 The UMW tried hard -- but with little success -- to make
Judge Elbert H. Gary of U.S. Steel the evil genius of the
association's antilabor policy. See Kenyon Hearings,
vol. 2, 604, 611, 640-47, 649-52, and Samuel Untermyer's
testimony, 697-719. For Gary's reply, see New York Times,
October 26, 1921. A pertinent anti-U.S. Steel article is
"Garyism in West Virginia," The New Republic 22 (September 21, 1921), 86-88. See also Gompers's interview published in New York Times, September 5, 1921; and Lauck and
Owens, Investigation by the Baltimore Sun, 16.

73 The madcap marches on Logan illustrate the control problems inherent in a splintered organizational structure.
See also the account of factions and infighting in Mooney,
Struggle in the Coal Fields, 67-69; New York Times, May 12,
1921; and Lane, Civil War in West Virginia, 94-98.

74 A representative sampling of the support includes: the
international UMW's financial aid (between two and three
million dollars by October 1922, as noted in New York
Times, April 12 and October 28, 1922, and in Thomas E.
Posey, "Some Significant Aspects of the West Virginia Labor Movement," Proceedings of the West Virginia Academy of

Science, 1950 22 (June 1951), 119; legal counsel, for example, see "Correspondence Folder," Box 4742-91, Lauck MSS,
and _New York Times_, September 25, 1921; professional as-
sistance on the scene, Kenyon Hearings, vol. 1, 23; and
moral support in the press and elsewhere: Rand School of
Social Science, _American Labor Year Book_, 199; and _New
York Times_, January 10 and 24, July 17, and September 3,
1921. For examples of a variety of aid from the AFL, see
AFL Proceedings, 1921, 194; "Forty-first Convention of the
American Federation of Labor," _Monthly Labor Review_ 13
(August 1921), 151; and _New York Times_, September 15, 1922.
The support, material and otherwise, of the West Virginia
State Federation of Labor is discussed in Harris and Krebs,
From Humble Beginnings, 158-60.

75 Arthur Warner, "West Virginia--Industrialism Gone Mad,"
The Nation (October 5, 1921), 372. For other discus-
sions of this point see Fisher, "Cornwell," 383; Lane,
Civil War in West Virginia, 11, 15, 43, 124-25, and "Civil
War," 179; _New York Times_, December 5 and 6, 1920; and
Kenyon Hearings, vol. 1, 112-24, 130-31, vol. 2, 908-909,
999, and vol. 3, 4-6, 1036.

76 Kenyon Hearings, vol. 2, 605.

77 "Operators' Brief," 8, 9, Box 4742-93, Lauck MSS; and Kenyon Hearings, vol. 3, 6.

78 Kenyon Hearings, vol. 1, 10.

79 See notes 23-29.

80 Lane, _Civil War in West Virginia_, 22. See also notes 17
and 19.

81 Fitch, "West Virginia," 850-52; Gleason, "Company-owned
Americans," 794-95; Hindrichs, _UMWA and the Non-Union Coal
Fields_, chaps. 2-6; Lane, _Civil War in West Virginia_,
chaps. 2, 4, 6, and 18; Lauck and Owens, _Investigation by
the Baltimore Sun_, 9, 13-18; _New York Times_, September 19,
1920; and Kenyon Hearings, vol. 1, 16, 24-26, 76-79, 92-93,
241-47, 469-83, vol. 2, 636-38, 655, 694-97, 747, and
vol. 3, 4.

82 Olmstead's testimony, Kenyon Hearings, vol. 1, 241-45, and
his statement, _New York Times_, May 18, 1921.

83 See note 86.

84 Kenyon Hearings, vol. 1, 258.

85 An operator quoted in _New York Times_, February 7, 1921.

86 Kenyon Hearings, vol. 1, 250-63; "Operators' Brief,"

folder in Box 4742-93, Lauck MSS; Hindrichs, UMWA and the Non-Union Coal Fields, chap. 11; and Philip Murray's evaluation in Kenyon Hearings, vol. 2, 630-36. See also the variety of testimony in Kenyon Hearings, vol. 1, 18, 175, 187-91, 250-54, 393-468, vol. 2, 802-37, 908-909, 940-44, and vol. 3, 8; Thurmond, Logan Coal, 102; and the interview with William H. Coolidge of Boston, Boston Herald, September 8, 1921, Box 426, Lauck MSS.

87 Hindrichs, UMWA and the Non-Union Coal Fields, 13-16; "Operators' Brief" and "West Virginia Case--Press," folders in Box 4742-93, Lauck MSS; McCormick, New Kanawha River, 163; New York Times, February 7, May 18, August 30, and September 6 and 10, 1921; Ross, Machine Age in the Hills, 145-46; and Kenyon Hearings, vol. 1, 263-64. Also, see footnote 71 in the American Constitutional Association's incredibly rosy pamphlet, Life in a West Virginia Coal Field, and "Coal Facts," Special Collection, West Virginia State Department of Archives and History.

88 Clipping from the New York Journal, April 7, 1922, in Box 425, Lauck MSS.

89 Ambler and Summers, West Virginia, 449-51; Coleman, Men and Coal, 84; Charles B. Fowler, Collective Bargaining in the Bituminous Coal Industry (New York, 1927), 138-39; and Felix Frankfurter and Nathan V. Greene, The Labor Injunction (New York, 1930), 15-16, 37-39.

90 Quote is that of Circuit Judge John J. Parker cited in Irving Bernstein, The Lean Years: A History of the Worker, 1920-1933 (Boston, 1960), 211. See also Frankfurter and Greene, Labor Injunction, 100, and appendix I, item 7, and Lunt, "The Struggle Against the Law."

91 AFL Proceedings, [1922], 40-43; Charles F. Carter, "Murder to Maintain Coal Monopoly," Current History 15 (January 1922), 597-603; "Enjoining the Check-off System of the United Mine Workers," Monthly Labor Review 14 (February 1922), 128-31; Frankfurter and Greene, Labor Injunction, 100, and appendix I, item 8; Lane, Civil War in West Virginia, chap. 10; New York Times, October 30 and November 1, 1921, and February 11, 1923; Perlman and Taft, Labor Movements, 480; and Kenyon Hearings, vol. 2, 754-57, 781.

92 "Interference with Union Organizers: West Virginia," Monthly Labor Review 16 (June 1923), 227-28; and New York Times, December 23 and 29, 1920, and February 18, 1923.

93 New York Times, December 8 and 20, 1920, and February 7, 1921; Kenyon Hearings, vol. 1, 8, 13, 100-101, 158; Pocahontas Operators Association pamphlet, The Bill, The Answer, The Injunction (Bluefield, W. Va., 1921?), pass.;

Lane, <u>Civil War in West Virginia</u>, chap. 9; <u>New York Times</u>, December 6, 1920; and Kenyon Hearings, vol. 1, 12, 26-27, 292.

94 Kenyon Hearings, vol. 1, 159.

95 <u>New York Times</u>, December 8 and 20, 1920, February 7, March 15, May 18 and 20, and July 13, 1921; Ross, <u>Machine Age in the Hills</u>, 150-51; and Kenyon Hearings, vol. 1, 249-50.

96 Kenyon Hearings, vol. 1, 555. The Mingo operators were paying an estimated $25,000 monthly merely to protect their mines and workers, according to the <u>New York Times</u>, May 25, 1921.

97 See sources in note 44.

98 <u>New York Times</u>, July 7, 1920; Ross, <u>Machine Age in the Hills</u>, 149; and Kenyon Hearings, vol. 1, 27, 64-69. The operators apparently tried to buy off such UMW leaders as Keeney and lawyer Harold Houston (Spivak, <u>Man in His Time</u>, 106), and union-sympathizing local officials as well. (A bribe attempt might have figured in the preliminaries to the Matewan Massacre. See note 36.)

99 See pp. 104-106 and notes 27-29, pp. 128-29.

100 <u>New York Times</u>, December 11-13, 1920, and June 6 and 15, 1921.

101 See p. 108 and note 40, p. 132.

102 <u>New York Times</u>, December 13, 1920; and Kenyon Hearings, vol. 1, 158.

103 See pp. 108-109 and notes 41 (p. 132), 49 (p. 133), and 67 (pp. 135-36).

104 Examples of the variety -- in sources, media, and targets -- of this attempt to bring intervention by a third party, are: (1) John L. Lewis's: (a) public letter to President Harding, August 27, 1921, in <u>New York Times</u>, that date, (b) conference with Secretary of Labor James J. Davis on May 19, 1921, in <u>New York Times</u>, May 20, (c) wire to Governor Morgan, summer 1921, in Cecil Carnes, <u>John L. Lewis, Leader of Labor</u> (New York, 1936), 74, 75; (2) International UMW's: (a) executive board's public statement on December 5, 1920, in <u>New York Times</u>, December 6, 1920, (b) Mingo officials' public statements on May 14, 1921, in <u>New York Times</u>, May 15, 1921, (c) committee conference with Harding, in October 1921, in <u>New York Times</u>, October 3, 1921; (3) AFL Convention

Resolutions, see note 72; (4) Samuel Gompers's: (a) con-
ference with Harding on September 3, 1921, in New York
Times, September 4, 1921, (b) public letter to Senator
Kenyon, in New York Times, May 23, 1920, (c) conference
with Senator Johnson on February 5, in New York Times,
February 5, 1921; (5) District 17 UMW's: (a) officers'
conference with Secretary of Labor Davis and several
United States senators in Washington, May 20, 1921, in
New York Times, May 21, 1921, (b) public call by Keeney
for a United States Senate investigation, Washington Post,
February 5, 1921, and proposal for settlement in letter
from Keeney to Governor Morgan, New York Times, July 12,
1921, (c) convention resolutions submitted to Governor
Morgan, New York Times, August 8, 1921, (d) officers' and
executive board's call for congressional investigation,
in New York Times, November 8 and 28, 1919, and June 21,
1921, (e) officers' appeal to Kentucky and West Virginia
governors to intervene to end strike on December 5, 1920,
in New York Times, December 6, 1920, (f) officers' telegram to Secretary of Labor reporting evictions, in New
York Times, March 29, 1922, (g) officials' call for and
cooperation with Department of Labor mediators, in New
York Times, July 1 and 4, 1920, and Kenyon Hearings,
vol. 1, 106-11; (6) Senator Hiram Johnson's call for a
Senate inquiry, in New York Times, February 8, May 25,
and June 25, 1921; (7) The American Civil Liberties
Union's: (a) public statement, in New York Times, December 2, 1920, (b) director's letter to Kenyon Committee,
dated September 13, 1921, Kenyon Hearings, vol. 1, 558;
(8) the West Virginia State Federation of Labor's telegram appeals to President Harding, Secretary Davis, and
the United States Senate, as well as its pressure on Governor Morgan -- as noted in Harris and Krebs, From Humble
Beginnings, 159; (9) the letter sent September 19, 1921,
by the Federated Crafts of the City of Huntington (West
Virginia) to the Kenyon Committee, in Kenyon Hearings,
vol. 1, 558-59; (10) the dispatching to Washington by the
UMW in West Virginia and the State Federation of Labor of
an authorized spokesman who presented the miners' case in
a White House meeting with Joseph P. Tumulty, in Spivak,
Man in His Times, 73-85.

105 For examples, see Boxes 4742-91 and 4742-92, Lauck MSS.
Walsh, Lauck, and Kenyon all urged federal intervention
in the form of an industrial code defining fundamental
rights for both sides and establishing machinery to
settle disputes. See Kenyon Hearings, vol. 2, 604-605,
and vol. 3, 9-27, 1036-38, 1046-49; "Report of Senate Committee on West Virginia Coal Fields," Monthly Labor Review 14 (March 1922), 28-30; and Zieger, Republicans and
Labor, 217. Kenyon later drafted such a bill, which the
AFL promptly opposed! See AFL Proceedings, 1922, 103;
and William S. Kenyon, "A Code of Industrial Law," The

Annals of the American Academy of Political and Social Science 111 (January 1924), 305-13. The operators had not participated in the hearings for the purpose of proposing federal intervention in any form. Nevertheless, their views were sought on several occasions. Senator Kenyon himself asked William H. Coolidge, a distinguished Boston lawyer and board chairman of a Logan coal company, if he could suggest specific remedies for the West Virginia disorders. Mr. Coolidge replied bluntly: "In the first place ... 'More business in government and less government in business.' That is my first. My second is that there are no new laws needed and there are no new Government bureaus needed, and I do not believe there are any reports needed." Kenyon Hearings, vol. 2, 920.

[106] Kenyon Hearings, vol. 3, 1054.

[107] Hindrichs, UMWA and the Non-Union Coal Fields, 173, 176.

[108] Taft, Organized Labor in American History, chaps. 26 and 27.

[109] Edward E. Hunt, F. S. Tryon, and Joseph M. Willits, eds., What the Coal Commission Found: An Authoritative Summary by the Staff (Baltimore, 1925), 34.

[110] Perlman and Taft, Labor Movements, chap. 26; U.S. Geological Survey, "Coal, 1919-1921," 512-14, 518-19.

[111] Spero and Harris, Black Worker, 370.

[112] Corwin D. Edwards, "The Dilemma of the Coal Union," in American Labor Dynamics in the Light of Post-War Developments, ed. Jacob B. S. Hardman (New York, 1928), 183-85; Perlman and Taft, Labor Movements, chap. 12; and Taft, Organized Labor in American History, 398-404.

[113] Ambler and Summers, West Virginia, 460-61; Anson, "History of the Labor Movement," 126-33; Harris and Krebs, From Humble Beginnings, 156-58; James P. Johnson, "Drafting the NRA Code of Fair Competition for the Bituminous Coal Industry," The Journal of American History 53 (December 1966), 526; and Mooney, Struggle in the Coal Fields, 127-28. According to F. Ray Marshall, in 1931 the UMW could claim a mere forty dues-paying members. Labor in the South (Cambridge, Mass., 1967), 76.

[114] Ross, Machine Age in the Hills, 51.

[115] Perlman and Taft, Labor Movements, chaps. 33-38, 41; and Taft, Organized Labor in American History, chaps. 26 and 27.

[116] Perlman and Taft, Labor Movements, chaps. 33-38, 41; and Taft, Organized Labor in American History, chaps. 26 and 27; but see especially Table 6, in "Strikes and Lockouts in the United States, 1916 to 1924," Monthly Labor Review 20 (June 1925), 185.

[117] There is no treatment of the Mingo War in recent accounts of violence in America by Richard Maxwell Brown, Strain of Violence: Historical Studies of American Violence and Vigilantism (New York, 1975); and Richard Hofstadter and Michael Wallace, eds., American Violence, A Documentary History (New York, 1970); and only two pages on it in Hugh Davis Graham and Ted Robert Gurr, eds., The History of Violence in America: A Report to the National Commission on the Causes and Prevention of Violence (New York, 1969), 337-38.

[118] Lane, Civil War in West Virginia, 99.

[119] Spivak, Man in His Time, 77. The newcomer was Spivak himself, a young civil libertarian-journalist, who later acquired two guns.

[120] Lane, Civil War in West Virginia, 99; and Kenyon Hearings, vol. 1, 543, and vol. 2, 782-84.

[121] Quote is from Walter Graham, New York Times, September 3, 1921.

[122] Quote is from Ross, Machine Age in the Hills, 140. See also New York Times, May 19 and 20, 1921; and Kenyon Hearings, vol. 1, 230, 344, and vol. 2, 945.

[123] Pertinent to this was the belief in Mingo during the winter of 1920-1921 that "when 'Judge Green' arrives the shooting will begin again" -- "Judge Green" being the spring foliage necessary for cover, ambushes, and so forth. Quoted in Literary Digest, "Battle of the Tug River," 16.

[124] U.S., Bureau of the Census, Fourteenth Census, vol. 3, 1107, 1039.

[125] "Economic Condition of the Negro in West Virginia," Monthly Labor Review 16 (April 1923), 21-23; Fisher, "Cornwell," 284; Harris and Krebs, From Humble Beginnings, 162, 164; New York Times, February 17, 1921; Mooney, Struggle in the Coal Fields, 53; Posey, "Labor Movement," 110; Spero and Harris, Black Worker, 208, 213-17, 220, 223, 366-74; and Kenyon Hearings, vol. 1, 26-38, 470, 559-60, 573, and vol. 2, 635. Silent on Mingo is Julius Jacobson, ed., The Negro and the American Labor Movement (Garden City, N.Y., 1968).

126 For samples of attempts to pin a red label on the UMW and
its supporters, see Frederick A. Barkey, "The Socialist
Party in West Virginia from 1898 to 1920" (Ph.D. diss.,
University of Pittsburgh, 1971), 215-16; Fisher, "Cornwell," 378; Lane, Civil War in West Virginia, 83; New
York Times, August 27, and September 3 and 5, 1921; Ross,
Machine Age in the Hills, 145-47; Swain, who called a
visiting ACLU delegation "parlor bolshevists," Logan
County, 178; Thurmond, Logan Coal, 102; Kenyon Hearings,
vol. 1, 556, vol. 2, 888, 938-39, 1001, and vol. 3,
1056-57, 1062.

127 See Keeney's statement in Kenyon Hearings, vol. 1, 197;
and also Posey, "Labor Movement," 125-26.

128 U.S., Bureau of the Census, Fourteenth Census, vol. 3,
1105, 1107, 1039.

129 The "no evidence" view is confirmed, indirectly, by the
absence of any comment on these West Virginia disorders
in such likely sources as Stanley Coben, A. Mitchell
Palmer: Politician (New York, 1963); Paul Brissenden,
The I.W.W.: A Study of American Syndicalism (New York,
1920); Joseph R. Conlin, Bread and Roses Too: Studies of
the Wobblies (Westport, Conn., 1969); Melvyn Dubofsky, We
Shall Be All: A History of the Industrial Workers of the
World (Chicago, 1969); John S. Gambs, The Decline of the
I.W.W. (New York, 1932), which also excludes it in the
list of strikes involving the I.W.W. between 1917 and
1930, on pp. 230-32; Robert K. Murray, Red Scare: A
Study in National Hysteria, 1919-1920 (Minneapolis, 1955);
William Preston, Jr., Aliens and Dissenters: Federal
Suppression of Radicals, 1903-1933 (Cambridge, Mass.,
1963); Patrick Renshaw, The Wobblies; the Story of Syndicalism in the United States (Garden City, N.Y., 1967);
and Fred Thompson, comp., The I.W.W.: Its First Fifty
Years, 1905-1955 (Chicago, 1955). As one liberal journalist put it, "The [national] communist scare and the
rounding up of aliens left little imprint in the state's
non-union fields; there were no aliens or communists
there." Spivak, Man in His Time, 102. The historian of
the West Virginia labor movement concludes that it developed and continued within the capitalistic system and not
as an attempt to displace it with communism or socialism.
Posey, "Labor Movement," 167, 301. Apparently, during
the second march on Logan, "two communists had ensconced
their hides ... safely behind the walls of the Washington
Hotel in Charleston," from which they printed and disseminated circulars. Mooney, Struggle in the Coal Fields,
122. Mother Jones, of course, had a minor role; and a
recent dissertation on Socialism in West Virginia notes a
tie between the party and a few UMW leaders. Barkey,
"Socialist Party," 190 ff., 205, 241, but barely mentions
the Mingo War, 215.

"Frank Keeney Is Our Leader, and We Shall Not Be Moved": Rank-and-File Leadership in the West Virginia Coal Fields

David A. Corbin

> Frank Keeney is our leader, and
> We shall not be moved,
> Frank Keeney is our leader, and
> We shall not be moved,
> Just like a tree that stands beside
> The water, we shall not be moved.

The song was sung in union meetings and along the picket lines by nearly 20,000 hungry miners in southern West Virginia during their massive wildcat strike in the summer of 1931.[1] The song was to become famous; but the man to whom the stanza was a tribute, Frank Keeney, has been largely neglected in labor history. Herbert Gutman has reminded us that "until we know more fully the world of ... [rank-and-file labor leaders], we shall not clearly comprehend the tragedy and hope embedded in recent American history."[2] The story of Frank Keeney and his coal diggers challenges many popular myths: that American workers are oriented toward "bread and butter issues"; that the miners, especially in West Virginia, were organized from top down; and that Appalachians have failed to develop their own folk heroes.[3] Most importantly, the story of Keeney and his coal diggers reveals that the recent "Miners for Democracy" revolt was not unique but typical of a people who have resisted oppression and corruption, whether in the coal camps or in their union.

Keeney was born in 1884, in a small coal camp on Cabin Creek, Kanawha County, West Virginia, as the railroads were opening the state's coal fields. Frank's father died when he was six months old, and his mother was forced to support the family by "taking in sewing." At ten, Keeney went to work in the mines. After a year, his mother forced him to quit the job and finish school. Six years later, Keeney married and returned to work in the mines.[4]

Keeney's career as a rank-and-file leader began during the protracted and violent Paint Creek-Cabin Creek strike of 1912-1913. After a year of struggle, United Mine Workers' (UMW) officials attempted to end the strike with a compromise settlement. Keeney believed that total victory was near, however; and though he held no official union position, he persuaded the rank and file to reject the compromise and continue the strike until the operators met all of the miners' demands.[5]

This victory for the miners led to problems for their leader. Blacklisted and his family evicted from its company house, Keeney moved to Charleston and then to other states in search of work. After a year of traveling, Keeney persuaded a mine superintendent to hire him, and he returned to Cabin Creek.[6]

Once settled, he began to study law, taking extension courses from LaSalle University of Chicago and reading with a local attorney who promised him a partnership. Within the year, however, Keeney accepted positions in the local union and abandoned thoughts of becoming an attorney.[7]

The year 1916 witnessed the blossoming of Keeney's career as a labor leader. In late 1915, the southern West Virginia miners revolted against their district officials, who they claimed had failed to obtain good contracts and "permitted grievances to be settled with the checkbook and made working agreements behind closed doors." The miners demanded the suspension of the officials and an investigation by the international union, demands which the international executive board of the UMW promptly rejected.[8] Thousands of angry miners withdrew from the established union districts, formed a "rump" organization, and elected Keeney president. The executive board refused to recognize the new district; and UMW leaders, including Mother Jones, made appeals to the miners to return to their old union. Guided by Keeney, the miners refused.[9]

Keeney's actions forced the executive board to intervene. On February 21, 1916, it withdrew the autonomy of the involved districts and began to investigate the insurgents' charges. Satisfied with these acts, Keeney brought his coal diggers back into the regular union.[10]

The executive board's investigation revealed that the insurgents had been correct. Several of the district officials were stockholders in coal companies, the report revealed, and better contracts could have been obtained.[11] The executive board dismissed the corrupt officials and, in December, conducted new district elections. By a substantial majority, Keeney was elected president of District 17, UMW, which included almost all of West Virginia. "Brothers," he told the coal diggers, "if you will give me your cooperation and your

support I don't think that you will ever have to regret it.
You need never be ashamed of the trust reposed in me."[12]

Within three months, 2,000 new members were enrolled, twelve
new locals organized, and a new contract negotiated with the
Kanawha County Coal Operators' Association. A national UMW
organizer called the new contract "the greatest victory ever
achieved by any district in the history of our organization,"
and a rank-and-file miner described it as the "culmination of
everything that we have struggled for the past twenty
years."[13] By March 1918, the district had the largest membership in its history; and later that year Keeney negotiated
the Fairmont Agreement, which the United Mine Workers Journal
called "the biggest single step that has been taken toward
the creation of a complete organization ... in W. Va." In
his address to the UMW's 1919 convention, John L. Lewis
stated: "District 17 within the past two years has done itself proud. Its membership should be inspired by the work
and accomplishments of its most competent officials."[14]
After Keeney had overwhelmed his opponent in the 1920 district election, he began preparations to organize the only
nonunion sections of West Virginia, Logan and Mingo counties,
an area which Samuel Gompers called the "last remains of industrial autocracy" in the United States.[15]

Keeney's success as a labor leader was largely attributable
to his personality. In 1921, a New York journalist claimed
the small, soft-spoken Appalachian possessed the "force and
alert watchfulness of a tiger," which made the miners respect
him and the operators "smell of brimstone." Over a decade
later, an observer described Keeney's charisma as dynamism
that gave a "hypnotic influence" and a "natural bond with the
state's miners."[16]

Equally important was Keeney's continuing closeness to the
coal diggers. He attended nearly all the local union meetings throughout the Kanawha coal field and as many as he
could throughout the state. "We would have our meetings and
he would be right there with us," recalled an eighty-seven-
year-old ex-miner. "He believed in district autonomy and
practiced it, not like John L. Lewis." Another veteran of
the coal wars recalled, "He was never too proud to shake your
hand." Any unemployed or blacklisted miner could get a meal
and bed at the Keeney house. "I haven't left the class I was
born into yet," Keeney once declared, "and I hope I never
will."[17]

Keeney spoke the coal miners' language. His impromptu
speeches were salted with "By Gods" and "God almighties" and
with folk analogy and humor. "I am a native West Virginian,"
Keeney explained, "and there are others like me working in
the mines here. We don't propose to get out of the way when
a lot of capitalists from New York and London come down here

and tell us to get off the earth. They played that game on
the American Indian. They gave him the end of a log to sit
on and then pushed him off that. We don't propose to be
pushed off."[18]

Keeney understood, because he shared the miners' sense of dignity and their anger at a world -- New York, Charleston, the
local "elite" -- that seemed both to take advantage of and to
look down on them. "Who are you, you dirty despised people
who can't walk into Charleston because you'd give them a dis-
ease? That's what they say," Keeney harangued. "It's no
disgrace to dig coal. Coal makes civilization possible. You
ought to know that. Quit hanging your heads." And he shared
their dreams as well as their pride. During a major coal
war, Keeney consoled his fellow unionists, "One day there
will be no more gun men, no tent colonies, because right now
you people are going through what you are."[19] And because
the miners were a part of him, he led but never dictated to
them. For example, Keeney always urged the union miners to
honor their contracts; but he never suspended any person or
local for a work stoppage, because he believed they knew what
the problems were and what had to be done. Under Keeney,
District 17 enjoyed the most democratic and open administration in its long and bloody history.[20]

Keeney possessed a flair for the dramatic, and he well understood the tactics and politics of "confrontation." In apa-
thetic areas, where UMW organizers long had failed to persuade the miners to join the union, Keeney purposefully
called organizing meetings on company grounds, knowing that
within a few minutes the mine guards would break up the
gathering and force him off the grounds. After the officials
had served Keeney's purpose, the miners, annoyed at the in-
justice, were ready to accept the union.[21] When federal
soldiers were sent into the Mingo County strike in 1920 to
perform strikebreaking activities, Keeney threatened a general strike of over 100,000 miners unless the troops were
withdrawn. The governor withdrew the soldiers.[22] During the
same strike, a Mingo County coal operator spotted Keeney in
front of a bank in Charleston and called him and the UMW "a
gang of criminals and outlaws." Before an audience of fifty
people, Keeney approached the operator, hit him twice, and
kicked him down the steps of the bank. Those blows resounded
through the striking miners' tent colonies ninety miles away
in Mingo County.[23]

Acts like that gave Keeney a reputation as a radical, although, like most miners, he had neither the education nor
leisure for theoretical political thinking. He joined the
Socialist party in 1912 and flirted with leftist organizations during the 1930s. But Keeney never felt comfortable
with the Communists nor trusted the Socialists after their
betrayal of the miners' efforts during the Paint Creek-Cabin

Creek strike.[24] His radicalism, little involved with system,
was an indigenous product of his trust in the rank-and-file
coal miners and his belief that the meaning of America had
something to do with justice and human dignity for all.
Winthrop Lane rightly said of Keeney, "His experience is his
philosophy." "Employers want to measure wages in cold dollars and cents," Keeney once explained, "while the miners in-
sist that they be measured in human values.... miners take
the position that low wages deprive children of education, of
good food, destroy self-respect." When asked about his image
as a radical, Keeney replied, "Who made me a radical? I've
seen the time when I didn't have the right to eat in this
state. I've seen the time when I was refused a job. I've
been served with eviction papers and thrown out of my house.
I've seen women and children brutally treated in mining camps.
I've seen hell turned loose!"[25] Keeney simply wanted to remove the hell from the coal diggers' lives.

Keeney normally opposed industrial violence because he understood its dangers and costs to the miners. In 1919, he personally persuaded 3,000 miners bent on the overthrow of the
mine guard system to lay down their guns and await the
union's efforts to organize the involved area and negotiate
an end to "thug rule."[26]

Keeney did not believe in peace at any price, however. When
the Logan and Mingo County operators refused to negotiate
with District 17 officials, Keeney proceeded with his plans
to organize the area, warning: "If our organizers come back
in boxes, neither heaven nor hell will be able to control the
miners. Organize Logan County we will, and no one shall stop
us."[27] The operators responded with hundreds of mine guards
to intimidate the miners and to threaten, beat, and murder
the union organizers.

Consequently, on August 7, 1921, Keeney called a meeting of
union miners in the Kanawha Valley to tell them about the
atrocities committed against the miners and the governor's
refusal to protect the striking miners. "You have no recourse
except to fight," he shouted; "the only way you can get your
rights is with a high-powered rifle." He then advised the
miners to return home and await the call to mobilize. On
August 20, Keeney gave the call; and during the next three
days, over 10,000 miners responded and began a sixty-mile
"armed march."[28] The announced intentions of the marchers
were the overthrow of two county governments that were controlled by the coal operators, the destruction of the mine
guard system, and the "liberation" (unionization) of the miners.[29]

Although Mother Jones shared responsibility for the uprising,
upon learning about the "armed march," she rushed to the coal
fields and begged the miners to return home. For the second

time during a major union crisis, the miners chose to follow
Keeney rather than the legendary national leader and continued the march.[30] The insurrection was halted only by the
federal government's intervention, which involved the United
States Army and the Air Service. It ended with the indictment and trial of Keeney and 550 other miners for murder, insurrection, and treason against the federal government.[31]
The failure of the "armed march" and later the Mingo County
strike signified the collapse of the UMW in the Mountain
State.

In the early 1920s, the UMW in West Virginia and throughout
the nation began losing ground largely because of the postwar
depression in the coal industry. Unable to pay the war-
inflated union wage rates, the coal operators appealed to the
UMW and the government for a reciprocal lowering of wages
during the recession. President Harding and the president of
the British Miners Federation told UMW officials that it
would be impossible to keep their war-inflated scales.[32]
They were right; in West Virginia, coal operators in two
counties were unable to pay the union wage rates and had already declared an open shop.[33]

Keeney and his associates recognized the predicament of the
coal industry and its threat to the union; therefore, they
formulated a "solution that would have as its chief aim the
perpetuation of the union." For the only time in his career,
Keeney agreed to accept temporarily wage cuts, provided that
the companies maintained the union and preserved the miners'
jobs.[34]

John L. Lewis, however, strongly disapproved of Keeney's approach. As national president, Lewis believed that the union
needed to present a solid, united front in the time of economic crises in order to obtain justice for the most miners.
He feared that a wage reduction in one district would undermine the union's efforts in others. Further, he was afraid
that any "temporary reduction" would become permanent. Consequently, when Keeney persisted in his independent ways,
Lewis withdrew the autonomy of District 17, suspended its officials, and issued strike calls in a fruitless effort to
prevent wage cuts.[35]

Frank Keeney, exiled from the UMW, refused to give up the
cause of the rank-and-file worker. He turned down a lucra-
tive position as a mine superintendent because he believed it
would be a "betrayal of his people" and instead led the fight
for industrial unionism in the West Virginia State Federation
of Labor.[36] A few years later, he went to Illinois to work
in John Brophy's "Save the Union" movement and to serve as
editor of its newspaper.[37]

Meanwhile, in the West Virginia coal fields, economic

conditions grew worse for the coal operators and their employees. Unable to find markets for their stockpiles of coal,
companies laid off thousands of miners, while scores declared
bankruptcy, and others worked on a part-time basis. Unemployment and hunger became widespread in the southern West Virginia coal fields.[38]

By the late 1920s, one-third of the state's 112,000 miners
were jobless; and another one-third worked only one or two
days a week, "not enough for a corn-bread living," according
to one miner. Another miner in southern West Virginia wrote
the United Mine Workers Journal: "I don't know what is going
to happen here. Families are crying for bread and can't get
it.... Beaten out of wages, we don't know what to do, as we
need help in every way.... When the men ask the superintendent about payday he will say tomorrow. But tomorrow never
comes."[39]

Tomorrow came to the miners in early 1931, when Frank Keeney
returned to West Virginia for what was to be his greatest effort and greatest defeat. Believing that under Lewis the UMW
was incapable of solving the miners' problems, in March 1931,
Keeney brought together his assistants from the days when he
was president of District 17 and established a dual union,
the West Virginia Mine Workers Union (WVMWU). Keeney's return revived the union spirit, seven years dead in the southern part of the state. According to Edmund Wilson, the coal
diggers came out with "tremendous enthusiasm to meet their
old leaders and ... sign up for the union. The miners hail
the organizers as wrecked men hail a ship."[40] Within a few
weeks an estimated 20,000 miners joined the independent union.
The WVMWU conducted two "hunger machines" into Charleston to
protest the state government's depression policies and to demand food. Its presence, moreover, forced the operators to
place union checkweighmen on the tipples and to maintain wage
rates well above those which the UMW officials were negotiating in northern West Virginia.[41]

On July 6, Keeney made his boldest move; he declared a general strike in the Kanawha field to force a collective bargaining agreement with the Kanawha County Coal Operators.
The strike was undertaken against overwhelming odds; but as
Keeney stated, "What the hell are you going to do when nobody
knows any other language?" and a contract was needed if the
nascent union was to help the miners.[42]

Probably the most serious obstacle the union faced was the
need to house and feed the striking miners. The union could
not collect dues because the miners did not have any money,
and the Red Cross refused to provide assistance because the
miners' troubles were not "acts of God." Therefore, union
officials accepted aid from Northern liberals; and Keeney
sold his house in Charleston to finance the strike.[43]

A number of rival organizations attempted to undercut Keeney
and his union. The Communist party sent organizers, including William Z. Foster, to West Virginia to persuade the dissident miners to align with the Communist National Miners
Union. The Socialist Party of America sent Normal Thomas and
other major party officials to the area in an effort to obtain an alliance with Keeney's union. Failing to obtain the
desired alliance, local Socialists attempted unsuccessfully
to "overthrow" Keeney.[44] Most important, the UMW, inactive
in the state for seven years, suddenly came to life. National UMW officers denounced the WVMWU as a "renegade scab
outfit" and called Keeney a "gangster," "bushwhacker," and
"double crosser" who "took money from pinks and reds."[45]
District 17 officials, particularly Van Bittner and Percey
Tetlow, entered the coal fields and employed the red-baiting
tactics of their national president. One official told a
miners' meeting in Charleston, "This little union that has
been misrepresenting ... the UMW of A -- who's at the head of
it? Short-haired women and long-haired men -- Bolshviks
[sic] and crank professors."[46]

By mid-August, the strike was doomed. Impoverished and
sniped at by all its rivals, the WVMWU could not overcome the
economic and political power of the coal barons. Keeney refused to make excuses or rationalize this, his first strike
defeat. According to Malcolm Ross, "Unlike outside union
organizers, who often vanish from a strike area when disaster
looms ahead, Keeney rode up the creeks on empty food trucks
to tell his people that he had failed."[47] In one of his
final appearances before his coal diggers after the strike,
Keeney told them, "We've had our parades, songs and strike --
and we got left damned good. Nothing left but debts and memory of defeat. The greatest thing you have done is to stick
together and take it on the chin." Afterward, he asked the
miners to return to work. A few months later, following the
passage of the National Industrial Recovery Act, Keeney asked
the miners to return to the UMW, although he never did. The
UMW executive board rejected Keeney's application for membership. A few years later, however, he served as an organizer
for the Progressive Mine Workers of America. Following its
demise, he retired from the coal fields.[48]

Keeney ended his career as a parking lot attendant in
Charleston, ostracized by the UMW and denounced as a "false
prophet" of the labor movement by the court historians of the
West Virginia State Federation of Labor. Nevertheless,
Keeney's name is still revered by the elderly miners who
fought with him. An eighty-nine-year-old black miner who accompanied Keeney on the "Armed March on Logan" recalled that
"Keeney was a good man, trustworthy and honest ... a good
president and leader. Since he had [sic] been gone, things
have been tough in the mines -- for a long time."[49]

Notes

[1] Archie Green, Only a Miner: Studies in Recorded Coal-Mining Songs (Urbana, Ill., 1972), 245.

[2] Herbert Gutman, "The Negro and the United Mine Workers of America," The Negro and the American Labor Movement, ed. Julius Jacobson (Garden City, N.Y., 1969), 127.

[3] See the works of John R. Commons, Philip Taft, and Selig Perlman; and Edward Knipe and Helen Lewis, "The Impact of Coal Mining on the Traditional Mountain Subculture," The Not So Solid South, ed. J. Kenneth Morland, Proceedings, Southern Anthropological Association, no. 4 (Athens, 1971); Jack Weller, Yesterday's People (Lexington, 1966), 82-94; and Harry Caudill, Night Comes to the Cumberlands: A Biography of a Depressed Area (Boston, 1962), 112, 121, 132-34. For a commendable but somewhat unsuccessful effort to break free from these myths, see David Whisnant, "The Folk Hero in Appalachian Struggle History," New South 28 (Fall 1973), 30-47.

[4] Letter from Syble K. Phillips, daughter of Frank Keeney, Hilton Head Island, S.C., August 7, 1975; interview with C. B. Keeney, son of Frank Keeney, Alum Creek, W. Va., July 20 and December 30, 1975.

[5] David A. Corbin, "Betrayal in the Coalfields, Eugene V. Debs and the Socialist Party of America, 1913" (paper in preparation); and Fred Mooney, Struggle in the Coalfields: The Autobiography of Fred Mooney, ed. J. W. Hess (Morgantown, W. Va., 1967), 27.

[6] Letter from Syble K. Phillips, August 7, 1975; Winthrop Lane, Civil War in West Virginia (New York, 1921), 86; and A. F. Hinrichs, The United Mine Workers and the Non-Union

Coal Fields (New York, 1923), 64.

7 Letter from Syble K. Phillips, August 7, 1975; C. B.
Keeney Interviews; and U.S., Congress, Senate, Committee
on Education and Labor, Hearings, The West Virginia Coal
Fields, 67th Cong., 1st sess., 1921, 174.

8 Mooney, Struggle, 44-46; Argus-Star (Charleston, W. Va.),
March 30, 1916; Joe Bruttaniti to the editor, United Mine
Workers Journal, May 11, 1916 (hereafter cited as UMWJ);
Joseph Diana to the editor, UMWJ, December 28, 1916; and
George Norman to the editor, UMWJ, May 11, 1916; see also
UMWJ, September 16 and 23, and October 28, 1915. The
charges of corruption actually appeared in early 1914,
Coal Age 5 (May 9, 1914), 787. The miners believed their
contracts should have included the "check off" and higher
wages.

9 The Argus-Star (Charleston, W. Va.), March 30, 1916;
Mooney, Struggle, 45; and UMWJ, April 6, 1916.

10 Evelyn Harris and Frank Krebs, From Humble Beginnings:
West Virginia State Federation of Labor (Morgantown,
W. Va., 1960); and "Official Circular: To Settle W. Va.'s
Internal Differences," UMWJ, February 10, 1916; see also
UMWJ, April 6, 1916. The executive board's withdrawal of
district autonomy at this time should not be confused with
withdrawal of autonomy under John L. Lewis. The executive
board apologized for its action and constantly announced
that suspension of the autonomy of District 17 would be
temporary. See UMWJ, February 19, 1916; May 18, 1916; and
April 6, 1916.

11 Mooney, Struggle, 41-42; and UMWJ, January 4, 1917, and
March 21, 1918; see also UMWJ, September 1, 1924, for
copies of eviction notices sent out by Haggerty, as a company official.

12 "Official Circular," UMWJ, January 4, 1917; and "Report of
the International Teller on Elections Held, District
No. 17, UMW of A.," UMWJ, January 4, 1917.

13 Lawrence Dwyer to the editor, UMWJ, March 29, 1917; G. H.
Edmunds to the editor, UMWJ, April 12, 1917; and UMWJ,
March 29, 1917, June 28, 1917, and March 29, 1917.

14 UMWJ, April 4, 1918, August 1, 1918, and January 1, 1919;
and "Lewis' Report to the National Convention," UMWJ, September 15, 1919.

15 Keeney defeated his opponent by a vote of 17,705 to 1,360.
UMWJ, February 15, 1921; and Charleston Gazette, September 2, 1921.

16 Lane, _Civil War_, 85; Malcolm Ross, _Machine Age in the Hills_ (New York, 1933), 155; and Edmund Wilson, _The American Jitters_ (New York, 1932), 169.

17 Interview with Ike Peters, Eskdale, W. Va., June 24, 1975; interview with Rogers Mitchell, Institute, W. Va., May 27, 1975; and Lane, _Civil War_, 87.

18 John Brophy, _A Miner's Life_, ed. John O. P. Hall (Madison, 1964), 74; C. B. Keeney interview; and Lane, _Civil War_, 87-88.

19 Ross, _Machine Age_, 157-60.

20 Lane, _Civil War_, 92-93, 96; _UMWJ_, December 27, 1917; and U.S., Congress, Senate, _W. Va. Coal Fields_, 198-99.

21 Interview with William Miller, Alum Creek, W. Va., August 3, 1975.

22 _UMWJ_, October 1, 1920; _New York Times_, September 24 and 25, 1920; and _Charleston Gazette_, September 25, 1920, and November 10-25, 1920.

23 U.S., Congress, Senate, _W. Va. Coal Fields_, 198-99.

24 Corbin, "Betrayal"; David A. Corbin, "Charleston Socialist Local: Reflections on the Rise and Fall of a Regional Socialist Movement, 1928-1940" (M.A. thesis, Marshall University, 1972), chaps. 1 and 2.

25 _The Charleston Gazette_, February 11, 1925; and Lane, _Civil War_, 87-88.

26 _UMWJ_, November 15, 1919.

27 Arthur Gleason, "Private Ownership of Public Officials," _Nation_ 110 (September 14, 1920), 724-25.

28 _Charleston Gazette_, August 8, 1921; and Howard Lee, _Bloodletting in Appalachia_ (Parsons, W. Va., 1969), 96. Keeney's role in organizing and ordering the armed march on Logan will be treated more thoroughly in the author's forthcoming dissertation at the University of Maryland.

29 Interview with Frank Blizzard, Dry Branch, W. Va., June 24, 1975; _Charleston Gazette_, August 20-29, 1921; and Lee, _Bloodletting_, 95-97.

30 Interview, Ike Peters; interview, Rogers Mitchell; interview, Frank Blizzard; and Mooney, _Struggle_, 90-92.

31 For narratives of the "armed march" on Logan and Mingo

counties, see Cabell Phillips, "The West Virginia Mine War," American Heritage 25 (August 1974); Mauer and Calvin Senning, "Billy Mitchell, the Air Service, and the Mingo War," The Airpower Historian 12 (April 1965); and Lee, Bloodletting, chap. 4.

32 Heber Blankenhorn, The Strike for Union (New York, 1923), 153; and Rex Lauck, John L. Lewis and the International Union (Washington, D.C., 1952), 11. A more thorough analysis of the collapse of the UMW in West Virginia during the 1920s is given in the author's forthcoming dissertation at the University of Maryland.

33 UMWJ, February 15, 1924; and Black Diamond, December 24, 1922, 54.

34 Mooney, Struggle, 127.

35 Technically, the District 17 officials, after a closed door session with Lewis, "resigned" in order to "protect and preserve ... the integrity" of the union in West Virginia. UMWJ, July 1, 1924. This was the fourth district charter revoked by Lewis while he was on his way, as Brophy states, to "crushing union democracy." Brophy, A Miner's Life, 213.

36 Letter from Syble K. Phillips, August 7, 1975; Harris and Krebs, Humble Beginnings, 172-73; and Proceedings, West Virginia State Federation of Labor, 1924, p. 264.

37 Harris and Krebs, Humble Beginnings, 198-99; and Selig Perlman and Philip Taft, History of Labor in the United States, 1896-1932, vol. 4 (New York, 1966), 564.

38 William Houston to the editor, UMWJ, January 1, 1932; UMWJ, December 1, 1924, March 15, 1927, and May 1, 1937; and Irving Bernstein, Lean Years: A History of the American Worker, 1920-1933 (Baltimore, 1960), 381-84.

39 Member of Local 4019, Enterprize, W. Va., to the editor, UMWJ, June 15, 1930, and August 1, 1927; and Bernstein, Lean Years, 381-84.

40 Bernstein, Lean Years, 382-83; A. J. Muste, "Slavery in West Virginia," Labor Age 20 (May 1931), 8-10; Wilson, American Jitters, 156; Cara Cook, "The Union Returns to Kanawha," Labor Age 20 (May 1931), 5-8; and Tom Tippett, "The Miners Try for a Clean Union," Labor Age 20 (April 1931), 5-7.

41 Charleston Gazette, June 5-10, 1932, and August 20-26, 1931; Wilson, American Jitters, 160; Tippett, "Miners Try," 5; and Tom Tippett, "Hungry Miners March in Charleston,"

Labor Age 21 (July 1932), 5.

[42] Katherine Pollak, "Life-or-Death Struggle Looms in Coal Fields of W. Va.," Labor Age 20 (July 1931), 5-7; Muste, "Slavery," 19; Bernstein, Lean Years, 384; and Ross, Machine Age, 163.

[43] Bernstein, Lean Years, 383-85; letter from Syble Phillips, August 7, 1975; and Muste, "Slavery," 9-10.

[44] Corbin, "Charleston Socialist Local," chaps. 1 and 2; Marcus Kornstein to Clarence Senior, April 25, 1932, Socialist Party Papers, Duke University; and Labor and Socialist Press Service, October 10, 1931, Socialist Party Papers, Duke University.

[45] UMWJ, October 15, 1931, and February 1, 1931.

[46] William Houston, president of District 17, to the editor, UMWJ, August 14, 1931; and Wilson, American Jitters, 166. For Lewis's red-baiting tactics, see Saul Alinsky, John L. Lewis: An Unauthorized Biography (New York, 1949), 49-51.

[47] Helen Norton, "Outcome of West Virginia Miners' Strike," Labor Age 20 (September 1931), 9-10; Ross, Machine Age, 158; and Charleston Gazette, August 26, 1931.

[48] Ross, Machine Age, 160; Charleston Gazette, August 26, 1931, and June 20, 1933; and The Progressive Miner, August 15, 1931, and September 1, 1938.

[49] Harris and Krebs, Humble Beginnings, 241; and Roger Mitchell interview.

Comment

A synopsis of the remarks by Warren R. Van Tine, Ohio
State University, Columbus (Corbin), and John W.
Hevener, Ohio State University, Lima (Jordan).

In attempting a survey of Frank Keeney's career in a short
paper, perhaps David Corbin tries to do too much. Such a
dynamic and important figure deserves better than cursory
treatment. Moreover, Corbin's study, which requires a more
fully developed analytical structure, projects an interpretation that well might be misleading. Following the lead of
Herbert Gutman and the Lynds, Corbin pursues the critically
important task of exploring the life of a rank-and-file labor
leader. Unfortunately, the author has a tendency to replace
the study of "great figures" in labor history with an analysis of "greater lesser-figures." The result is still a
"great man" approach but from a radical perspective. Corbin
portrays the rank-and-file coal miner as essentially passive,
emerging from the depression under Keeney's leadership. In
attributing the growth during 1917-1919 of West Virginia's
District 17 largely to Keeney's personality, Corbin negates
the contributions of the rank and file and ignores the social
and economic dynamics of World War I. With a broader understanding of the larger economic forces affecting the coal industry and with a better knowledge of the social and political environment, the "great radical figure" approach to labor
history will also fade. In its place will emerge a more
sophisticated radical analysis of the dynamics of social
change and the role of organizational leadership.

Daniel Jordan's paper on the Mingo War reflects thorough
analysis and research extending well beyond the immediate
time and place. Extensive notes provide reading almost as
interesting and informative as the text, while demonstrating
an abundance of relevant sources. In fact, Jordan may well
have encountered "too much" controversial content. But the
author judiciously selected from the variety of contentious
materials, relying especially on such new sources as the
papers of UMWA economist W. Jett Lauck, the published memoirs

of District 17 secretary-treasurer Fred Mooney, and the book
on West Virginia's mine wars by a former state attorney-
general, Howard B. Lee. While the documentation is exceptional, Jordan could also have utilized more local newspapers,
trial transcripts, and indictments. These additional sources
might reveal that much of the reported violence was unrelated
to the labor struggle.

The paper's only notable shortcoming appears in Jordan's
somewhat superficial treatment of the causes of labor violence. The explanations offered are valid. But possibilities other than gun toting, habitual violence, and escalating
violence might be explored. Jordan should consider that miners engaged in direct action because they had come to expect
nothing from law enforcement and the judicial system. Workers either counted on the intervention of an outside third
party or took the law into their own hands. Furthermore, as
Jack Weller and Warren Van Tine observe, Appalachians regarded a strike as a "blow out"; and such occasions sometimes
exploded into festivals of death. Finally, Jordan should
consider Sheldon Hackney's model of a "paranoid South" which
views all change as a conspiracy forced upon the region by
Yankee intruders. Because the Southern operators viewed
unionism as a Northern conspiracy, active local unionists became fair targets for retaliation.

CHAPTER IV

OIL:
Labor Organizing
During Two World Wars

Organized labor's battles with the oil industry during two
World Wars illustrated what tough adversaries the oil companies could be despite administrations in Washington ostensibly friendly to labor. During both periods, producers
could count on solid support from local communities; and as
high profit firms with relatively low labor costs, they could
further undermine the unions with well-timed wage concessions
to the workers. Interestingly, unions with the support of a
bare majority of the workers could prevail against the industry during World War II with adequate federal involvement,
while during the earlier period their strikes failed even
with a massive 97 percent of the oil workers unionized.

Of the two periods, labor's most difficult time came during
World War I, as James C. Maroney points out in an essay on
the 1917 strike in the Texas-Louisiana oil fields. Determined to make no concessions to labor despite the policies of
the Wilson administration, oil producers themselves organized
into an association that successfully resisted union recognition and federal mediation and smeared the union with charges
of disloyalty and radicalism. Perhaps a harbinger of later
struggles in steel and other industries, the oil producers'
victory was so complete that the union never offered another
serious challenge until the 1930s.

Clyde Johnson writes of the unionization efforts during World
War II as a former participant. Although lacking academic
precision, his essay reveals interesting insights into union
organizing. The important role of the professional organizer
particularly stands out, as does the hectic pace such men had
to pursue during long periods of confrontation. The essay
also reminds the reader of the serious gap sometimes existing
between stated national CIO policy and local Southern practices when race relations were at issue.

James C. Maroney has served on the faculty of Lee College
since 1964 and received the Ph.D. in history in 1975 from the
University of Houston. His dissertation dealt with "Organized Labor in Texas, 1900-1929." He is the author of several articles and has read papers at the conventions of the
Southern Historical Association (1976) and the Southwestern
Social Science Association (1977). Clyde Johnson, while working as a draftsman for Western Electric in Kearney, New
Jersey, became involved with Donald Henderson and a student
group at City College of New York interested in organizing
farm workers. Thereafter, he served as secretary of the Alabama Share Croppers Union and, successively, as research director, international representative, and international vice-
president of the United Cannery, Agricultural, Packing, and
Allied Workers of America, CIO. He joined the CIO Oil Workers Organizing Campaign in Texas in 1942. After serving in
the merchant marine during World War II, he became a local
union business agent for the United Electrical, Radio, and
Machine Workers and later the United Brotherhood of Carpenters and Joiners. Currently retired, he published Organize
or Die in 1970.

The Texas-Louisiana Oil Field Strike of 1917

James C. Maroney

By World War I, labor unions were beginning to make significant progress in the South, an area experiencing dramatic
developments in manufacturing. Although most Americans
balked at mass unionism until the 1930s, skilled craftsmen in
the South, like their counterparts in the rest of the nation,
frequently attained middle-class status during the initial
decades of the new century and thereby shared in the fruits
of prosperity. Too, during World War I, the American Federation of Labor (AFL) achieved the benefits accompanying an unprecedented degree of collaboration with government and business. As the 1917 strike of Texas and Louisiana oil field
workers vividly illustrates, however, some employers remained
inexorably opposed to organized labor and greatly resented
all concessions made to labor by the administration of
Woodrow Wilson.

Labor unions initially came to the East Texas oil fields in
the wake of the mighty Spindletop gusher in 1901.[1] Jay H.
Mullen of Bowling Green, Ohio, secretary of the International
Brotherhood of Oil and Gas Well Workers, indicated to Samuel
Gompers his organization's interest in the East Texas workers
as early as February 1902. Gompers sent an organizer into
the fields, and locals soon appeared at such sites as Spindletop, Batson, Sour Lake, Saratoga, and Humble. In 1905, the
J. M. Guffey Petroleum Company -- later to become the Gulf
Oil Corporation -- reduced wages for the standard twelve-hour
day from $3 to $2.50. Widespread dissatisfaction led to
rapid union growth, and workers chose an executive board to
act on behalf of the Spindletop, Saratoga, Batson, and Sour
Lake locals. Although a ten-day strike preserved the $3 wage
scale, union membership soon declined.[2]

A new attempt by operators to cut wages in the spring of 1907
revived union membership. Employers initially refused all

demands, including union recognition; and another ten-day
strike followed. Upon notification of the "critical" situation in Batson, AFL organizer James Leonard rushed to the
scene and helped negotiate a settlement in which the union
won all but its most important demand -- union recognition.[3]

Oil workers, however, remained committed to unionism only
during periods of crisis; with little prior knowledge of
organized labor, "they could see no need for paying dues to a
union unless they were in immediate distress and needing
strong assistance." This lack of interest, along with the
effects of the 1907 panic, virtually eliminated unionism in
the Texas oil fields until World War I.[4]

Wartime demands during the presidency of Woodrow Wilson, however, led to the development of close ties between the national government and the American labor establishment. The
U.S. Conciliation Service, established within the Department
of Labor and strongly supported by President Wilson and Secretary of Labor William B. Wilson, a former official of the
United Mine Workers Union, was created to mediate labor disputes.[5] During World War I, the Conciliation Service overcame much of the initial suspicion on the part of both business and labor. Ultimately, wartime collaboration of government, business, and labor resulted in an industrial code administered by the War Labor Board, which recognized labor
unions but forbade strikes or lockouts.[6]

Disputes between employers and organized labor in Texas referred to the Conciliation Service after failure to achieve
settlement locally included a 1918 streetcar strike in Waco
and disputes with shipbuilding contractors in Orange, Beaumont, and Houston. The latter disputes arose over the practice of contractors paying carpenters, electricians, caulkers,
and other skilled tradesmen from 5 to 20 percent below the
prevailing area wage rate, even though organized labor previously had been assured by representatives of the secretary of
the navy and other government agencies that the local wage
scale would be paid. Former Texas Labor Commissioner C. W.
Woodman, serving as a commissioner of conciliation for the
Department of Labor, helped to adjust the shipyard disputes
whereby all employees received the union scale retroactive to
the beginning of the controversy.[7]

The promise of a new era of labor-management accommodation
offered by successful conciliation of these disputes proved
illusory, however, when would-be conciliators confronted the
united opposition of oil producers during the Texas-Louisiana
Gulf Coast oil field strike of 1917-1918.[8] In their adamant
stand, the producers not only undermined attempts at conciliation, but also inflicted a defeat upon organized labor from
which it did not recover until the 1930s.

Rising costs of living, poor working conditions, and paternalistic company policies prompted Goose Creek oil field
workers, aided by the Texas State Federation of Labor and the
Houston Trades Council, to form a local in December 1916. By
the spring of 1917, oil field workers throughout the Texas-
Louisiana Gulf Coast area had established locals affiliated
directly with the AFL since no national union for oil workers
existed.[9]

When Gulf Coast locals invited producers to meet with them in
Houston to discuss worker grievances on October 15, 1917, the
producers refused and sent letters of explanation to their
employees. Representative of the employer stance, Ross
Sterling, president of the Humble Oil & Refining Company,
wrote in part: "We see no reason why we should confer with
outsiders or strangers upon matters which concern our employees and ourselves." In regard to union labor, Humble Oil expected "from every employee loyalty to the company and con-
scientious and competent performance of his duty. So long as
membership in a labor union does not in any way interfere
with or prevent an employee from rendering this character of
service," Sterling continued, "we have no objection to his
being a member of such labor union." However, "this company
will continue to exercise the right to select its own employees and to deal with them directly and not through the medium
of a 'labor union' or other organization."[10]

Such an unequivocal declaration of employer position prompted
the union to issue a set of formal demands and to call a
strike vote. The demands included replacing the standard
twelve- to fourteen-hour day with an eight-hour day, a minimum daily wage of four dollars, a revision in the bonus system, and union recognition.[11] In the strike vote which followed, 5,992 of the oil field workers, representing 97 percent of those participating, voted to strike; and on November 1, 1917, approximately 10,000 men in some seventeen oil
fields in Texas and Louisiana walked out.[12]

When the strike was more than a month old and U.S. Commission-
ers of Conciliation James J. Barrett and George W. Musser
were unable to effect a settlement, the President's Mediation
Commission, a specially created branch of the Conciliation
Service, previously assigned to deal with a similar dispute
in California and headed by President Wilson's personal representative, Verner Z. Reed, arrived in Houston, charged with
responsibility to bring about a settlement. A number of factors, however, worked against an equitable solution for the
oil field workers. Basic to all else was tenacious employer
opposition to unionism. Management tactics included a determination to defeat worker solidarity, featuring the full use
of economic resources at their disposal and an identification
of the workers' cause with radicalism and disloyalty. Associated producers initially denied workers the same right of

association they enjoyed themselves by refusing to meet with
representatives of the Gulf Coast oil field workers, although
each individual company proclaimed a willingness to meet with
its own employees. Furthermore, the producers subsequently
displayed an ill-concealed contempt for the agents of the U.S.
Conciliation Service, James J. Barrett and George W. Musser.
Finding himself unable to establish a basis for negotiations
with "the chief officer of one of the largest [oil] companies," Musser offered to send for Secretary of Labor William
B. Wilson. The oil man, however, quickly replied with utter
disdain that even if Musser secured the services of President
Wilson, the producers fully intended to run their own busi-
nesses. Barrett reported that he was being followed, presumably by agents of the companies, and that producers had
spread the word among the workers that he was affiliated with
the Industrial Workers of the World (IWW).[13] With the onset
of the strike, certain producers informed Attorney General
T. W. Gregory that IWW agents and German spies representing
the "mailed hand of [the] enemy" had secretly infiltrated the
union and suggested that Gregory send Justice Department
agents to ferret out the enemy agents.[14] The Gulf Coast Oil
News, a mouthpiece for the producers, claimed that the "average American workingman," making up 80 percent of the oil
field workers, had enunciated no real complaints until the
arrival of outside agitators several months before and that
ordinary American workmen, now bitter toward union leaders,
feared to return to work in the oil fields because of a
"reign of terror" imposed by a "vicious class" which included
"the arch enemy of our Nation, the I.W.W."[15] Employer propaganda notwithstanding, the men continued to support the union
leadership. Little evidence of IWW influence during the
strike exists; moreover, the union firmly denounced the IWW
on numerous occasions.[16]

The none too subtle propaganda disseminated by the producers
found a sympathetic ear in the person of Texas Governor
William P. Hobby, who requested the army to send troops into
the oil fields to guard company property "from enemies and
trouble makers."[17] While some evidence exists to indicate
that the army initially maintained an impartial stance, the
very presence of government troops could not help but lend
credence to employer claims of subversive influence within
the ranks of the strikers.[18] Furthermore, some military officials displayed a hostile attitude toward the strikers.
Colonel D. J. Baker, of the Fifty-seventh Infantry, charac-
terized the majority of the strikers as "Americans of the ir-
responsible type which, when it feels itself aggrieved is
prone to violence and disorder." While recognizing little
violence had actually taken place, Colonel Baker warned that
"there is much latent hostility to the operators which, whatever the outcome of the strike, ... must be for some time
taken into account and guarded against." Complaints against
troops came not only from strikers but from local citizens

who charged soldiers with indiscriminate destruction of property, slaughtering of stock, and a cavalier attitude toward disturbing citizen sensibilities.[19]

Influenced by producer insistence that IWW agents and German spies infested the union and constantly reminded that the nation was at war, public opinion remained hostile to the strikers. The Houston Post branded the wartime strike "a blow below the belt"; and Sydney J. Smith, chairman of the Exemption Board of Appeals for the Selective Service's Southern District of Texas, threatened to use his position to induct strikers into the army.[20]

The ready availability of strikebreakers, resulting in part from a lengthy drought affecting West Texas farmers and ranchers, an influx of job applicants from across the state attracted by the $3.60 daily wage, and the importation of skilled drillers from other states, severely damaged the strike's effectiveness. Within two weeks, producers were maintaining near normal production levels, which convinced them the strike would soon be over.[21]

In dramatic contrast to the unity of purpose achieved by the producers, the inability of the oil field workers to win the support of the refinery workers in Texas and Louisiana sealed the fate of the strike; only by enlisting the support of the refinery workers could production be significantly affected, a necessary condition for union victory. While expressing sympathy for the strikers' cause and undoubtedly influenced by producer propaganda and public opinion and more firmly entrenched in middle-class society than the itinerant roughnecks, Beaumont and Port Arthur refinery workers voted against a sympathy strike on November 26, 1917.[22]

These, then, were the conditions greeting Verner Z. Reed and his colleagues comprising the President's Mediation Commission upon their arrival in Houston on December 17, 1917. After several hurried meetings with representatives of management and labor, Reed issued the commission's findings on December 21 after wiring Felix Frankfurter, counsel for the President's Commission, that he would suggest government take-over of pipelines and refinery properties if the operators "continue in their arbitrary and autocratic attitude."[23]

While rebuking the strikers for walking out before granting the government an opportunity to mediate, the findings approved most of the union demands and, in doing so, infuriated the producers. The findings of the commission called off the strike "without prejudice" on or before December 24, 1917; approved the eight-hour day in all branches of the industry effective March 1, 1918; granted immunity against intimidation or discrimination to members of any AFL-affiliated union; and charged representatives of operators, employees, and the

Texas and Louisiana state federations of labor to devise a uniform minimum wage scale for the entire Gulf Coast district by February 1, 1918. If they failed to reach a settlement, the matter should be decided by a government-appointed board of arbitration.[24]

Apparently unaware of the limits of the commission's authority, Reed appeared to dictate the terms as he "respectfully requested and directed [both parties] to accept the ... findings without delay."[25] While operators registered an official complaint with Reed, a committee representing the Louisiana and Texas oil workers endorsed the commission's findings and declared the strike over. His task apparently accomplished, Reed left for his Colorado home.[26]

On January 2, 1918, some 241 producers, representing 95 percent of area production, met in Houston, organized a formal association of oil and gas producers of Texas and Louisiana, arrogantly questioned Reed's authority, and refused to accept the findings of the President's Commission. In a letter to Reed, the producers took exception to the wording in the commission's findings "directing" them to comply:

> If we may do so with courtesy, permit us to suggest
> the limits of your authority.... The President never
> intended that your Commission should undertake to
> order the settlement of strikes, but merely to nego-
> tiate between the parties and endeavor to get them
> to dispose of the differences by agreement; his pur-
> pose is manifest from the name -- Mediation Commis-
> sion -- which he gave to your body.[27]

The producers' rebuttal to the findings of the Reed Commission argued the following points: an eight-hour day, reducing the labor supply, and increasing production costs would be "unpatriotic" in wartime; union demands represented the work of outside agitators who claimed a strike would force the government to compel the producers to grant the union demands, and to give in at this point would represent an endorsement of such tactics; oil field workers already received better pay than other workingmen, although "[i]f we could believe that an increase in this minimum wage would be of benefit to our Nation, we would cheerfully add this to the other ever growing burdens of enhanced cost ... from which the oil industry now suffers"; and the companies presently employed a sufficient labor force to maintain normal production, rendering government interference unnecessary -- in fact, implementation of the commission report would require the dismissal of current employees "to make room for the strikers." Finally, the producers appealed to the Department of Labor for a hearing before the full mediation commission to protest the Reed Commission's report.[28]

Between January 21 and January 28, representatives of the producers' association and the union men met with the officials
from the Department of Labor in negotiations leading to an
agreement which "superseded" Reed's report. With all parties
ultimately signing the new agreement, albeit with reluctance
on the part of the union men, the settlement, announced on
January 30, 1918, by the secretary of labor, vetoed the
eight-hour day and left a decision on wages and hours up to a
proposed committee on complaints of the oil and gas producers'
association. Only employees -- not "paid agitators" or union
organizers -- could present grievances to the committee on
complaints. No current employees would be dismissed to make
room for strikers, but former employees would be shown pref-
erence when openings occurred. But "[i]t is understood ...
that no employer shall be expected to re-employ any man who
is personally objectionable to the foreman or superintendent
of the employer under whose direction such applicant would
have to work if so employed." Provision was made whereby
either party could appeal a decision made by the complaint
committee to a three-man board of appeals composed of a producer representative, an appointee of the secretary of labor,
and the federal district judge of the Southern District of
Texas. In practice, however, the board proved totally ineffective. At producer insistence, the final settlement took
the form of an agreement between the producers' association
and the government in order to avoid recognition of the oil
workers' union.[29]

The final settlement represented almost a total victory for
the producers and killed union effectiveness. Approximately
one-fourth of the strikers lost their jobs as a result of the
strike, including R. E. Evans, president of the Goose Creek
local and one of the union's guiding lights. Within two
months of the settlement, Gulf and Humble granted wage increases equivalent to the union request; and the executive
committee of the employer association recommended another increase a short time later which became effective on June 1,
1918. Furthermore, several of the oil companies soon inaugurated housing programs and stock-purchasing plans for employees, all of which thoroughly undermined any effective demand
for unionism. Such activity represented an adaptation of the
so-called Rockefeller Plan, which has been called "a hybrid
form of organization somewhere between the various alterna-
tives of a company union, open shop, and union shop."[30]

Failure to win the support of refinery workers and the success of employer solidarity convinced members of the Gulf
Coast oil field locals and their counterparts in California
of the necessity to form a national union. Upon application,
the 1918 AFL convention issued a charter in June to the International Association of Oil Field, Gas Well, and Refinery
Workers of America (OFGWRWU), with the full understanding
that the charter did not entitle the new organization to

infringe upon the jurisdiction of any existing craft union.[31]

Continued division in the ranks of union members, in stark
contrast with employer unity, remained abundantly clear in
the sixteen-day organizational convention of the OFGWRWU
which began late in November in El Paso. Sharply divided between moderate and radical factions, the convention enacted a
resolution demanding nationalization of the oil, railroad,
communication, shipping, coal, water, and electric power industries; but it elected R. E. Evans, representing the moderate faction, as president by a slim three-vote margin. While
the new international grew rapidly for a time, the combined
effects of the failure to attract refinery workers because of
craft union hostility, internal conflicts, employer-initiated
benefits, and a new open shop offensive led to a near total
decline of the OFGWRWU until its reincarnation under the New
Deal.[32]

Notes

1 On the beginnings of the Texas oil industry, see John O.
King, "The Early Texas Oil Industry: Beginnings at Corsi-
cana, 1894-1901," Journal of Southern History 32 (November
1966), 505-15; and Seth S. McKay and Odie B. Faulk, Texas
After Spindletop (Austin, 1965), 1-16. For colorful
glimpses of life in oil field camps, see Mody C. Boatright
and William A. Owens, Tales From the Derrick Floor: A
People's History of the Oil Industry (Garden City, N.Y.,
1970); and Charlie Jeffries, "Reminiscences of Sour Lake,"
Southwestern Historical Quarterly 50 (July 1946), 25-35.

2 Samuel Gompers to George J. Jordan, February 14, 1902, and
Gompers to E. P. Lord, January 30, 1906, in Samuel Gompers
Letterbooks, Manuscript Division, Library of Congress,
Washington, D.C. Hereafter cited as Gompers Letterbooks.
Dallas Laborer, December 16, 1905; and American Federation-
ist 13 (February 1906), 107.

3 Telegram, Samuel Gompers to James Leonard, April 27, May 1,
1907, Gompers Letterbooks; and Ruth A. Allen, Chapters in
the History of Organized Labor in Texas (Austin, 1941), 222.

4 Grady L. Mullennix, "A History of the Labor Movement in the
Oil Industry" (M.S. thesis, North Texas State Teachers Col-
lege, 1942), 10; and Harry O'Connor, History of Oil Workers
Intl. Union (CIO) (Denver, 1950), 4-5.

5 The Conciliation Service was officially established in 1917,
although Secretary Wilson put Department of Labor mediators
into the field early in President Wilson's administration.
The U.S. Conciliation Service, within the Department of
Labor, was a forerunner of the Federal Mediation and Conciliation Service, established as a separate government
agency in 1947 by the Taft-Hartley Act. Popular usage

during the World War I era, however, commonly referred to
the U.S. Conciliation Service as the "Federal Mediation
Commission" or the "Federal Mediation Service."

6 John S. Smith, "Organized Labor and Government in the
Wilson Era, 1913-1921: Some Conclusions," Labor History 3
(Fall 1962), 265-86, sees the wartime collaboration as
beneficial to organized labor. For a much different view,
see Ronald Radosh, "The Corporate Ideology of American
Labor Leaders," in The Twenties: The Critical Issues, ed.
Joan Hoff Wilson (Boston, 1972), 73-83.

7 Federal Mediation and Conciliation Service Records, files
33/1068 and 33/1634, record group no. 280, National
Archives. Hereafter cited as Federal Mediation Records.
Proceedings, Texas State Federation of Labor, 1918, 34.

8 The best account of the strike is William Lee Greer, "The
Texas Gulf Coast Oil Strike of 1917" (M.A. thesis, Univer-
sity of Houston, 1974). See also Allen, Chapters, 221-48;
O'Connor, History of the Oil Workers Intl. Union, 5-8, 204;
Henrietta M. Larson and Kenneth W. Porter, History of
Humble Oil & Refining Company: A Study in Industrial
Growth (New York, 1959), 66-71; and Harold F. Williamson
et al., The American Petroleum Industry: The Age of
Energy, 1899-1959 (Evanston, Ill., 1963), 831-35.

9 Proceedings, Texas State Federation of Labor, 1917, 16,
112-13; ibid., 1918, 4; and O'Connor, History of the Oil
Workers Intl. Union, 204.

10 W. A. Campbell to Oil Producers and Operators of Texas and
Louisiana, October 2, 1917, Federal Mediation Records,
file 33/754; and Gulf Coast Oil News, October 20, 1917,
11, 13.

11 The wage demands demonstrated that neither the earlier employer action instituting the bonus as a solution to the
rising cost of living nor the increasing of the minimum
wage rate from $3.40 to $3.60 per day satisfied worker demands.

12 Oil and Gas Journal, November 1, 1917, 18; and Houston
Labor Journal, November 3 and 31, 1917.

13 James J. Barrett to E. J. Cunningham, November 2, 1917,
Federal Mediation Records, file 33/754; Barrett to H. L.
Kerwin, November 12, 1917, ibid.; Barrett to Kerwin, Octo-
ber 31, 1917, ibid., file 33/754-A; and G. W. Musser and
Barrett to William B. Wilson, December 8, 1917, ibid.

14 F. C. Proctor to T. W. Gregory, October 29, 1917, ibid.,
file 33/754; and telegram, J. B. Rogers to Gregory,

November 6, 1917, ibid.

15 Gulf Coast Oil News, November 3, 1917, 1, 4, 31; and December 1, 1917, 1.

16 E. P. Marsh to James L. Rodier, February 24, 1918, Chief Clerk's Files, file 130/14A, Department of Labor Records, National Archives; Greer, "Texas Gulf Coast Oil Strike," 40-41; Allen, Chapters, 224-25; and Houston Labor Journal, August 25, and November 31, 1917.

17 Hobby acted after receiving an appeal from Houston Sheriff M. Frank Hammond, who telegramed Hobby that he could not protect nearby oil fields from "I. W. W. or alien enemies." Telegram, Hammond to Hobby, October 31, 1917, United States Army, Southern Department, Records, file 370.6, record group no. 393, National Archives, Washington, D.C. Hereafter cited as Southern Department Records. Telegram, Hobby to Commanding General, Southern Department, Fort Sam Houston, Texas, November 2, 1917, ibid.; Brigadier General H. L. Todd to Commanding General, Southern Department, Fort Sam Houston, November 2, 1917, ibid., file 370.61; and Hobby to Major General John J. Ruckman, November 16, 1917, ibid.

18 Greer, "Texas Gulf Coast Oil Strike," 44; and O'Connor, History of the Oil Workers Intl. Union, 6.

19 Colonel J. D. Baker to Commanding General, Southern Department, Fort Sam Houston, December 22, 1917, and March 13, 1918, Southern Department Records, file 370.61; F. M. Jordan to Hon. J. B. Daily, February 8, 1918, ibid.; and Sheriff W. C. Jordan to General Ruckman, February 11, 1918, ibid.

20 Houston Post, October 30, 1917; and Minutes, Houston Labor Council, November 6, 1917, January 15, and February 5, 1918 (Division of Archives and Manuscripts, University of Texas at Arlington).

21 Allen, Chapters, 223; Williamson et al., The American Petroleum Industry, 833-34; Oil and Gas Journal, November 15 and 22, 1917, 16; and Greer, "Texas Gulf Coast Oil Strike," 59.

22 Greer, "Texas Gulf Coast Oil Strike," 29, 47-51, 86-87; and Gulf Coast Oil News, November 3, 1917, 3.

23 Allen, Chapters, 225; and telegram, Verner Z. Reed to Felix Frankfurter, December 21, 1917, Federal Mediation Records, file 33/754-B.

24 "Findings of the President's Mediation Commission,"

December 21, 1917, Federal Mediation Records, file
33/754-B.

[25] Ibid. On Reed's authority see Greer, "Texas Gulf Coast
Oil Strike," 55-58; and Allen, Chapters, 225.

[26] R. E. Brooks, Underwood Nazro, W. S. Farish, and F. C.
Proctor to Hon. Verner Z. Reed, December 21, 1917, Federal
Mediation Records, file 33/754-B; telegram, Reed to Felix
Frankfurter, December 22, 1917, ibid.; Charles T. Connell
to H. L. Kerwin, December 22, 1917, ibid., file 33/754;
and Houston Labor Journal, December 29, 1917.

[27] Oil Producers to Verner Z. Reed, January 2, 1918, Federal
Mediation Records, file 33/754.

[28] Ibid.

[29] "Report of the Executive Committee of Texas Gulf Coast and
Louisiana Oil and Gas Association and Agreement with the
President's Mediation Commission," February 12, 1918,
ibid., file 33/754-C; and Gulf Coast Oil News, February 2,
1918, 3-5.

[30] Larson and Porter, History of Humble Oil, 70-71; and
O'Connor, History of the Oil Workers Intl. Union, 7.
Quote from Williamson et al., The American Petroleum In-
dustry, 832.

[31] Williamson et al., The American Petroleum Industry, 834;
and O'Connor, History of the Oil Workers Intl. Union, 13.

[32] The decline can be followed by OFGWRWU membership: 1919 --
4,500, 1920 -- 20,900, 1921 -- 24,800, 1924 -- 2,000,
1929 -- 1,100, 1933 -- less than 300. Williamson et al.,
The American Petroleum Industry, 834-35; O'Connor, History
of the Oil Workers Intl. Union, 15-21, 29-35; and Oil and
Gas Journal, December 20, 1918, 51, 58.

CIO Oil Workers'
Organizing Campaign in Texas, 1942-1943

Clyde Johnson

In 1940, the oil workers ousted John Coulter and elected
O. A. Knight president of the Oil Workers International Union
(OWIU). This action cleared the way for an organizing drive.
Vice-President Sam Beers said later that "this union at that
time [1940] had the reputation of entering into more NLRB
[National Labor Relations Board] elections and losing them
than any other International Union in existence."

At the next (1941) convention, John Crossland from the Houston
Shell local chaired a special organization committee. The
committee proposed a CIO-directed drive in the oil industry
with Standard Oil as the main target. The delegates approved
it.

In November, the CIO convention adopted an "Organize Oil"
resolution. After the delegates voted, CIO President Philip
Murray introduced Edwin S. Smith as national director of the
CIO Oil Workers Organizing Campaign (OWOC). Smith, a former
member of the NLRB, was highly respected by CIO unions for
his landmark decisions that formed early NLRB policy.

Smith appointed Travis K. Hedrick, a veteran journalist and
Newspaper Guild activist, as publicity director. Hedrick had
organized and led the guild strike at the Chattanooga News,
the first white-collar strike in the South.

Several OWIU representatives were put on the OWOC staff, including Ben Schafer as Southern director. When Smith asked
Schafer for a list of CIO unions to invite to a Houston conference to launch the Texas campaign, the National Maritime
Union (NMU) was ignored. The NMU was concerned with the oil
industry. They lost their Standard Oil tanker agreements in
the ill-timed 1939 strike. Smith invited them.

On January 6, 1942, a Houston conference heard Smith outline
the aims of the CIO Oil Workers Organizing Campaign. Frederick N. (Blackie) Myers, dynamic young vice-president of the
NMU, was there to tie in tanker organizing with the refinery
workers campaign.

During the conference, John Crossland and Rocky Davis, officers of the Houston Shell local, asked me to accept a job
with the OWOC. They said the campaign needed an organizer
with a successful record in that area. I had led a tough but
successful strike of pecan shellers in San Antonio and organized 1,200 cotton compress and flour mill workers along the
Houston Ship Channel. Blackie Myers also asked me to accept
a job with the campaign.

Smith hired me. Schafer assigned me to organize the Pan
American Oil refinery in Texas City (Standard Oil of Indiana).

THE TEXAS CAMPAIGN IN PORT ARTHUR

An organizing campaign was already under way at the Texas
Company refinery in Port Arthur. The OWIU had started it,
and Smith sent Hedrick to work on publicity. The Port Arthur
City Council and Police Department were viciously opposed to
unions. Organizer F. H. Mitchell was beaten by Chief Baker
and two cops just before the NLRB election. NMU pickets were
beaten and jailed repeatedly during the 1939 tanker strike.

OWIU Local 23 in Port Arthur was Jim Crow. Black workers
were segregated in Local 254. This was contrary to official
CIO policy, but it was common practice for reactionary white
CIO officials.

In mid-January, the Texas Company election was won: CIO --
1,351, no union -- 781, and AFL -- 67.

THE PAN AMERICAN CAMPAIGN

The first thing I was told upon arrival in Texas City was
that the City Council, Police Department, and Chamber of Commerce were meeting to decide on how to run the CIO out of
town. The secretary of Local 449, Foy Hopkins, seemed to
tremble as he repeated the rumor. Next, he said there were
only 7 of the 150 members signed up at Pan American still in
good standing. Pan Am employed 1,100 workers.

A few days later I was shocked to learn that Local 449 had
petitioned the NLRB for an election at Pan Am. Schafer had
not told me, and I was sure Smith didn't know about it. We
were in a bad spot. Later I was told OWIU representatives
had a bad reputation for rushing unprepared into elections

and then deserting the workers when the going got tough.

The next day I met with F. A. (Doc) Yoas, president of Local 449, Ernest Hebert, Hoskins Foster, and a few more Pan Am members to work out an organizing plan. I wrote Smith proposing the 150 members who had paid initiation fees at Pan Am be declared in good standing without payment of monthly dues until the NLRB election. I also requested three organizers.

Jack Frye, a student radical from the University of Texas, and John Roe, a young machinist from Denver, Colorado, were hired away from District 50, United Mine Workers, in Houston. A few days later Clyde Jones arrived from Oklahoma. He was a militant strike leader in the oil fields and president of the Sinclair local in Gainesville, Texas. We worked well as a team, so the Pan Am campaign took shape quickly. Seniority and job classifications were issues as we gathered department lists and started home visits.

THE SOUTHPORT CAMPAIGN

We were making good progress at Pan Am when another surprise jolted us. The United States Supreme Court ruled that change of ownership was no reason Southport Petroleum should not deal with Local 449. This meant an NLRB election would be ordered soon, and the local was not prepared. We decided to take on Southport along with Pan Am rather than risk leaving it to OWIU representatives. I was assigned to the job. Southport employed 140 workers.

We had a small nucleus of active members. By the time of the election hearing, aided by Southport's nasty, arrogant treatment of the workers, Local 449 recruited a good majority as members.

On March 11, Southport workers voted 105 to 21 for the CIO. Meanwhile, the NLRB had ordered the Pan Am election hearing. We were under heavy pressure to increase membership fast.

PAN AM WIN-THE-WAR ACTIVITIES

The AFL and company union had started red-baiting rumors about the CIO, but Smith and Hedrick were publicly attacking Standard Oil's close ties with Nazi Germany. Hedrick played up Senator Truman's charge of treason against Standard Oil. He also publicized government charges that Standard Oil gave I. G. Farbenindustrie the patents for synthetic rubber and other oil products.

We drew attention to oil tankers being torpedoed off the

coast of Florida and in the Gulf of Mexico, which placed the
Nazis close to the refineries. We proposed a twenty-four-
hour patrol on the lonely road behind the Pan Am tank farm.
We played up CIO member Tom Bludworth's plan for concrete
barges to haul oil products on inland waterways.

Our attack on Standard Oil's collaboration with the Nazis
helped discredit the use of red baiting against the CIO and
radical organizers in the campaign.

Another major issue was race prejudice.

BLACK WORKERS AT PAN AM

Pan Am employed about 120 blacks. We worked out a minimum
program to appeal to them: one local union, one seniority
list, equal pay on jobs, open job bidding by seniority, and
seniority to govern layoffs and shutdowns. That was a revolutionary program in Southeast Texas. Local 449 accepted it.

Rock Richardson, president of the CIO Cotton Compress local
in Houston, spoke to CIO meetings in the black community of
La Marque. He was a tall, dignified, militant black man who
created confidence in people. He was the black president of
a mixed local -- perhaps the first in Texas.

Edwin Smith, Blackie Myers, John Crossland, Travis Hedrick,
and the Sinclair Negro Quartet were featured speakers at the
La Marque meetings. Some white Pan Am workers attended these
meetings and learned more about the race issue.

The company union and AFL seized upon the race issue for
their rumor mill, warning white workers the CIO stood for
equality.

THE WAGE AND JOB ISSUES

Standard Oil bragged they paid the highest wages in the industry. We investigated this claim with the help of Bill
Glazier, a brilliant young economist out of Harvard, who
Smith hired as OWOC research director. The top-rated man in
a Pan Am department did get a few cents more per hour. But
in a pipe gang, for example, Pan Am had one first-class pipe-
fitter, one or two second-class, and about twelve helpers.
At Shell or Sinclair, under union contract, there were two or
three first-class pipefitters, three or four second-class,
and five or six helpers.

The average hourly wage for a Pan Am pipe gang was five cents
an hour less than Shell or Sinclair. The same was true of
other departments. We broke the illusion of Standard Oil's
high wages.

We attacked Pan Am's system of job classifications; the suc-
tion system for promotions, layoffs, and shutdowns; and other
inequities.

BOIL HITLER IN TEXAS OIL—CIO

As a high point for the campaign, we planned an "Oil for Victory" parade and rally about two weeks before the election.
Local 449 members pitched in, and NMU port agent Jack Duchere
mobilized support for it.

The parade started in La Margue and grew as it passed through
outlying communities. It went by the refinery and into Texas
City. As we reached Texas Avenue, most community organizations joined in, including the Central High Band, the Fire
Department, and Mayor E. A. Johnson (who had just been
elected with CIO support).

As the parade reached City Hall, people saw a sixty-foot banner stretched across the front advocating "BOIL HITLER IN
TEXAS OIL -- CIO." The rally that evening in the Texas City
Auditorium featured Edwin Smith, O. A. Knight, president of
the OWIU, George Roberts of the War Production Board, and the
mayor.

It was a great windup for our campaign. Two days later, the
company union withdrew from the ballot.

RUNOFF ELECTION NECESSARY

On May 5, Pan Am workers voted: CIO -- 353, AFL -- 354,
neither -- 136. A runoff election was necessary. The race-
baiting rumor campaign and the Pan Am strategy of withdrawing
the company union had hurt more than we expected.

Doc Yoas, our main poll watcher, protested the intimidation
of black voters by NLRB agents. Yoas demanded that they stop
using insulting language with Negro voters. He refused to
sign the NLRB form certifying the vote count. After a long
argument, Doc asked to see me at the plant gate. I told him
that signing did not interfere with an election protest.
Edwin Smith sent a sharply worded protest to NLRB Regional
Director Elliott based on Yoas's report of the anti-Negro
bias.

During the next four weeks, we concentrated on the lack of
democracy in competing AFL unions. The Hod Carriers had not
held a convention in thirty years. The Operating Engineers
relegated refinery workers to Class C locals which never got
to vote.

The night before the June 5 runoff, I drove Smith to the air-
port. He told me if we lost the election, the whole campaign
was over. I didn't tell the staff.

The next day we won: CIO -- 462, AFL -- 375. Doc Yoas said
the chastised NLRB agents were polite to Negro voters. The
devastating criticism of the AFL swung the "neither" vote to
the CIO. Also, the former company union president, Mel Johnson, swung to the CIO.

John Roe stayed in Texas City to help prepare for Pan Am contract negotiations. Jones and I moved to Baytown to open the
Humble Oil (Standard of New Jersey) campaign. Jack Frye went
to Ingleside to organize the small Humble refinery.

PAN AM CONTRACT NEGOTIATIONS

The Pan Am members chose Doc Yoas, Ernest Hebert, and six
more members to work with Edwin Smith, Bill Glazier, John Roe,
and me on the negotiating committee. When negotiations deadlocked, our dispute went to the War Labor Board (WLB) in
Washington, where Smith and Glazier represented us.

The WLB awarded us plant-wide seniority, job bidding, the
grievance procedure we preferred, overtime for hours worked
over eight in a twenty-four-hour shift period, time and a
half for Negroes on Emancipation Day, and the mechanical
shift handyman rate for Negroes on shutdowns. Classifications
were sent to arbitration, and we faired well in the decision.

On December 17, the Pan Am members approved their contract.

We anticipated provocations by Pan Am on the new rights for
Negroes under the contract. Clyde Jones reported that Foy
Hopkins, secretary of Local 449, was denouncing the Pan Am
agreement to Pan Am members, mainly on Negro issues. He said
the International was coming in to tear up the contract. He
got a few disgruntled members to petition for a special meeting on the contract. When Doc Yoas opened the meeting, he
asked for a motion stating the purpose of the meeting. A
long silence was broken when a member who had helped circu-
late the petition got up and moved to adjourn. Roe, Jones,
Yoas, Hebert, Jerome Peek, Hoskins Foster, Al Grospiron, Tom
Bludworth, and others had worked hard to counteract Hopkins's
dirty work.

Hoskins Foster left Pan Am to work for the OWOC in Baytown.
Bucky Aylor moved from Borger to Port Arthur and the Gulf
campaign.

THE INGLESIDE HUMBLE CAMPAIGN

Meanwhile, Jack Frye had found members of Local 316 in Ingleside raring to go with the organizing drive. Local leaders
like Henry (Slick) Wier, Red Hydrick, and J. D. Hickman were
fed up with the company union and Humble paternalism. Seniority and a grievance procedure with teeth were key issues.

On July 8, Smith, Hedrick, Clyde Drake, NMU port agent in
Houston, and I spoke to a good-sized rally in the Local 316
hall. It was obvious Frye had the campaign in high gear.

The race issue in Ingleside involved Mexican-Americans, and
they were already active in Local 316. On October 13, Ingleside Humble workers voted 212 to 68 for the OWOC-CIO. The International sent their staff man, Bill Trombley, to help negotiate. The members had drafted contract proposals patterned
after the Pan Am agreement. Trombley argued against the proposals in front of Humble management. In a special membership
meeting, Trombley was rebuked by Local 316 and fired.

Local 316 approved an agreement reached through the WLB on
May 17, 1943.

THE BAYTOWN CAMPAIGN BEGINS

Late in June 1942, I met with members of Local 333 in Goose
Creek to discuss the Baytown Humble Oil campaign. This was
the big one, the heart of the Standard Oil of New Jersey operation in Texas. The members agreed to set up a campaign
local.

Dedicated union men like Cap Rawson, W. A. (Hot Shot) Rogers,
Big Jim Dunman, C. T. Bonner, C. C. Fogarty, N. O. Carnes,
Emmett Shumway, E. Hoffpauer, and others were ready to give
their all to the campaign.

Smith had removed Schafer as Southern director in March and
appointed Hedrick in his place. After the Pan Am election, I
was given the title, plus that of assistant to the national
director. My main work was directing the Baytown campaign.

On July 3, 1942, the first issue of the CIO Campaigner, a
tabloid we published for the next seventeen months, announced
the opening of the Baytown campaign. Two weeks later, the
AFL staked a claim with a small ad in the Goose Creek (Texas)
Daily Sun.

We played up the NLRB decision outlawing three Standard Oil
of New Jersey company unions in New Jersey (at the Bayway,
Bayonne, and Jersey City refineries). Jones, Foster, and I
were busy setting up department membership drives and ferret-
ing out issues for the campaign.

Smith had to report to the OWIU convention just nine months after the OWOC began. If delegates expected miracles, all Smith could report were the Texaco, Pan Am, and Southport election victories, plus a certain victory soon at Ingleside. There was not much to report for California or New Jersey. He said the Gulf Oil and Baytown campaigns were going well, and he made a strong appeal for full support to get the broad campaign in high gear.

THE BAYTOWN CAMPAIGN GOT HOT

Back in Baytown, we got into an overtime pay fight for shift workers. Humble declared Saturday the first day of the week to avoid paying overtime, and the company union agreed.

Then the company union announced it had assigned a professional propagandist, Clifford Bond, to write their bulletins. Humble Oil put him on their payroll. His first target was the CIO position on black workers.

Their Bulletin number 9 used isolated quotes from "The CIO and the Negro Worker," a pamphlet put out by the CIO national office. The quotes were selected to inflame prejudice among white workers. They followed with a few more bulletins filled with race-baiting diatribes about how white workers would be hurt by the CIO policy on black workers. About 500 of the 4,000 workers at the refinery were black.

One of our replies quoted ex-Governor Allred: "The resistance of our own people to Hitler ... depends on how well we stand together in our own country ... Negro and white, Jew and Gentile, native and foreign born."

Edwin Smith talked to members of the War Manpower Commission and the president's Fair Employment Practices Commission (FEPC) in Washington. On October 29, the FEPC wired the company union that Bulletin number 9 was an "incitement to violence against Negro workers ... an act of gross irresponsibility ... retarding the war effort." They demanded a retraction. The company union defied them, saying "no retraction ... under any circumstances."

We hired Ewart Twine, a Negro organizer. Clive Knowles and Herman Meddler were transferred from New Jersey to the Baytown staff.

In our equal pay for women handbill, we said, "The Fed condemned the CIO ... for its policy on colored labor. They turned around and 'Negotiated' $100 for white women to do the same type work Humble pays $157 to colored janitors." We again demanded equal pay for Negroes in the labor department. Humble replied by taking white workers out of the ditches.

There were no defections by CIO members, but recruiting
slowed down.

RACIAL PROVOCATIONS DURING TENSE PERIOD

Clive Knowles got his first contact with the white problem in
the South. Most of our staff were Texans. I had been organizing in the South for ten years. Some of the incidents related here could have triggered riots if the CIO members had
not kept clear heads.

When Twine got his first paycheck, he realized he had equal
status on the staff. He proceeded to decorate his hat with
CIO buttons. On Saturday night he was having a beer in a Ne-
gro bar in McNair. Three deputy sheriffs entered. One saw
Twine with his hat on and yelled, "Nigger, take off that hat."
Twine sat still and looked at him. The deputy then threat-
ened to blow his head off. Twine sat and looked at him.
Then the deputy fired, and the bullet slammed into the wall
near Twine's head. He sat there and stared at the deputy.
The three of them went outside; then their car roared away.
They had made Twine a local hero.

Jones, Knowles, and I were covering a midnight shift change.
A Negro member told us there might be racial trouble on the
trolleys. About the time Bulletin number 9 came out, the
Missouri Pacific (MP) withdrew cars from the line. Hundreds
of white and black workers used the service. Now sixty to
eighty workers were crowding into cars built to carry forty.
We each rode a trolley that night. It was a tinderbox situation, but there were no incidents. We raised hell with MP
publicly and rode the trolleys now and then. Finally, MP put
more cars back in service.

During the same period, Knowles got a call at night asking
him to come out to a bar in a Negro community. We went.
There were two white women sitting at the bar. We suggested
they leave. They did. Knowles took their license number.
The next day, he checked them out. They were whores from
Houston obviously planted in the bar to create an incident.

Hervis Bradley was fired by Humble in November. He was a
black CIO member. We filed a charge with the NLRB. Unusual
interest developed in the case because of the race issue. Attorney Herman Wright presented our case. The NLRB decision
on January 20 forced Humble to rehire Bradley, pay his wages
for time lost, and post notices saying workers were free to
join CIO Local 1002.

WE GAMBLE ON "CIO IN JANUARY"

We were winning skirmishes with Humble, but we were also

suffering demoralization from the racial tension. To shake
up the campaign, I suggested we set a goal of "CIO in January." The staff and executive board agreed, so the CIO Campaigner announced it on December 5.

We had won a Christmas bonus for shift workers; the Bradley
case won regular status for over 1,000 workers (most of them
white) whom Humble classified "temporary," and we won equal
pay for women. A worried company union was pleading, "Don't
kill the goose that laid the golden egg."

THE GULF OIL CAMPAIGN

Meanwhile, in Port Arthur the Gulf campaign was moving ahead.
We got a campaign charter installed because Local 23 insisted
on a separate Local 254 for blacks. Joe Sherwood (from New
Jersey) and Bucky Aylor were not raising issues in their
handbills. Jack Frye and John Roe spent some time at Gulf.
The sign-up campaign had gone well. On November 10, Aylor
notified Gulf the union represented a majority.

The notice triggered action by company stooges. They met at
the Goodhue Hotel. They ran a full-page ad in the Port
Arthur News attacking CIO "outsiders." An unsigned handbill
headed "CIO Promises Negroes Equality With Whites" warned of
"serious trouble" and a "secret" campaign among Negroes.

Clyde Ingram of Sinclair Local 227 told me some officials of
Local 23 were spreading the word we had organized mainly Negroes. Bucky phoned to ask that I spend the two weeks before
the election in Port Arthur doing publicity.

Congressman Martin Dies, chairman of the House Un-American
Activities Committee, took time on Radio Station KPAC to
blast the CIO as a Communist front. We ran spot announcements
on the same station timed for the shift changes. We issued
handbills every day and ran a full-page ad in the Port Arthur
News.

Two officers of Local 23, Morris Akin and J. Elro Brown,
joined me on KPAC to appeal to Gulf workers for their support.
The wives of Akin, Brown, and L. W. Hoelzer did an interview
with me on the same station. We watched carefully for racial
provocations. Because the race issue had been ignored by the
staff, we were in no position to counteract provocations in
the final days of the campaign.

On March 6, the 3,700 Gulf Oil workers gave the CIO a 60 percent majority in the election. The white workers went to
Local 23 and the black workers to Local 254, contrary to official CIO policy.

BAYTOWN ELECTION REQUESTED

In Baytown we ran a New Year's Day ad in the Daily Sun reviewing the campaign at Humble and reciting our victories in
Southeast Texas. Then, on January 19, Smith presented Humble
with the CIO demand for bargaining rights. On February 11,
seven months after opening the drive, Smith announced filing
an election petition with the NLRB. Our membership drive was
still dragging.

Jack Montgomery was sent to Baytown from the California staff
to see if he could suggest ways to pep up our campaign. Jack
was seasoned in the longshore, farm, and auto worker union
campaigns on the West Coast. At that time we were busy ex-
posing Humble's claim to paying the highest refinery wages.

SMITH FIRED, CAMPAIGN UPSET

On March 23, Edwin Smith wrote he had been fired. The CIO
turned the campaign back to the OWIU executive council and
hired W. B. Taylor, an Auto Workers organizer, in Smith's
place. Hedrick and Glazier were fired, and Smith said our un-
dated resignations were requested.

The Baytown staff was shocked. We felt a great loyalty and
respect for Smith. Knight's letter to local unions on
March 28 gave no reasons for the action. We knew sharp differences existed on organizing practice, but they were hidden
behind official lip service to the policies we advocated.
The main differences were on equal rights for Negroes and mo-
bilizing all workers to battle the corporations as class
enemies.

Smith had hired dedicated radical unionists to direct the
Standard Oil organizing, men like Morgan Hull and Jack Mont-
gomery in California, Clive Knowles and Milt Kaufman in New
Jersey, and Jack Frye and me in Texas. Bill Glazier wrote me,
"Those bastards are so insecure that they simply had to kill
us off." The Baytown staff refused to submit resignations.
Knight and Taylor did not fire us. They knew our draft
boards would take care of us soon.

Our immediate concern was the Baytown election. I sent Jack
Montgomery with six members of Local 1002 to Fort Worth to see
Knight and Elliott of the NLRB. They returned believing we
would get the election. On April 6, Jack returned to California.

HUMBLE'S ANTI-NEGRO CAMPAIGN CONTINUES

The April 27 company union bulletin carried the heading, "A

VOTE FOR THE CIO IS A VOTE FOR ABSOLUTE EQUALITY BETWEEN THE
WHITE AND COLORED RACES ON EVERY JOB IN BAYTOWN REFINERY FROM
LABOR GANG TO DEPARTMENT HEAD." This headline was repeated
in their next ten bulletins, in addition to warnings that
blacks would take white workers' jobs and that riots and
other disasters would occur.

Basically, the headline was true. In using it to rally opposition to any improvement for blacks, the company union was
fanning the flame of race hatred. We announced that we would
challenge the right of the company union to appear on an NLRB
ballot.

We denounced Humble for hiring white workers at the seventy-
six-cent Negro labor rate. This move by Humble was the preliminary for setting seventy-six cents as the labor rate for
all. We demanded the eighty-nine-cent white labor rate for
all workers in the department.

The NLRB election hearing was finally set for July 15.
Elliott let us sweat out five months of racist propaganda that
hurt our sign-up campaign. Elliott claimed the NLRB had to
check out whether the company union contract signed January 26 was a bar to an election. The information we supplied
was so clear that we felt sure there was sabotage in the NLRB
regional office.

THE BAYTOWN ELECTION HEARING

On July 15, the Pelly courtroom bulged with spectators for
the hearing. Our attorney, Herman Wright, challenged the
right of the company union to appear on the ballot because of
its racist propaganda. Trial Examiner Bliss Daffan refused
to accept a motion to hear argument on the issue. This was a
serious setback for the CIO.

That same day, an AFL handbill invited Humble workers to examine their record. Their local unions were lily-white,
which was what they wanted known without saying it. It was
the first we'd heard of them in a year. They petitioned to
represent machinists, electricians, and railroad workers. We
withdrew from those departments to improve our representation
in the big unit of 3,900 workers.

One lively bit from an otherwise dull eight-day hearing was
the testimony of Jack Jones on the Humble payroll deductions
for company union dues. Wright asked to look at the book.
For the next four or five minutes, we examined as many departments as we could. The book showed foremen and clerks
were members of the company union, and in no department we
checked did they have a majority of the workers. When Gordon
Farned, the Humble general manager, realized what we were

finding out, he roared his demand for the return of the book.
Then Daffan allowed a Humble motion to have Jones's testimony
and reference to the book stricken from the record. Instead,
he accepted the unsupported recollections of another Humble
official. At the end of the hearing Wright tried again to introduce the anti-Negro bulletins, and again Daffan refused to
accept them as evidence.

WE CHALLENGE TEXAS ANTI-LABOR LAW

For a preelection high point, our new national director proposed we invite R. J. Thomas, president of the United Auto
Workers, to a mass meeting to make a test case of the new law
in Texas requiring the licensing of organizers. We set it
for September 25. Over 1,000 workers came to Pelly City Hall.
The meeting had to be moved outside. Thomas got his biggest
applause when he said, "Standard Oil has its headquarters in
New York and its hindquarters spread all over the world."

The deputies scheduled to make the test case arrests were
worried about the prounion crowd and asked me to guarantee
them safe conduct. I got Knowles and Jones to stand by while
the arrests were made. John Crossland and C. M. Massengale,
Taylor's assistant, were also arrested.

BEHIND THE ELECTION SCENES

By the beginning of October, the NLRB had not ordered the
election. We had filed in February. (The army had taken
Jack Frye, and the Seabees got John Roe. A Boston draft
board was after Clive Knowles. Jones, Foster, Twine, and I
remained as staff.) We were very worried about the election.
We sent a wire to the NLRB in Washington. We also wired the
CIO general counsel, Lee Pressman.

On October 4, Clive Knowles got a wire from Gene Cotton,
Pressman's assistant, saying the NLRB decision would be out
soon and would be adverse. We were gathering for a board
meeting; so Jones, Knowles, and I had a quick conference. I
presented the telegram to the board and recommended we send a
man to Washington to make one last appeal to the NLRB. They
agreed and designated me. I said we would have to bear the
expense. Big Jim Dunman immediately put $10 on the table. So
did Hot Shot Rogers. Within two minutes, there was $200 on
the table.

An amazed Gene Cotton greeted me at the CIO offices in Washington the next morning. We went right over to see Ivar
Peterson, secretary to the NLRB. He showed us a damp copy of
the adverse decision, still undistributed. I asked if we
could talk to him about it. For the next two hours I

reviewed our campaign, the ugly racist propaganda of the company union, and the strong desire of the Local 1002 members
to challenge Standard Oil in an election. We left Peterson
feeling we would get the election if we could produce another
100 cards.

I wrote to Jones, Twine, and Knowles. Then I wrote a long
letter to the NLRB reviewing our case, as I had with Peterson.
I said one of the worst anti-Negro handbills had been passed
out the day of the Beaumont race riot not fifty miles away.
I also charged we were in effect being penalized for supporting Executive Order 8502. I emphasized that many white workers supported the CIO, and this was a major factor in preventing a race riot in this key war production plant.

On October 27, the NLRB ordered the election.

MAGNOLIA VICTORY IN BEAUMONT

In Beaumont, F. H. Mitchell had plugged away at the Magnolia
refinery (Standard Oil of New York) for almost two years.
The handbills had never been much more than notices of meetings. No effort was made to integrate white and black members. Taylor sent me down to handle the election hearing.
E. C. Byerly, secretary of Local 243, wrote me saying I had
done a good job.

In September there was a race riot in Beaumont, originating
in a shipyard. Discrimination against blacks had been ignored
completely, and nobody raised the issue of the CIO program.
Neither a company union nor the AFL was involved. On October 25, the 1,200 Magnolia workers voted three to one for the
CIO.

THE BAYTOWN ELECTION

Jones, Twine, Foster, and I had tried our best to revive the
spirit of the campaign. Members were loyal. There were no
defections. But the spark was missing.

Then, two days before the election, local newspapers ran the
headline: "CIO Broke Pledge--Elliott." The company union
complained the CIO raised the race issue in violation of a
preelection agreement with the NLRB.

They referred to the tenth paragraph of a story on page 2 of
the CIO Campaigner. A white refinery worker who had written
to the company union was bitter against Negroes and denounced
the "Goebbels" who wrote their bulletins.

The racist attacks on the CIO by the company union continued right up to November 11, just fourteen days before the election. A few days later, Elliott got the preelection agreement to lay off the race issue. Elliott's statement condemned the CIO and in effect praised the company union for suspending its racial attacks. Elliott had failed to block the election due to our alert action, but he had stalled NLRB procedures for ten months while the company union carried on constant racial provocations. If Edwin Smith had still been national director, we felt sure the company union would not even have been on the ballot. This last jab by Elliott would have been reason to void the election. Nobody among Baytown CIO leaders had any confidence in Knight or Taylor.

On November 25, Humble workers voted two to one for the company union. Out of 3,900 workers, 3,200 voted. The CIO got 35 percent, just about our membership strength.

The staff had kept its promise to the members. Standard Oil had been forced to go through an NLRB-supervised election. Our failure was due, basically, to the loss of Edwin Smith and the backing he supplied in tough situations.

We won six of the seven refinery elections during the two years 1942 and 1943. That meant eleven of the twelve refineries in Southeast Texas were CIO.

Jones and Twine went on to work for the OWIU elsewhere. Knowles and I sailed oil tankers for the duration.

Comment

A synopsis of the remarks by Charles H. Martin, University
of Alabama, Gadsden Program.

The papers of Maroney and Johnson on labor in the oil fields
share a common geography, a similar social milieu, and several
unifying themes. Both studies demonstrate the tenuousness of
the wartime compromise between labor and management, as well
as the latter's willingness to manipulate the highly emotional
issue of patriotism to undermine unionization. Likewise, they
expose the way management exploited local fears of political
radicalism. Finally, each paper discusses a most frequent
phenomenon in Southern labor history, charges of outside agitation.

Regarding Johnson's paper specifically, the former organizer's
reminiscences clearly reveal management's exploitation of the
race issue in its struggle against the union. Unfortunately,
Johnson does not provide adequate information, such as the
percentage of black workers in each refinery, to assess fully
the effectiveness of the racial appeal. Also, further delin-
eation of the geographical and cultural origins of the oil
workers might clarify difficulties in organizing and union
dissension.

Maroney's paper needs further amplification. The author might
explain the inconsequence of the race issue in the 1917 strike
of Texas-Louisiana oil fields and more fully consider the impact of public opinion and the roles of church and press.
Likewise, information on the percentage of the total work
force involved in the strike and the immediate effect of the
strike on production would strengthen the study. Equally important, greater utilization of local newspapers and state
documents might well provide a more complete picture.

CHAPTER V

URBAN TRANSPORTATION: Transit Strikes in New Orleans and Atlanta

Public transportation assumed major importance in Southern urban centers by the 1890s and, as in the North, facilitated expansion into the suburbs. Although sporadic labor disputes occurred, transit workers' unions did not become a serious threat to management until well after World War I. The following essays examine labor disputes on the streetcars of New Orleans (1929-1930) and Atlanta (1949-1950). In many respects, the two strikes seem to have little in common beyond regional identification. The New Orleans dispute occurred before the automobile made noticeable inroads among the streetcar's patrons. Moreover, in New Orleans the strike was strongly supported, while in Atlanta the reaction was generally hostile.

In writing about New Orleans, Gerald Carpenter found that widespread public support for the transit workers' position was crucial in the final determination of the strike, thus challenging the conventional wisdom that Southerners were always hostile to labor unions. Bitter confrontation between labor and management was typical of the textile South, Carpenter argues; but outside the mills there was a long tradition of Southern craft unionism which seemed to enjoy considerable favor.

James W. May, Jr., finds no such support for the transit workers in Atlanta. Indeed, the strike was barely under way in the spring of 1949 before a hostile Atlanta power structure including Georgia Power Company (which owned the transit company), the press, the downtown business interests and Chamber of Commerce, and state and local governments had lined up solidly against the strikers in an attempt to supplant the collective bargaining process with overwhelming public pressure. Yet, beyond the differences in public behavior between the two cities, May's account provides support for

Carpenter's interpretation. The Atlanta confrontation certainly differed from the Southern textile strike pattern if
for no other reason than the fact that the union in the end
prevailed. Like New Orleans, the opponents of the Atlanta
workers never made an issue of union recognition and bar-
gained with union representatives collectively, if not always
in good faith.

Gerald Carpenter received the M.A. (1968) and Ph.D. (1973)
degrees from Tulane University. Both his master's and doctoral theses dealt with Southern labor in the post-World War I
period. He is currently research associate with the Tulane
Center for Business History Studies.

James W. May, Jr., received the M.A. degree from Georgia
State University in 1976. His master's thesis dealt with
"The Atlanta Transit System: Labor-Management Relations,
1946-1950." May presently teaches history at Peachtree High
School in Northeast Atlanta.

Public Opinion in the
New Orleans Street Railway Strike of 1929-1930

Gerald Carpenter

Recently the North Carolina Anvil began an account of the
difficulties faced by textile union organizers at J. P.
Stevens & Co. with this observation: "One of the greatest
gaps between the South and the rest of the country is the attitude toward labor."[1] This statement is notable for two
reasons. First, it shows the unfortunate but persistent tendency to generalize about Southern labor from the experience
of textile workers. The result of that tendency has been the
establishment of a stereotype of Southern labor which virtually ignores the experience of urban craft unions in the
South. The second point about the Anvil's statement is that
it correctly points out the importance of attitudes toward
labor to that stereotype.

One of the most universally accepted elements of the standard
generalizations about the South and organized labor has been
the idea that Southern society presented a united front
against the alien doctrine of trade unionism. Not only industrial employers but the business and professional middle
class and even the workers themselves have been pictured as
violently opposed to unionization, a principle they considered to be "against the American and Southern way of life."[2]

According to the generalization, community hostility derived
from a variety of sources, but the primary explanation has
usually been the desire for more industrialization. "Southern
patriotism ... was dedicated to progress, progress meant new
industry, and industry in the South was based on cheap labor.
Thus, labor unions were anathema to the established order, so
much so that even working men themselves were generally antagonistic to unions."[3]

The idea of pervasive hostility toward unions has seldom been
directly contradicted, largely because strikes by urban

unions almost never touched the general population in the
same devastating manner in which textile strikes involved the
entire community. In the summer of 1929, in New Orleans, a
strike of street railway employees began that had a direct
and profound impact upon the city and which brought forth
positive evidence of urban attitudes toward organized labor.

During the night of July 1-2, 1,500 carmen, members of Local
Division 194 of the Amalgamated Association of Street and
Electric Railway Employees of America, struck against the operators of the city's transit system, the New Orleans Public
Service Incorporated (known locally as NOPSI). After more
than a decade under a union shop contract, the carmen walked
out, charging NOPSI with trying to destroy their union by
fostering a dual organization, the Protective Benevolent Association. For two weeks riots and the threat of riots kept
the cars in their barns, but finally the company began restoring transit service. Public opinion then became the crucial element in the strike. The company had to lure the public back to the cars to break the strike, while union strategy depended upon forcing management to the bargaining table
through a boycott.[4]

In the emergency, most erstwhile trolley patrons had relied
on a motley collection of automobiles-for-hire known as jitneys. With the restoration of trolley service, the jitneys
became the backbone of a boycott that kept the streetcars
nearly empty for two months and operating well below capacity
even longer. A month after service resumed, rioting at City
Hall following a demonstration against a 1915 anti-jitney
ordinance cost the boycott a few supporters. However, the
first significant desertions came in reaction to the union's
rejection of an apparent settlement.

NOPSI General Manager A. B. Paterson reached a tentative
agreement with President William Green of the AFL in New York
on September 5, and many boycotters returned to the trolleys.
When Local 194 rejected the pact because of its vague reemployment clause, many more abandoned the carmen, charging
them with negotiating in bad faith. Nevertheless, the strike
and the boycott continued to be viable until a long court
battle finally eliminated the jitneys. The carmen maintained
their hopes until the election of January 1930 ended the possibility of a more sympathetic city administration, but their
chances -- and their union -- had died with the jitneys.

Even the briefest description of the New Orleans streetcar
strike illustrates the importance of public opinion in the
struggle and the contrast with the common stereotype of the
Southern strike. To appreciate the implications requires
closer scrutiny, especially of the boycott and the jitneys.

Although the carmen and their supporters had halted the

trolleys briefly, the resumption of service made the boycott
the central arena of the conflict. Strike leaders could only
be gratified by the public's response. A successful boycott
in any city of over 100,000 population was considered "practi-
cally impossible."[5] Yet weeks after virtually complete restoration of service -- after the City Hall riots -- a company
spokesman confessed that the boycott remained 90 percent effective. The trolley-riding public began returning to the
cars in appreciable numbers only after rejection of the Green-
Paterson settlement.[6]

Company statistics demonstrate the impact of the boycott. The
trolleys should have carried over 61,000 passengers in the
last six months of 1929, but the actual figure was scarcely
half that.[7] Even after the rejected settlement, the company
needed only half the usual number of cars during rush hour.
Despite a continual return to the transit system beginning in
September, conditions were still only "almost normal" by January.[8]

The success of the jitneys also attests to the public's support of the boycott. With a higher fare than the trolleys
and no transfers, schedules, or insurance, the illegal jitneys
should have disappeared when regular transit service resumed.
Instead, they continued to operate on a massive scale even
after the Green-Paterson fiasco and a police crackdown. Despite court orders against a thousand jitney drivers, company
spokesmen complained that over 400 still prowled the streets.[9]

Although partial evidence indicates that boycotters represented a cross section of the trolley-riding public, the specific composition of that group of strike supporters is impossible to determine. Nevertheless, participation by two
groups -- Negroes and organized labor -- should be noted. Although the carmen's local had only a few black members,[10]
George J. Theophile, a Negro minister, reassured strike leaders that 90 percent of his people supported the boycott.[11]
The Reverend Mr. Theophile's claim cannot be substantiated,
but the fact that black unions contributed to the strike fund
and ordered their members to boycott the trolleys supports
the idea of interracial cooperation.[12] Whether their support
was based on the class sympathies suggested by Theophile or
simply on union solidarity, the role of the black unions reflects the role of organized labor in all aspects of prostrike activities.

In the weeks after the walkout, local unions in all trades
passed resolutions endorsing the strike and pledging their
moral and financial support. Many levied fines of up to
fifty dollars against members seen riding the streetcars;
others agreed with the printing pressmen that fines were unnecessary "because good union men ... [would] not ride in
street cars operated by Scabs and Strikebreakers."[13]

Organized labor also took the lead in the fight against enforcement of the anti-jitney ordinance. Soon after the company began restoring service, a mass meeting of 15,000 strike
sympathizers unanimously called for repeal of the law, and
labor's representatives took the demand to the New Orleans
Commission Council. Following initial rejection, E. J. Foster and William Ruth, president of the Carpenters' Union and
active in the militant Organized Workers of Orleans Parish,
presented the city fathers with a 50,000-signature petition
calling for a repeal referendum.[14] Although labor ultimately
failed in its purpose, continued pressure on the council delayed strict enforcement.[15]

Official response to the jitney question showed indirectly
the strength of prounion sentiment. Rather than move quickly
to eliminate the jitneys, the administration, led by Acting
Mayor T. Semmes Walmsley, equivocated on the issue. Only
after reaction to the City Hall riots had convinced him that
popular support for the strike had waned did Walmsley respond
to demands by the city's business establishment for unrestrained enforcement of the law.[16]

The fight against jitney law enforcement was only one mani-
festation of organized labor's commitment to the carmen's
cause. Local labor's most dramatic attempt to aid the carmen
came when labor leaders representing the construction and
metal trades unions called on the Commission Council on
July 5. William Ruth, president of the carpenters' union,
informed city leaders of labor's solidarity behind the strikers, stressing the deep resentment of unionists toward the
imported strikebreakers brought in by the company. Finally,
to show that unionists were "'not going to stand for Public
Service importing strikebreakers to take the place of local
men,'" Ruth threatened to call a sympathetic strike of the
20,000 men for whom he spoke.[17]

By July 9, Ruth's threat had escalated to the dimensions of a
general strike. Paralysis and chaos seemed imminent. Union
officials representing over 45,000 workers met and authorized
a mass meeting of unionists to vote on a general strike.
Fortunately for the city, company directors agreed to meet
with a citizens' committee seeking a negotiated settlement,
and the mass meeting was called off. Ruth soon tried to revive the general strike idea but found no broad support among
unionists, who by then had found less dramatic ways to aid
the strike.[18]

Union members composed a large percentage of the participants
at mass meetings, where crowds cheered attacks on the jitney
law, NOPSI, and city officials.[19] Local unions also supported the carmen in identifiable and tangible ways. Of almost $43,000 contributed to the strike fund locally, over
$18,000 came from unions or their ladies' auxiliaries.[20]

Although the contributions did not quite substantiate the
pledge of one union leader to stand by the carmen "so long as
there is a dollar in the treasuries of ... organized labor,"
craft locals did provide the largest source of funds within
the city; and the use of regular assessments indicated their
intention to support the carmen in a sustained fight.[21]

Some unionists like the musicians offered their services as
well as their money in a variety of benefits held to enrich
the strike fund. These shows, dances, card parties, and
raffles afforded both unionists and the public opportunities
to support the strike cause. Most of the participants remained anonymous, but sponsorship of the events does allow
identification of another group of strike supporters.

Although a variety of individuals and groups sponsored benefits, these fund-raising activities spotlighted the role of
women in the strike.[22] Participants in every public demonstration of prostrike sympathies from boycotting to rioting,
women took the lead in sponsoring benefits, raising the bulk
of the almost $6,000 coming to the strike fund from that
source. In addition, ladies' auxiliaries at the five car
barns contributed over $9,000 from other activities.[23] In
two mass meetings at which they comprised most of the audience, women further demonstrated their active support of the
strike by pledging on one occasion to boycott gas and elec-
tricity as well as the trolleys and on another to picket
streetcars in the downtown area.[24]

Like boycotters, those who attended the benefits remained
largely anonymous; but many Orleanians did put themselves on
record as strike sympathizers through contributions to the
strike fund, resolutions by their organizations, and offers
of discounts or free services. The list of contributors
shows that unorganized labor, individual citizens, and social,
civic, and political organizations donated almost $7,700.[25]

For those individuals or organizations readily identifiable
with "the laboring class," such support does not seem surprising.[26] However, the record of support for the strike shows a
much broader base. Organizations representing all major factions in New Orleans politics pledged material and moral assistance in the fight.[27] Business groups like the Retail
Grocers Association and the Retail Ice Dealers added their
support, as did the "voters and property owners of the Jefferson Boosters Club."[28] Perhaps most surprisingly, the Young
Men's Business Club, while declaring its continued neutrality,
gave a vote of confidence to its strike committee, which had
publicly supported both jitney law repeal and binding arbitration.[29]

Contributions from individuals reinforced the picture of community support for the strike. Contributors included domestic

servants, secretaries, salesmen, government employees of all
sorts, skilled and unskilled workers, policemen, and a variety of businessmen.[30] Offers of discounts and free services
showed that business supporters even included some members of
the Association of Commerce, the organization the strikers
considered the company's chief ally. A large furniture store
offered to suspend the installment payments of strikers for
the duration, while a dry-cleaning establishment promised to
help keep the fight clean by pressing, free of charge, one
suit for any striker who presented his union card.[31] Even
professional men -- from dentists to lawyers -- offered their
services. Edward Rightor, described by newspapers as "a
millionaire attorney," donated his services as chief legal
counsel for the strikers, joining union officials in negotiations, speaking from union platforms, and even having his
chauffeur give free rides to pedestrians.[32]

The pattern of strike support, then, seems clear. Centering
in all phases on the city's organized labor movement, it cut
across social, economic, political, and even racial lines.
The contrast with the stereotyped Southern strike seems obvious, but showing the depth of the difference necessitates
analysis of the basis for prostrike and antistrike sympathies
in New Orleans.

Unlike many Southern employers, New Orleans Public Service
admitted that the strikers enjoyed considerable public support; but the explanations management offered ignored the
possibility of prolabor or prounion sentiments. Instead, it
insisted that strike support actually represented animosity
toward the corporation based on two past incidents: the
bankruptcy of NOPSI's predecessor and the conflict over introduction of natural gas in the city.[33]

The contention that New Orleans investors held the new corporation responsible for losses due to the failure of an earlier company is patently untenable. On the other hand, the
widely held belief that Public Service had resisted the introduction of cheap natural gas did represent a source of
strong anticompany feeling. The corporation's role in the
natural gas controversy was used regularly to elicit an anticompany response at rallies.[34]

Consistent with the practice of Northern-based employers in
the South, company spokesmen failed to note one final, important source of anticompany sentiment: sectionalism. Strike
sympathizers clearly resented NOPSI as a "foreign" corporation. That New York firms controlled the company was well
known, and the use of strikebreakers from Northern cities ac-
centuated the idea of foreign control. The opportunities
suggested were recognized by strike leaders and exploited in
statements to the press and at rallies.[35] Letters to strike
headquarters confirmed the existence of this prejudice. One

accused "North Capital [sic]" of exploiting New Orleans.
Others, blaming the city's problems on "Wall Street, New
York," and a "bunch of kikes up in New York," suggested that
the carmen benefited from established Southern biases.[36]

The issue of outside control gave anticompany sentiment a
sectional cast which partially carried over to prounion
strike support. While prounion feelings centered on the
rights of labor, a cause often assumed to be outside the pattern of Southern labor disputes, strike sympathizers often
mixed endorsements of unionism and vague class feelings with
animosity toward outsiders. Letters to the carmen shifted
easily from assurances that "the working class ... [could]
beat the Capitalists to a frazzle" to condemnation of "Northern Capital," then back to the "Labor-Capital fight" and the
virtues of unionism in the same letter.[37] However, the feeling of class animus also existed independently. Some strike
supporters simply stated their "sympathy for the oppressed"
or called for economic sanctions against "the Rich Man's
Union, the Association of Commerce."[38] Other messages revealed much stronger class hostility; but this remained a
minor component of prostrike sentiment, usually coming from
sympathizers who had left the state for strongholds of more
radical unionism.[39]

By far the most common expressions of prolabor feeling among
strike sympathizers referred explicitly to the rights of
organized labor. The carmen had struck for contractual provisions they deemed essential to the continued existence of
their organization. The issue was clearly their right to
organize and bargain collectively.

Coming at the end of a decade in which New Orleans unionists
had seen several strong organizations prostrated by hostile
employers,[40] the carmen's strike symbolized organized labor's
fight for survival against the city's open shoppers. Labor's
response showed not only the strength and extent of the movement but also its commitment to the basic principles of
unionism. While strike leaders broadened their appeal to include "labor in general,"[41] they depended most heavily on the
organized crafts' response to the "name and principle of
Union Labor."[42] Their appeal succeeded. Not only did unionists come to their aid, but they came with the fervor of men
fighting for "a cause that is as holy as the cause which
moves one who dies for his country in the time of war, the
right of Organized Labor to exist."[43]

The local unions' strong advocacy of the carmen's cause on
the basis of union principles is certainly significant but
does not necessarily mean that overall support for the carmen
rested on that base. However, union correspondence reveals
active endorsement of the rights of organized labor by individuals and groups not connected with unions.

Nonunion organizations of all descriptions passed resolutions
calling on their members to support the carmen's fight for
the rights of organization and collective bargaining and the
principle of arbitration.[44] Letters from individuals confirmed the public's awareness of union principles as the fundamental issues of the strike. Unionists and former unionists regularly mentioned their affiliations and commitment to
the cause; but even sympathizers who explicitly denied any
union connection often signed their messages: "Yours for
Unionism, ... Friend of Labor" or "We are in favor of the
union shop."[45]

Analysis of procompany sentiment in the strike also reveals a
departure from the stereotyped Southern labor dispute. Obviously, NOPSI did not enjoy the almost universal support presumably given employers in Southern strikes. In fact, public
support for the company seemed to be limited to a few commercial and financial organizations and most of the city's newspapers. However, the difference went far beyond this narrow
support. Even the statements of those considered NOPSI's
allies avoided any explicit defense of the company or attack
on the principles of organized labor. The Cotton Exchange
and the Association of Commerce professed neutrality while
calling only for jitney law enforcement and return to normal
conditions. They expressed no concern for employers' prerogatives or the future progress of the city, themes presumably
fundamental in Southern strikes.[46] Even after the riots at
City Hall, they avoided linking the outbursts with organized
labor, asserting only their concern for "law and order."[47]

The editorial postures assumed by the newspapers also demonstrated the tendency toward guarded support of the company.
In the first editorials following the strike call, only the
Times-Picayune echoed the company's contention that the strikers had tried to maximize the inconvenience to the public;
and even that paper stopped short of openly siding with management. The Item's "A Striking Strike" more accurately reflected initial editorial reaction, blaming both sides for
abusing the public.[48] Later, the Times-Picayune led the way
in editorially condemning the inconvenience and violence of
the strike but still kept arm's length from the company.[49]
The paper limited its public stance, as did the business
groups, to a demand for return to normal conditions.

In a further contradiction of the stereotype, one of the
city's newspapers, the Daily States, actually championed the
strikers' cause. With editorials like its front page "What
Says Public Service?"[50] the States reveled in its role as the
friend and defender of union labor. Significantly, the paper
suffered no apparent loss of advertising as a result of its
stand.

Although presumed by strikers to be controlled by Public

Service, the city administration, like the _Times-Picayune_, carefully avoided any sign of hostility toward organized labor. Even when the City Hall riots raised antiunion feeling to a peak, the administration blamed the "political demagogues" who had helped stir the mob rather than labor leaders.[51] From the early days of the strike through the last attempt at a settlement in September, the administration's proposals had included recognition and protection of the union and abolishment of the Protective Benevolent Association.[52]

The appeals of management and labor for public support bore out the significant differences between the New Orleans situation and the "typical" Southern strike, although in a few instances company appeals were reminiscent of the calls-to-arms that were supposed to rally the Southern public. A. B. Paterson, NOPSI general manager, early accused strike leaders of virtually demanding control of the company's property.[53] Later he struck more familiar notes, declaring on July 10 that the corporation "'could no longer negotiate with the association'" and would take the men back only as individuals.[54] On two other occasions, the company spokesman seemed to raise the shibboleth of progress by pointing out that New Orleans was the largest of only five American cities with a closed shop in its transit system.[55]

Company appeals primarily reflected the public's acceptance of unionism. At no time did management attack the principle of organization. Even accusations of usurping management prerogatives carefully blamed only specific power hungry union leaders.[56] Despite its avowals to the contrary, the company continued to seek a settlement with the union, declaring its final determination to cease those efforts only in October.[57] As late as August 3, management declared in a full-page newspaper ad that it had "never made an attack on organized labor or the Union" and that it had offered the union a renewal of the closed shop agreement before the walk-out.[58] Responding to editorials in the _Daily States_, Paterson vigorously denied any intention of destroying the union and declared management's continued willingness to sign an open shop contract recognizing Local 194.[59] A few days later the company retaliated against the _States_, attacking the paper as a false friend of labor that had destroyed the union in its own composing rooms.[60]

The act of signing an agreement with William Green to recognize the union signified management's acceptance of organized labor, however grudging and pragmatic. Paterson's statement on the settlement made manifest his rejection of traditional attitudes toward "outside" labor leaders by presenting Green's role in the negotiations as its greatest asset.[61] NOPSI did not dare challenge local attitudes toward organized labor but sought instead acquiescence to the settlement by portraying it as labor's own.

For the carmen, reference to organized labor in public appeals seems more natural; but even here, specific allusion to
abstract principles denotes a sharp divergence from the sectional stereotype. Where prejudice against unionism prevailed, strike leaders usually took pains to submerge the issue of recognition in favor of more acceptable "bread-and-
butter" demands. In New Orleans the carmen placed recognition first and consistently presented themselves as strug-
gling for the existence of organized labor in the city.[62]

Even before the strike began, union leaders had charged that
the company sought to destroy their organization. The suspension-of-work order that inaugurated the strike repeated
that theme, and union spokesmen called on the public to support "the great AMERICAN PRINCIPLE (ARBITRATION)."[63] From
the first, the union made recognition and arbitration the
sine qua non of negotiations, while wages and hours were for-
gotten.[64]

Throughout the strike, union appeals for support rested
jointly on positive concern for the principles of organized
labor and negative objections to outside control. Significantly, strike leaders appealed consistently to the cause of
labor unity and the "life-and-death" threat to unionism and
seized on the prejudice against outside control only when the
corporation presented an opportunity that could not be ignored.[65]

The crucial struggle for public support in New Orleans presented opportunities for both sides to show the patterns of
appeal associated with labor conflict in the South. Yet for
the most part, conflict was avoided. Management touched on
the theme of progress and property rights but could never
make those elements the center of its attack. Union leaders
kept even further from the traditional Southern strikers' appeals to the public. In fact, their reliance on public support seems entirely alien to the regional pattern. Their use
of local prejudice against outside corporations had sectional
overtones, but overtones seldom found in the stereotyped
South where management traditionally enjoyed immunity from
such charges. Moreover, they restrained their use of that
sectional element, favoring instead their role as champions
of organized labor.

The New Orleans public's response to those appeals and to the
entire strike not only demonstrated an exception to the presumed unanimous animosity toward organized labor in the South
but suggests something broader. Although the New Orleans
strike did not fit the stereotype, it did evince certain sectional attributes and implied others. The possibility of a
mixed pattern in the region's urban labor disputes seems

evident, as does the necessity of considering those urban conflicts in reevaluating generalizations about the history of
Southern labor.

Notes

[1] Gerry Cohen, "Stevens Stonewalls N.C. Textile Workers," North Carolina Anvil 9 (December 20, 1975-January 3, 1976), 1-2.

[2] Francis B. Simkins, A History of the South, 2nd ed. (New York, 1959), 596.

[3] Thomas D. Clark and Albert Kirwan, The South Since Appomattox: A Century of Regional Change (New York, 1967), 133. See also John S. Ezell, The South Since 1865 (New York, 1963), 207; George B. Tindall, The Emergence of the New South, 1913-1945, A History of the South, ed. Wendell Holmes Stephenson and E. Merton Coulter, 10 vols. (Baton Rouge, 1946-67), vol. 10, 351; Robert L. Brandfon, The American South in the Twentieth Century (New York, 1967), 99; and Francis B. Simkins, The South Old and New (New York, 1947), 371.

[4] This brief outline of the events of the strike is based chiefly on coverage in the New Orleans Times-Picayune (hereafter referred to as Times-Picayune) and the New Orleans Item (hereafter referred to as Item).

[5] Walter Weyl, "Street Railway Employment in the United States," Labor Department Bulletin, vol. 10, House Documents, 80 (March 1905), 626.

[6] Noel Sargent, New Orleans Street Railway Strike of 1929-1930 (New York, 1930), 29.

[7] New Orleans Public Service Company, Incorporated, Annual Report (1929).

[8] Sargent, Street Railway Strike, 6, 29.

9 Ibid., 24; and Times-Picayune, November 5, 6, 8, 9, and December 12, 1929, and January 17, 1930.

10 Gus Bienvenu to William Fitzgerald, September 16, 1930, Street Railways Collection, Special Collections Division, Howard-Tilton Memorial Library, Tulane University, New Orleans, La., Box 8. Hereafter referred to as Street Railways Collection.

11 George J. Theophile to Edwin Peyroux, n.d., Street Railways Collection, Box 7.

12 Maurice Lynch, "Special Report on Strike Financing" [1930], Street Railways Collection, Box 6. See also Arthur Raymond Pearce, "The Rise and Decline of Labor in New Orleans" (M.A. thesis, Tulane University, 1938), 30; and Times-Picayune, July 22, 1929.

13 Louis Sahuque to Edwin Peyroux, July 30, 1929, Street Railways Collection, Box 6. Among the unions pledging support of the carmen were those of the telegraphers, railway shopmen, garment workers, plasterers, carpenters, railway conductors, longshoremen, stereotypers, electrotypers, railway clerks, butchers, musicians, typographers, photoengravers, bookbinders, printing pressmen, theatrical stage employees, motion picture operators, bakers, operating engineers, retail clerks, machinists, teamsters, pilers, dotters and helpers, barbers, elevator constructors, billposters and billers, railway trainmen, and electrical workers (Letters, Street Railways Collection, Box 6; and Times-Picayune, July 3, 8, 10-12, 17, and 22, 1929).

14 Times-Picayune, July 25, 1929; and Item, August 14, 1929.

15 "To the Public," handbill, Organized Labor Committee, September 20, 1929, Street Railways Collection, Box 6.

16 Times-Picayune, August 14 and 15, 1929.

17 Ibid., July 6, 1929.

18 Ibid., July 6, 10, 17, and 23-25, 1929.

19 Ibid., July 8, 9, and 25; August 13; and September 13, 1929.

20 Lynch, "Report on Strike Financing," Street Railways Collection, Box 6.

21 Times-Picayune, July 25, and August 28, 1929. See also A. S. Johnstone to Local 194, August 5, 1929; R. L. Chabao to E. J. Foster, August 15, 1929; and Edward L. Janckler to Edwin Peyroux, August 5, 1929, Street Railways Collection, Box 7.

22 Organizations sponsoring benefits included the Gretna Swimming Pool Committee; Crusaders' Athletic Club; Kingsley House Woman's Club; Third Precinct, Tenth Ward, Old Regular Democratic Club; Fifth Ward Old Regular Choctaws; and Friends of the Second Ward. Times-Picayune, August 8, 15, September 1, and November 29, 1929; and Letters, Street Railways Collection, Boxes 6 and 7.

23 Lynch, "Report on Strike Financing," Street Railways Collection, Box 6.

24 Times-Picayune, July 19, and September 18, 1929. The strong support of women for the strike contrasted sharply with the typical strike in which women often acted as a strong force for settlement, urging their men to reestablish the security of a regular paycheck. Neil Chamberlain, Social Responsibility and Strikes (New York, 1953), 80, 191.

25 Lynch, "Report on Strike Financing," Street Railways Collection, Box 6.

26 Ibid.; Frank LeCourt to Local 194, August 14, 1929, and G. L. Barbin to Gus Bienvenu, August 22, 1929, Street Railways Collection, Box 7.

27 Mrs. J. F. Smyth to Local 194, n.d., Street Railways Collection, Box 6; Fred C. Huff to Local 194, July 3, 1929, and Frank LeCourt to Local 194, August 14, 1929, Street Railways Collection, Box 7.

28 Frank J. Jara to Edwin Peyroux, July 20, 1929, and M. R. Heintz to Local 194, July 12, 1929, Street Railways Collection, Box 6; and A. A. Larose to Local 194, August 14, 1929, Street Railways Collection, Box 7.

29 Times-Picayune, July 31, 1929.

30 Lynch, "Report on Strike Financing," Street Railways Collection, Box 6.

31 Charles M. Lepow to Edwin Peyroux, July 10, 1929, and R. G. Fernandez to Local 194, July 25, 1929, Street Railways Collection, Box 6; and Times-Picayune, July 5, 1929.

32 Dr. Ralph B. Tudbury to Local 194, July 6, 1929; E. A. Russell to Times-Picayune, July 19, 1929; and Constant J. Marquer to Gus Bienvenu, July 26, 1929, Street Railways Collection, Box 6.

33 Sargent, Street Railway Strike, 8.

34 Ibid.; and Times-Picayune, July 19, 1929.

35 *Times-Picayune*, July 10, 19, and 27, 1929.

36 Anonymous sympathizer to Local 194, August 1, 1929, and "A
Friend of ole 194" to Local 194, n.d., Street Railways
Collection, Box 7; and "Jack K." to Local 194, July 26,
1929, Street Railways Collection, Box 6.

37 Anonymous sympathizer to Local 194, August 1, 1929, Street
Railways Collection, Box 7.

38 G. C. Comstock to Edward Rightor, July 8, 1929, Street
Railways Collection, Box 6; and E. Vernon to Edwin Peyroux,
August 10, 1929, Street Railways Collection, Box 7.

39 J. M. Caravella to Local 194, August 7, 1929, and Sam
Wright to Gus Bienvenu, September 6, 1929, Street Railways
Collection, Box 7; Charles Mills to Edwin Peyroux, n.d.,
and Joe Templet to Local 194, July 23, 1929, Street Railways Collection, Box 6.

40 Pearce, "Rise and Decline of Labor in New Orleans," 76-85.

41 Suspension-of-work order, July 1, 1929, Street Railways
Collection, Box 6.

42 Gus Bienvenu to A. Bernier, November 30, 1929, Street Railways Collection, Box 7.

43 John F. Golden to Edwin Peyroux, July 5, 1929, and Carl F.
Metzner to Local 194, July 10, 1929, Street Railways Collection, Box 6; and Jesse W. Ford to A. J. O'Keefe, July 2,
1929, Street Railways Collection, Box 2.

44 Fred C. Huff to Local 194, July 3, 1929, Street Railways
Collection, Box 6; A. A. Peterson to Local 194, August 19,
1929, and G. L. Barbin to Gus Bienvenu, August 22, 1929,
Street Railways Collection, Box 7; and Resolution, n.d.,
Street Railways Collection, Box 7.

45 Ida Giefers to Gus Bienvenu, July 22, 1929; and Karl W.
Dietz to Local 194, July 12, 1929, Street Railways Collec-
tion, Box 6. See also E. J. Burvant to Edwin Peyroux,
July 6, 1929; and "A Friend of Union Labor" to Local 194,
July 24, 1929, Street Railways Collection, Box 6.

46 *Times-Picayune*, July 31, 1929.

47 Ibid., August 14, 1929.

48 Ibid., July 3, 1929; and *Item*, July 3, 1929.

49 *Times-Picayune*, July 6, 1929.

[50] New Orleans <u>Daily States</u>, August 2, 1929. See also the <u>States</u> editorial, "Let's Have an End of It," July 31, 1929. Hereafter referred to as <u>States</u>.

[51] <u>Times-Picayune</u>, August 14, 1929; and <u>Item</u>, August 14, 1929.

[52] <u>Times-Picayune</u>, September 1, 1929.

[53] Ibid., July 3, 1929.

[54] Ibid., July 10, 1929.

[55] Ibid., July 10 and 20, 1929. (Birmingham, Ala., was one of the other four.)

[56] Ibid., July 3, 1929.

[57] Ibid., October 17, 1929.

[58] Ibid., August 3, 1929.

[59] <u>States</u>, July 31, and August 2, 1929.

[60] <u>Times-Picayune</u>, August 6, 1929.

[61] Ibid., September 12, 1929.

[62] Local 194 to New Orleans Commission Council, July 2, 1929, Street Railways Collection, Box 7.

[63] Suspension-of-work order, July 1, 1929, Street Railways Collection, Box 6.

[64] Local 194 to Commission Council, July 2, 1929, Street Railways Collection, Box 7.

[65] Ibid.; <u>Times-Picayune</u>, July 10, and September 18, 1929; and "Notice," Edwin Peyroux and Edward Veillon, September 19, 1929, Street Railways Collection, Box 7. The Green-Paterson agreement brought the two elements of union appeals into conflict, and the resolution of that confrontation demonstrated the preeminent commitment of New Orleans unionists to the preservation of their movement. Realizing that the reemployment clause of the New York agreement represented the means for slow destruction of the carmen's union, local unionists supported the strikers' rejection of the pact. While asserting the superiority of local men in evaluating the threat to unionism, they avoided the temptation to make their movement provincial by reverting to sole reliance on the "antioutsider" prejudice. A few labor leaders sought censure of both Green and Amalgamated Association of Street and Electric Railway Employees President William Mahon; but the carmen's appeals

to the public simply presented Green as "a staunch and
true blue union man," somehow misled by Paterson. In the
end, the agreement served as new evidence of the corporation's determination to destroy unionism in New Orleans.
Carl F. Metzner to William Green, telegram, September 26,
1929, Street Railways Collection, Box 7; and Times-
Picayune, September 16, 1929.

Atlanta Transit Strike, 1949-1950, Prelude to Sale

James W. May, Jr.

In June 1950, shortly before the commencement of the Korean conflict, the Georgia Power Company sold its recently modernized Atlanta transit properties to the newly organized, locally controlled Atlanta Transit Company. The sale not only enabled Georgia Power to comply with the Securities and Exchange Commission's 1947 order to divest itself of its transportation properties but also ended the longest transit strike in Atlanta's history. For thirty-six days prior to the June 22 sale, members of Division 732, Amalgamated Association of Street, Electric Railway and Motor Coach Employees of America had stayed off the job in an effort to win higher wages, a better pension plan, and improved working conditions. The sale ended nearly fifty years of operation of Atlanta's public transportation system by Georgia Power and its predecessors. The last years before the sale had been highlighted by the increasingly stormy relationship between the company and the South's largest transit workers' local.[1] Ironically, the sale also inverted the original relationship of Atlanta transit and the power company. The streetcars that had once fostered the development of the state's electric utility industry were virtually discarded in 1950 as the troublesome partner of the booming electrical division.

The transfer of Atlanta's transit franchise, still valuable despite the decline of the industry nationally, evolved from the events of the interwar era from 1946 to 1950. Marked deterioration of labor-management relations followed increasingly aggressive union activity occasioned by the end of wartime restrictions on collective bargaining. By 1950 there had been three strikes, a controversial arbitration, and two fare increases. A six-day strike in May 1946 (the first walkout by Division 732 in over a quarter of a century) produced a long-delayed 17-cent wage hike to $1.07 an hour, a $225,000 company contribution to the union's new pension fund,

and an eight-hour day.[2] In 1947, labor and management again
experienced difficulty in agreeing on a wage rate, and
Georgia Power suggested arbitration. A three-man arbitration
board, whose chairman was selected by the company, awarded
another 17-cent increase to the union amid bitter management
denunciation.[3] The basic wage rose to $1.24 an hour, the
highest among transit workers in the South and only 3 cents
below the nationwide average rate for unionized properties of
a size comparable to Atlanta.[4] As a result of the 1947 arbitration award and a negotiated 7-cent raise the following
year, Georgia Power requested the first fare increases since
1928. Although the company twice sought permission from the
Georgia Public Service Commission to eliminate tokens in
favor of a straight 10-cent cash fare, the commission's final
order on March 16, 1949, only adjusted the price of tokens to
eleven for $1.[5]

With the conclusion of the 1948 annual negotiations, Division
732's contract with the Georgia Power Company clearly exhibited the tremendous improvement derived from three years
of unfettered collective bargaining. Not only were Atlanta's
transit workers the highest paid in the South, but the union
negotiated improvements in working conditions and fringe
benefits reflecting the most progressive trends in the transit industry. However, the 1948 negotiations also evidenced
a subtle shift of momentum in management's favor. The pace
of contract revision noticeably lessened in 1948, as the
union weighed the possible implications of the Taft-Hartley
Act of 1947, and Georgia Power President Clifford B. McManus
stiffened management's resistance to union demands.

Furthermore, hostile strains ominously surfaced during the
1948 negotiations, introducing new tensions to labor-
management relations which had historically remained placid.
Dissatisfied with the 1947 arbitration award, Georgia Power
announced it would agree to future arbitration only under re-
strictive and self-serving provisions.[6] Faced with substantial increases in the cost of labor and the continuing decline in customer patronage, the company insisted that "ability to pay" be the primary consideration in all contractual
modifications. Management complained that the Atlanta transit system not only operated in the red but had also become a
public relations liability for the whole company, attracting
community disfavor and statewide charges of transit subsidi-
zation by the electric division.[7] Routine bargaining was
further complicated by the uncertainty surrounding possible
divestment and the union's insistence that the Atlanta contract should conform to national standards.

Despite extensive contractual improvements gained in the
first three rounds of postwar bargaining, Division 732
entered the 1949 negotiations intent on making further modifications. Union President Jesse Walton, labor's chief

negotiator throughout the interwar era, insisted that Georgia
Power sought to unduly restrict concessions on the basis of
regional standards. Utilizing statistics from Division 732's
successful presentation in the 1947 arbitration, union representatives argued that because North-South wage differentials
were crumbling and Atlanta was experiencing such remarkable
prosperity and population growth, the transit workers' contract should rightfully compare to national standards.
Equally as important, Walton argued that despite seemingly
beneficent wage boosts during the previous three years, real
wages increased only minimally in an inflated economy.[8]
Georgia Power continued its hard-line opposition initiated
the previous year by citing increases in the costs of labor.
Management viewed the union's 1949 requests as unreasonable
and unwarranted and proposed instead certain regressive contractual changes that would require the union to relinquish
prior concessions.[9]

Union demands centered around a nineteen-cent wage boost, a
negotiated, joint-contributory pension to replace the two
separate plans in effect, and amelioration of certain burden-
some working conditions peculiar to the transit industry.
Among his primary goals, Walton specifically asked for additional uninterrupted runs for trolley and bus operators, better overtime provisions for men working split shifts in the
morning and afternoon, a daily guarantee for extra men hired
to operate buses during peak traffic periods, three-week vacations after five years of service, and fifteen days of sick
leave.[10] Walton also reintroduced an important and controversial old age retirement and disability allowance plan
closely resembling another plan initially suggested three
years earlier. Under its provisions, an employee with twenty
years of service at age sixty-five could collect a monthly
retirement income of seventy-five dollars, exclusive of social security. Unlike the company's master pension unilaterally instituted in 1944, Division 732's proposal included a
badly needed disability provision. Funding of the plan would
incorporate employee contributions of 3 percent of monthly
earnings, with company contributions "as are required."
Transit employee assets accumulated in the existing Georgia
Power pension would be transferred to the trust fund of the
old age retirement and disability allowance plan, as would
the assets accrued under a supplemental union pension established in 1946.[11]

Predictably, the company rejected all of these demands, insisting that even a mere six-cent-an-hour increase, or its
equivalent, would result in losses. Additionally, Georgia
Power continued its strong opposition to the principle of a
joint-contributory, mutually administered pension and would
not even discuss alteration of its master pension or any plan
posing new financial obligations. Instead, the company would
work with the union to establish a nonmandatory, deferred

annuity plan to operate separately from the existing pension.[12] Cost was certainly a factor in the company's rejection of the union's pension proposal. Georgia Power attorney
Harlee Branch argued the new plan called for two and one-half
times the minimum benefits under the existing master pension,
while reducing required service by one-third.[13]

As negotiations approached the April 30 deadline for a new
contract, the two sides were no closer to settlement than on
March 21 when the opening session began. On April 26, company and union officials turned to consideration of wages,
having failed to produce even the slightest hope for compromise on any other union requests. International Amalgamated
counsel Bernard Cushman, who acted as adviser to Division 732,
insisted that Atlanta must be responsive to wage trends
throughout the country. Georgia Power maintained that operators were well paid in relation to Atlanta workers with comparable skills. Indeed, postwar wage increases had out-paced
the rising cost of living, exceeding the company's ability to
pay.[14] Like the prior discussions of the pension and working
conditions, the wage talks deadlocked despite the efforts of
D. K. Jones of the Federal Mediation and Conciliation Service.
Continuous bargaining by labor and management on April 29 and
30 still produced no agreement. When Division 732, in accordance with the policy of the International, offered to
submit the contract and pension to final and binding arbitration, President McManus demurred, insisting that working conditions in the transit industry were far too complex for an
arbitrator. The two sides must first "clean up" working conditions, then reach an accord on the pension, and finally,
submit only wages to arbitration.[15] Walton subsequently offered to extend negotiations another sixty days, with all un-
settled issues to be arbitrated; but McManus refused. Negotiation ended, and the transit workers walked out. The May 1
strike did not alter Georgia Power's implacable bargaining
stance; and despite the continued efforts of the Federal Mediation and Conciliation Service, strike negotiations deadlocked on May 3.[16] Although the participants could not possibly have foreseen the future, the failure to negotiate a
settlement during the first days of the strike would have mo-
mentous effects. Indeed, subsequent events would relegate
collective bargaining to an empty ceremonial display.

While labor and management still conducted perfunctory negotiations, strike developments actually precluded any possibility of a settlement. Barely had transit workers walked
off the job when peripheral pressures, some carefully orchestrated, imposed an enervating strain on the collective bargaining procedure and specifically on Division 732. Two of
the most powerful and visible segments of Atlanta's civic establishment, the press and the mayor, quickly responded to
this perceived threat to Atlanta's prosperous "busy-ness."[17]
The Atlanta Constitution questioned the union's motive for

striking and called for the immediate resumption of service.[18]
At the same time, Mayor William Hartsfield labeled the strike
"absolutely unnecessary" and warned that Atlanta's citizenry
would not be made "the goats of this strike" through another
fare increase.[19] Atlanta's evening paper, the Journal, denounced the strike in even stronger terms: "We deny their
[Division 732's] moral right to beat the public over the head
with the bludgeon of strike in order to change conditions
which were acceptable to them one year ago."[20]

Similar sentiments, more subtly expressed, were also voiced
by the official spokesmen of Atlanta's powerful downtown
business interests. Obviously, the strike by dissident transit workers not only posed a serious threat to Atlanta's prosperous status quo but also represented an unorthodox incur-
sion into the traditional pattern of community decision making. The financial and commercial community responded vigorously and unanimously. Vulnerable to the crippling effects
of a protracted transit strike and unaccustomed to challenge
from Atlanta's reputedly docile labor community, the city's
economic leaders clamored for an immediate end to the strike.
Representing a delegation from the Atlanta Retail Merchant's
Association, Richard Rich, influential owner of the city's
largest department store, requested that transit service be
promptly restored. The strike was costing local business
$1 million a day.[21] Various other business, civic, and pro-
fessional groups repeated the call, including the Chamber of
Commerce, which Georgia Power President McManus served as a
director, the Atlanta Bar Association, and the Central
Atlanta Improvement Association.

While spokesmen for the central business district lent their
prestige to the call for immediate resumption of service, the
press and various other elements of a growing antistrike coalition contemplated direct intervention. Abrogating its alleged role of unbiased observer, the Journal proposed May 8
in a front-page editorial that a three-man citizens' committee investigate the strike and report its findings in order
that the public might assert its interests. Aware of the
tremendous public relations importance of this proposal, both
Walton and McManus agreed to cooperate and acquiesced to the
Journal's suggestion that the president of the Chamber of
Commerce and the president of the Atlanta Federation of
Trades represent business and labor, respectively.[22] The Atlanta Constitution, also eager to influence strike developments, urged the Georgia legislature to enact a state labor
law for public utilities which would permit seizure and operation of the transit system during a strike.[23] Within the
week, the speaker of the Georgia House of Representatives indicated that the next session of the General Assembly would
probably consider just such a bill.[24] Local politicians also
proposed punitive legislation. Councilman James Jackson
urged the city to break Georgia Power's monopoly over mass

transportation by authorizing jitney service.[25] And the
mayor, the most visible and vocal of all strike critics, continued his alternate tactics of conciliation and intimidation.
Having failed in all attempts to personally impose a settlement, Hartsfield unhesitatingly aligned with the antistrike
coalition. Either a long strike or a costly settlement would
undermine his political popularity among Atlanta's commercial
elite.[26] Thus, the mayor favored an immediate settlement on
company terms or, at least, a quick end to the strike.

As the various elements of Atlanta's power structure inter-
posed in the transit strike, Division 732 gradually lost control of strike developments. Georgia Power and the antistrike coalition of municipal government, the press, and the
downtown business community concluded that the strike could
best be handled outside the traditional channels of collective bargaining; instead, they would resort to the more easily manipulated public forum. Although Walton vigorously defended union demands on working conditions, wages, and the
pension, the company countered with warnings of imminent bankruptcy and threats of a 50 percent fare increase or radically
curtailed service. Charging that the union in the past had
"browbeat" Georgia Power into costly concessions, McManus
portrayed the company as the protector of the public interest
in resisting the union's exorbitant demands.[27] This equation
of company intransigence and the public interest, popularized
through an expensive advertising campaign, effectively ob-
scured the union's willingness to arbitrate all issues and
placed the onus of strike exclusively with Division 732.[28]
As its public relations campaign gathered momentum, Georgia
Power virtually abandoned direct negotiation, except for appearances, anticipating that a "test of will" and of finances
would force the union to succumb to company and community
pressure.

Developments during the second week of the strike confirmed
the wisdom of company strategy. While labor and management
met with federal conciliators, the Fulton County Grand Jury
announced a full-scale probe into the transit strike. The
Constitution, noting that the grand jury "might well provide
the vehicle for settlement," applauded its entrance into the
dispute: "whatever affects the affairs of the people ...
properly comes within its [grand jury's] province."[29] Almost
simultaneously, the Journal's "citizen's committee" prepared
for an opening session with officials of labor and management.
Faced with two major investigations, neither of which would
likely sustain the decision to strike, Division 732 reconsid-
ered its earlier pledge of support for the citizens' committee. Due to its total lack of authority and the inappropri-
ateness of fact finding, union leaders refused to submit evidence or participate in the investigation. To superimpose
another independent, fact-finding agency while the Federal
Mediation and Conciliation Service remained actively involved

only "muddied the waters." Furthermore, Division 732 would
never submit the merits of its position to a committee whose
chairman headed a corporation and whose "labor representative" had been appointed by the Atlanta Journal.[30]

Although the intercession of the grand jury on May 10 and the
union's rejection of the citizens' committee's investigation
on May 11 produced a minor crisis for Division 732, the latter decision initiated a strong, if somewhat belated, attempt
to reestablish union control of strike developments. As part
of the same strategy, President Walton called for a May 12
meeting of members to answer the mayor's charges of internal
dissension and to revitalize rank-and-file support for the
bargaining position of the leadership. Countering calls from
the press and City Hall for a secret ballot of members on the
proposition of immediately returning to work, Division 732
transit workers voted unanimously to hold to all their demands.[31] Refreshed by this vote of confidence, Walton and
the union leaders began to reassert their influence despite
continued community pressures. Unable to match the financial
resources of Georgia Power and compete for public favor
through extensive advertising, Walton and advisers from the
International Amalgamated escalated their criticism of the
company's refusal to arbitrate and insisted that company intransigence prevented settlement. However, lest anyone in-
terpret the union's drive for arbitration as a sign of weakness, Walton warned Georgia Power and its allies that the
union stood ready to stay out indefinitely to win its demands.

Despite new aggressiveness during the third week of the
strike, Division 732 failed to gain momentum at the bargaining table or significant public support. The Atlanta papers,
which had already generated pervasive conformity of public
opinion, attacked the union with new severity. Chagrined
over Division 732's refusal to cooperate with its citizens'
committee, the Journal accused Walton of playing "second
fiddle" to International officials and condemned the International's advisory role in Atlanta as part of a general effort
to "hammer all contracts into the same pattern." Journal editor Wright Bryan even hinted that the International Union
might be trying to bankrupt the Atlanta system and force it
into public ownership and insidiously suggested that the local
union, which had no such designs, reassume control of local
policy.[32] Likewise, several state and civic agencies involved in the dispute moved forcefully to suppress the union's
renewed assertiveness. On May 14, Governor Herman Talmadge
offered his services to labor and management, ostensibly to
improve chances for an arbitration agreement. Speaker Fred
Hand of the Georgia House of Representatives warned that con-
tinuation of the impasse might provoke a special session of
the General Assembly to consider appropriate antistrike legislation.[33] On May 16, Atlanta's City Council and Board of
Aldermen adopted a resolution condemning the strike and

warned operators to return to work within three days. Otherwise, the city of Atlanta "will be forced to authorize other
means of public transportation."[34] Furthermore, the citizens' committee and the grand jury, responding to Walton's
statement that the union was prepared to stay out indefinitely, expedited their investigations so that the public
might have their reports as soon as possible.

This last wave of threats and criticisms from the antistrike
coalition, coupled with growing public impatience with the
transit workers' walkout, persuaded Division 732 to seek a
more modest settlement. Anticipating calls for immediate resumption of service from the citizens' fact-finding committee
and the grand jury and anxious to avoid a showdown with the
City Council, Walton and his executive committee met with
McManus, grand jury foreman W. V. Crowley, and Fulton County
Solicitor-General Paul Webb in several closed sessions May 17
and 18.[35] At 1 A.M., May 19, labor and management announced
tentative agreement on a partial settlement featuring an immediate four-cent wage increase and further actuarial study
of the union pension proposal. Additionally, the union and
company agreed to extend negotiations on twelve disputed contractual provisions for sixty days, with no commitment to
arbitration or restriction on the union's right to strike at
the extension's expiration.[36] Shortly after noon, May 19,
union members voted to accept the terms of the agreement and
return to work. Almost immediately, the first Georgia Power
bus to run in nineteen days returned to the streets.

Soon after reaching an agreement with Division 732, Georgia
Power President McManus expansively observed that except for
the wage increase and minor adjustments of working conditions,
"the old contract has been renewed for another 12 months,
just as the company proposed in advance of the work stoppage."[37] Despite its provisional character, the May 19 agreement represented a difficult capitulation by Walton and his
International advisers, as the terms of settlement hardly
compensated for the sacrifice of a nineteen-day strike. Although the company granted a partial wage increase, the union
surrendered its key requests on pension, vacations, and sick
leave. Furthermore, the sixty-day extension offered little
hope for additional concessions. As one company negotiator
subsequently remarked, the May 19 agreement did not require
Georgia Power to make concessions but only to discuss twelve
proposed contract revisions.[38] Throughout the series of fourteen labor conferences during June and July, management offered only to sign the previous year's contract with those
alterations agreed to on May 19.[39] Despite the continuing involvement of federal and state conciliators, a second extension of talks, and the inexpensiveness of ten of the twelve
union demands, Georgia Power refused to compromise. Attempts
by the union to salvage an acceptable settlement from nearly
six months of negotiation ended August 24, when labor and

management agreed to make their tentative agreement binding
until April 30, 1950.[40]

The charade of negotiation after May 19 only aggravated
Georgia Power's rapidly polarizing labor-management relations.
When Walton returned to the bargaining table in the spring of
1950 with a similar list of demands, he confronted a still
intractable management. Although Georgia Power finally
agreed to discuss a joint-contributory pension, deadlocked
negotiations and the company refusal of arbitration again
forced the union to strike.[41] The dispute quickly assumed
the character and proportion of the 1949 confrontation. While
the company renewed extensive advertising and the Atlanta
papers very adroitly resuscitated the bogey of outside agitation, Mayor Hartsfield lambasted Walton as a labor tyrant and
a threat to democracy.[42] Unable to break the strike, the re-
consolidated antistrike coalition actively supported the company's attempts to sell the Atlanta transit system. After an
initial deal collapsed because the prospective purchaser
could not reach agreement with the union, a group of prominent
Atlantans, with the enthusiastic endorsement of the local
power structure, negotiated a settlement with Division 732
and immediately resumed transit operations. After thirty-
seven days of strike culminating five years of increasingly
antagonistic relations between Georgia Power and Division 732,
public transportation in Atlanta entered a new era, under new
ownership.

Although divestment was inevitable as a result of the Securities and Exchange Commission's order of 1947, Georgia Power
sold the Atlanta transit system in 1950 specifically because
of the total collapse of relations with Division 732. The
1949 confrontation played the pivotal role in this final es-
trangement. The company's willingness to desert collective
bargaining for power brokerage embittered the transit union,
with serious consequences for the final round of bargaining.
By enlisting the support of the powerful civic establishment,
Georgia Power successfully repulsed the union's drive for a
better contract, but the company's victory in 1949 proved no
more than a reprieve. In fact, the union's setback in 1949
was only a postponement of essential demands. Despite its
relative isolation in a "white-collar town" and growing public animosity, Division 732 again defied the phalanx of Atlanta influentials in 1950. On this occasion, the union imposed a settlement of its own design. By completing the
struggle begun in 1949, Division 732 not only forced the sale
of Atlanta transit; it successfully challenged Atlanta's traditionally impervious power structure.

Notes

1 Frederic Meyers, "Organization and Collective Bargaining in
the Local Mass Transportation Industry in the Southeast,"
The Southern Economic Journal 15 (April 1949), 429. Meyers
estimates that in 1949, Division 732 represented about
1,400 vehicle operators and maintenance employees.

2 Memorandum of Agreement Between Georgia Power Company and
Amalgamated Association of Street, Electric Railway & Motor
Coach Employees of America, Division No. 732, Effective
May 1, 1945: Expires April 30, 1946, Agreements and Con-
tracts, Georgia, Southern Labor Archives, Georgia State
University, Atlanta, Ga. This depository will hereafter be
cited as SLA.

3 Board of Arbitration Award, August 2, 1947, in the Matter
of Georgia Power Company, Atlanta, Ga. and Amalgamated Association of Street, Electric Railway and Motor Coach Employees of America, Division 732, M.A.R.T.A. Records, Atlanta Transit Company, Georgia Department of Archives and
History, Atlanta, Ga., hereafter cited as M.A.R.T.A. Records. Further description of this collection is limited
because of only partial inventory and cataloging.

4 Meyers, "Mass Transportation," 435.

5 Georgia Public Service Commission, Minutes, March 16, 1949,
67-71, Offices of the Georgia Public Service Commission,
State Office Building Annex, Atlanta, Ga.

6 Notes on Labor Negotiating Meetings, Conference no. 24,
April 26, 1948, 2, Atlanta Transit System Records, 1920
(1946-1969), Labor Relations Files, Georgia Power Company
Negotiations with Amalgamated Association Local 732,
1946-49 A, Box 274, Folder 7, SLA, hereafter cited ATSR.

[7] Interview, Clifford B. McManus, president of the Georgia Power Company, July 30, 1975.

[8] Notes, Conference no. 23, April 26, 1949, pass., ATSR, Box 275, Folder 10.

[9] John Gerson to J. L. Walton, February 29, 1949, M.A.R.T.A. Records.

[10] Jesse L. Walton to C. B. McManus, February 28, 1949, M.A.R.T.A. Records.

[11] Union's Proposal for Old Age Retirement and Disability Allowance Plan, Georgia Power Company, Atlanta, Georgia, February 1949, M.A.R.T.A. Records.

[12] Notes, Conference no. 13, April 18, 1949, 3, ATSR, Box 274, Folder 9.

[13] Notes, Conference no. 20, April 25, 1949, 5, ATSR, Box 275, Folder 10.

[14] Notes, Conference no. 23, April 26, 1949, 3-8, ATSR, Box 275, Folder 10.

[15] Notes, Early Morning Conference on April 30, 1949, 1, ATSR, Box 275, Folder 10.

[16] Atlanta Constitution, May 4, 1949.

[17] Floyd Hunter, Community Power Structure: A Study of Decision Makers (Chapel Hill, 1953), 8. In his study of Atlanta's power structure, Hunter uses "busy-ness" to describe the bustling importance of business to the city.

[18] Atlanta Constitution, May 2, 1949.

[19] Atlanta Journal, May 2, 1949.

[20] Ibid., May 4, 1949.

[21] Atlanta Constitution, May 5, 1949.

[22] Atlanta Journal, May 8, 1949.

[23] Atlanta Constitution, May 5, 1949.

[24] Ibid., May 12, 1949.

[25] Atlanta Journal, May 7, 1949.

[26] Kent Jennings, Community Influentials: The Elites of Atlanta (New York, 1964), 131; and Hunter, Community Power

Structure, 81.

27 Atlanta Constitution, May 3, 1949.

28 Frank Otwell, "Hush-Hush Theory Exploded: How Georgia
    Power Broke the Atlanta Transit Strike," Bus Transporta-
    tion 29 (August 1949), 43-45.

29 Atlanta Constitution, May 11, 1949.

30 Notes on Meeting of Fact-Finding Board, May 11, 1949, 1-3,
    ATSR, Box 275, Folder 10. Division 732's disavowal of
    Federation President Henry Chandler's participation re-
    ceived support from Atlanta's labor hierarchy. The Exec-
    utive Board of the Atlanta Federation of Trades, AFL,
    passed a resolution supporting striking transit workers.
    Although repudiated by his own organization, Chandler none-
    theless maintained that Division 732 should return to work.

31 Atlanta Journal, May 12, 1949.

32 Ibid., May 15, 1949.

33 Atlanta Constitution, May 15, 1949. Floyd Hunter notes in
    Community Power Structure, page 160, that Atlanta's power
    structure occasionally used the "special session" as a
    means of policy implementation.

34 Minutes, General Council and Aldermanic Board, City of
    Atlanta, vol. 46, 6, in Offices of the City Clerk, Atlanta
    City Hall, Atlanta, Ga.

35 Expanding his role as jury foreman, Crowley actively medi-
    ated the dispute. Federal and state conciliators played
    no part in the final agreement.

36 Atlanta Journal, May 19, 1949.

37 Ibid.

38 Notes, Eleventh Post-Strike Conference, July 6, 1949, 1,
    ATSR, Box 275, Folder 11.

39 Ibid.; see also Memorandum, ATSR, Box 275, Folder 11.
    This unsigned, undated memorandum summarizes the content
    of meetings held June 3 and June 8.

40 Notes, Labor Negotiations Meeting At Which Contract Became
    Binding, August 24, 1949, 11:25 P.M., 1, ATSR, Box 275,
    Folder 11.

41 Atlanta Journal, April 30, 1950.

42 Ibid., June 4, 1950.

Comment

A synopsis of the remarks by Jack Blicksilver, Georgia
State University.

Each of these studies of transit workers discusses substan-
tive matters important to an understanding of the history of
Southern labor beyond the immediate issues of the specific
disputes. Carpenter hypothesizes that the New Orleans strike
was a distinct exception to the usual community hostility directed against unions in the South. In demonstrating that
large segments of the community sympathized with the strikers'
cause, Carpenter follows in the pioneering tradition of
Herbert Gutman. Findings reveal that not only organized labor, but also businessmen and professionals, black and white,
supported the transit workers. Although the author fails to
identify sufficiently the sources and strengths of strike
support, he does include some pertinent factors in the mobilization of prounion sentiment. Labor rallied behind the cry
for preservation of the union and the right of collective bargaining, while nonlabor groups united in their dislike of a
monopolistic public utility with ties to Yankee capital.
Carpenter would do well to explore in more detail other elements of the strike situation that strongly favored labor:
(1) the fact that presumably the outcome of the strike would
not affect fares; (2) that the strike did not appreciably
diminish the profits of downtown merchants; and (3) that un-
named social or political issues account for the indifference
or neutrality of certain key, nonlabor interest groups. Carpenter might also expand his consideration of the major
strike issues other than the basic right to organize. Finally, the New Orleans experience may have been a clear exception to the general Southern rule. Only additional
studies of comparable labor-management conflicts in urban
settings will determine whether the New Orleans strike was
unique or in fact constitutes an extension of the Gutman model
to a twentieth century Southern urban setting.

James May also provides a perceptive account of a transit

strike in the urban South. This study of Atlanta transit
strikes in 1949 and 1950 attempts to show that the unsatisfactory resolution of the earlier controversy and the inability
of Georgia Power to end a month-long walkout the following
year played a key role in the company's decision to divest itself of the Atlanta transit operation. May concludes that
despite the absence of public support, the transit workers remained unified and held out long enough to force a sale of
the system and then wrested a highly favorable contract from
the new owners. Unfortunately, he does not fully explain
this anomaly. By focusing too narrowly on the direct participants and the overwhelmingly promanagement community power
structure, the author fails to consider possible support for
the strikers from organized labor, the professional middle-
class ministers, and the black community. Moreover, the public's indifference and hostility to the transit union might
have emanated from a general perception of the workers' true
status. The strikers, already the highest paid transit workers in the Southeast, could well have appeared as the selfish
aristocrats of labor, whose postwar demands had already imposed two fare hikes on the riding public. May's conclusion
that the transit workers emerged victorious in their battle
with Georgia Power needs further development. In view of the
Securities and Exchange Commission's 1947 order that the
power company dispose of its trolley operations and the declining profitability of transit operations, management could
conceivably have welcomed the sale. Without a more detailed
study of the 1950 strike, May cannot support his strong generalizations on the resolution and ramifications of the conflict.

CHAPTER VI

LABOR AND POLITICS:
The Southern Experience

In assessing the reasons for organized labor's failure to effectively organize much of the Southern labor force, most
historians have emphasized the hostile political climate in
which the labor movement had to function in the South. The
following two essays leave little doubt as to the accuracy of
this assessment. Government power at the local and state
level has often been exercised to the detriment of organized
labor by political leaders more sensitive to the wishes and
needs of businessmen than to the labor force.

In the first essay, John Allen describes events in Georgia
during the dramatic general textile strike of 1934. The
strike involved more than 400,000 textile workers nationwide,
making it the largest strike in American labor history. The
distinctive features of the strike in Georgia revolved around
the activities of the state's volatile governor, Eugene
Talmadge. The strike occurred during the midst of a primary
election campaign in which Talmadge sought renomination. Until the day of the primary election, the governor refused to
take any overt action against the strikers, instead attempting to portray himself as a friend of labor and a strong supporter of the popular Democratic President Franklin D. Roosevelt and his New Deal. Shortly after the primary, however,
Talmadge mobilized the National Guard and ordered the construction of concentration camp type enclosures to confine
strikers and strike leaders. Talmadge's action broke the
strike in Georgia as mills reopened and defeated and demoral-
ized textile workers drifted back to their demeaning and de-
bilitating jobs. Meanwhile, Talmadge attempted to resurrect
his populist image while continuing to serve the economic interests of the state.

Daniel Powell, whose active involvement in Southern labor
politics dates back to the days of the Congress of Industrial

Organizations' Political Action Committee, approaches the
topic from the perspective of electoral politics. Powell recalls earlier days in which a public labor endorsement was a
liability to a candidate. Powell, nevertheless, argues that
while organized labor suffered numerous defeats in the South,
it also had some notable victories. He identifies several
officeholders in the United States Congress and in state governments who have been sensitive to the needs of the working
class. Moreover, Powell sees a brighter future for organized
labor in Southern politics. He notes that candidates now actively seek a labor endorsement and that the labor movement
has increasingly been accepted as a legitimate participant in
the politics of the South.

John Allen received an A.B. in political science from the
University of North Carolina. He is presently employed by
the DeKalb County school system and along with his teaching
duties at Peachtree High School serves as chairman of the
Social Science Department. This essay is an outgrowth of an
M.A. thesis, "The Governor and the Strike," which Allen will
complete at Georgia State University. He hopes to expand his
study of the general textile strike to a Ph.D. dissertation.

Daniel Powell is director of Area number 5, Committee on
Political Education, AFL-CIO. Like Allen, he attended the
University of North Carolina. Thereafter, he had a varied
career, working as a reporter on several newspapers, a correspondent for the United Press, a salesman, and an account executive. A member of the American Newspaper Guild, Powell
became Southern director of the Congress of Industrial Organizations' Political Action Committee in December 1945. After the AFL-CIO merger in 1955, he assumed his current position. Powell is a member of several organizations outside
the labor movement, including the Academy of Political Science, the Center for the Study of Democratic Institutions,
the National Association for the Advancement of Colored
People, and the United Nations Association. He has served as
a vice-president of the Tennessee American Civil Liberties
Union, the Tennessee Council on Human Relations, and the
Memphis chapter of the United Nations Association. He has
been the recipient of several awards, including the Peter
Cooper Service Award from the Memphis Unitarian Universalist
Fellowship, the Outstanding Service Plaque from the Tennessee
State Labor Council, and the Bill of Rights Award from the
American Civil Liberties Union in West Tennessee.

Eugene Talmadge and the
Great Textile Strike in Georgia, September 1934
John E. Allen

Late summer of 1934 was a time of several ominous and momen-
tous events. August witnessed the death of President Von
Hindenburg and Adolf Hitler's consolidation of the offices of
president and chancellor; he thus became the German "Fuhrer."
In October, Mao Tse-tung began the Long March from south
China with 100,000 devoted companions, only 20,000 of whom
would live to reach Yenan in the north the following year.

In 1934, the United States was in the depths of the Great Depression, but there was hope. President Roosevelt's New Deal
had begun to restore confidence and some employment; and his
approval of the National Industrial Recovery Act in June 1933,
creating the National Recovery Administration, encouraged the
notion that perhaps the country had turned the corner. But
only the foundation for recovery had been laid; economic
stagnation still stalked the land.

The predominantly agricultural South, already the most economically depressed area in the United States, was especially
hard hit by the depression. Cotton textiles, one of the more
important industries in the region, actually had begun to
sink into a serious depression as early as 1923. During the
mid-1920s when most stocks doubled or tripled in value, textile securities declined. By 1929, most textile stocks sold
at less than one-half of their 1923 price.[1] The Great Crash
in the fall of 1929 greatly exacerbated this process. In
that year, the value of the industry's product was
$1,524,200,000; by 1931, this figure fell to $305,800.000.[2]

That the depression in textiles predated the national industrial depression by seven long years is indicative of the
severe structural problems characterizing the production and
distribution of cotton textiles. Chronic overproduction accompanied by low and irregular prices plagued the industry.

The basic problem was too many units of production.[3]

Because of increased union activity in New England and the South's own vigorous Cotton Mill Campaign, the textile industry in the South mushroomed during the last two decades in the nineteenth century. During this period it was easy to get into the cotton mill business. The average capitalization of the new Southern mills during this time was a mere $100,000.[4] Moreover, virtually every hamlet in the South viewed the erection of a cotton mill as a panacea for the multiple social and economic ills besetting the region in the post-Reconstruction era. The end of slavery, soil exhaustion, and plummeting cotton prices drove thousands from the land -- owners as well as tenants and sharecroppers. The mills were to be the South's salvation, and this message was preached with fervor from every pulpit and editorial desk in the region.[5]

New England mill owners quickly took advantage of the large and, so they believed, tractable labor surplus in the South, while Southerners aided by providing favorable tax breaks, lax labor laws, and cheap power. Along with the proximity to raw materials, these were powerful lures.

Local capital contributed significantly to the creation of numerous small mills in the South. Local tradesmen and cotton factors often invested, and subscriptions from local citizens were obtained through weekly installments as low as twenty-five cents.[6]

Because capital was often amassed by pooling of local interests, and because the factories were intended to absorb the unemployed and cure local economic stagnation, the mills often assumed the status of institutions of public benefaction in the eyes of the local community. The notion that the local public was indebted to the mill and should be protective toward it greatly influenced labor disputes in the industry.

Although many small, rural mills failed, many survived. In 1934, 588 of the country's more than 1,000 mills were located in towns of less than 5,000 people. After the turn of the century, the Southern industry grew as the New England industry declined. By 1930, the South consumed 80 percent of all raw cotton produced in the country.[7]

Too many factories, consequent overproduction, and cutthroat competition were the overriding problems contributing to the depression in textiles in the late 1920s; but there were other significant factors that should be considered. The price and quantity of cotton fluctuated wildly from year to year. Also, foreign competition and the use of synthetics played a significant part in determining the unhappy state of the industry at the onset of the depression.[8]

Wage rates reflected the depressed state of the industry.
Figures from a Bureau of Labor Statistics survey of fifty-
five major industries ranked average weekly earnings in cotton goods at the bottom of the list in seven months of the
year 1929. During the other five months, the industry was
next to the bottom. In July 1933, figures for seventy-four
industries reporting average hourly earnings showed cotton
goods second from the end with an average of 23.1 cents per
hour. In fact, the average wage paid in the cotton textile
industry since 1921 had been below that paid in any other
major industry; and during some periods, it was less than
half the average for all manufacturing industries.[9]

To attack the stagnant conditions existing throughout all
American industry as well as textiles, President Roosevelt
and his New Deal advisers initiated the National Recovery Act.
It was generally accepted doctrine among most New Dealers
that the imbalance between productive capacity and purchasing
power had caused the depression, and this could be remedied
only by bringing about a relative rise in the purchasing
power of the masses. Further, the authors of the National
Industrial Recovery Act (NIRA) believed that a better balance
between purchasing power and production could be realized
through cooperation between industry and organized labor
under governmental guidance and supervision. They intended
to raise the purchasing power of labor through increased
wages and shorter working hours by providing more jobs and by
encouraging collective bargaining. To encourage industry,
NIRA officials suspended enforcement of antitrust laws and
encouraged industries to organize in order to regulate production, raise prices, and eliminate cutthroat competition.

To carry out these aims, each industry was to devise a code
of fair competition under NRA supervision; labor was to assist in an advisory capacity. It was intended that these
codes should have the force of law, with infractions punished
by the federal courts. An individual code would become effective only when approved by the president, who could also
modify or cancel a code at any time.[10]

Aware of the chaotic conditions existing within their industry, textile executives were first to come forward with a proposed code. This is ironic since previous attempts at self-
rule within the industry had been abysmal failures. In the
late 1920s, a group of executives had formed the Cotton Textile Institute to promote cooperative efforts to restrict
hours of work and publicize the inherent dangers of selling
below cost. According to Thomas McMahon, president of the
United Textile Workers of America (UTW), an agreement by this
group limiting weekly working hours was "scarcely dry when
some of those who were signers of this proposition broke
it."[11]

Only two days after a fireside chat in which President Roosevelt cited the textile business as an example of voluntary
regulation failing because a small percentage did not cooperate, the Cotton Textile Institute proposed a forty-hour week
with two daily shifts to be enforced by the government. Led
by George Sloan, president of the Cotton Textile Institute,
prominent executives of the industry dominated hearings on
the code held under the auspices of the Cotton Textile Industry Committee (CTIC). Labor was not represented on this committee; this exclusion foreshadowed later conflict between
the UTW and the CTIC.

After four days of testimony, a document was produced containing these major provisions: (1) a minimum weekly wage of
$12 in the South and $13 in the North (30 cents per hour in
the South and 32.5 cents per hour in the North); (2) a maximum workweek of forty hours; (3) a maximum machine-hour week
of eighty hours, divided into two shifts of forty hours;
(4) abolition of child labor under the age of sixteen years;
and (5) collective bargaining in accordance with the terms of
Section 7(a) of the NIRA. In a most ominous addition, the
code provided for the Cotton Textile Industry Committee to
serve as the administrative agency for the code (the Code
Authority).[12] General Hugh S. Johnson, National Recovery Ad-
ministrator, approved the code and forwarded it to the president. The Code of Fair Competition for the Cotton Textile
Industry became law with the president's signature on July 17,
1933.[13]

Both owners and workers responded favorably to the code.
W. D. Anderson, president of the giant Bibb Manufacturing
Company, a concern with mills throughout Georgia, commented
"a new day has dawned for all who are in any way concerned
with the manufacture and distribution of cotton textiles."[14]
Francis Gorman of the UTW viewed the adoption of the code as
"the most progressive step in the industry in many years."[15]

In fact, the code did precipitate a short-lived speculative
boom in the industry as manufacturers accelerated production
in anticipation of higher prices when the code became effective. Producers and consumers alike sought to beat the impo-
sition of the Agricultural Adjustment Act (AAA) processing
tax that was to go into effect in the late summer of 1933.
This tax was especially heavy on cotton (4.2 cents per pound
of raw cotton to be processed) and proved to be a significant
burden on an already depressed industry. It is illustrative
of the unfortunate fact that some New Deal policies were at
cross purposes.[16] Nevertheless, the boom in textiles continued even after the code and the processing tax went into effect. General Johnson described the industry's performance
under the code as "one of the bright spots of the NRA."[17]

In the fall, however, things began to change. Prices leveled

off and then fell. Manufacturers complained about increased
costs. Labor costs had increased 100 percent in many mills
because of the code's minimum wage provisions, and labor costs
per unit of production rose 70 percent in the industry as a
whole.[18] The bitterest complaints were reserved for the AAA
tax, which had increased the manufacturing costs of individual
mills between 8 percent and 13 percent. Increased costs produced a concomitant drop in demand.[19] The South suffered
more from the wage and hour provisions of the code than New
England, and Northern mills expanded to meet the upsurge of
orders in 1933. Most Southern mills, however, were already
on a two-shift, 110-hour week and had to curtail production
to meet the NRA maximum of 80 hours.[20] By November 1933, the
industry again faced accumulating inventories and below cost
prices. As they watched their profits slip away, Southern
manufacturers became increasingly dissatisfied with the
code.[21]

In 1934 a general agitation began throughout the industry for
a further machine curtailment, and this was officially requested of General Johnson in May. Without holding public
hearings or consulting labor, Johnson granted a 25 percent
reduction in machine hours during June, July, and August.
There was no provision for the maintenance of wages, and textile workers watched with dismay as their meager pay was reduced another 25 percent as the workweek dropped from forty
to thirty hours. Leaders of the United Textile Workers of
America were angry enough to call a general strike for the
first week in June.

Prior to the adoption of the code, there existed little labor
organization in the textile industry. The UTW, the only
organization of national scope, claimed a probably exaggerated membership of 15,000 to 20,000 in an industry that normally employed over 450,000 workers. Shortly after the adoption of the code, UTW leaders took advantage of Section 7(a)
of the NIRA and began a vigorous organizing campaign in the
South. By May 1934, the union claimed a membership of
300,000.[22]

From the time of the code's inception until May 1934, there
had been few actual labor disturbances in the industry; but
there was much grumbling among the workers. Complaints centered around three main problems. There was a growing feeling that the rights granted to employees under Section 7(a)
of the NIRA were not being properly protected. The UTW's
Southern organizing campaign had met vicious employer resistance. A second source of dissatisfaction was the increasing
use of the "stretch-out," a common term for having an employee
operate or oversee a larger number of machines than previously
at the same or even reduced pay. Management increasingly employed this tactic as increased costs necessitated maximum
utilization of the labor force. Also, weekly earnings were

declining; by August 1934, average earnings were $11.46 a
week, 40 percent less than the average for all manufacturing
workers.23

The June strike was averted when the NRA granted the UTW representation on the Cotton Textile National Industrial Relations Board and promised to have their Research and Planning
Division investigate wages, the stretch-out, and productive
machine hours necessary to meet normal demand. Under the
terms of this agreement, the strike order was countermanded
by the UTW "without prejudice to the right of labor to
strike."24

The results of the NRA investigation bitterly disappointed
union officials. Authors of the report found "no factual or
statistical basis for any general increase in Cotton Textile
code wage rates." The findings on the other points of contention were equally unsatisfactory. The June settlement had
obviously not gone to the roots of the problem; consequently,
it was short-lived. Irritated with the outcome of the NRA
investigation and further incensed by the discharge of some
workers who had been participating in union activities, the
newly organized Alabama State Council of Textile Workers
called a statewide strike on July 16. Twenty-four mills were
involved; and on the first day, 20,000 Alabama textile workers walked off the job.25

In mid-August at the national convention of the United Textile Workers in New York, Southern delegates presented fifty
resolutions, all urging a general strike. President Thomas F.
McMahon and firey Vice-President Francis Gorman agreed. Opposition came from George L. Googe, Southern director of the
American Federation of Labor, who argued that the union's in-
sufficient treasury and the economic circumstances of the industry rendered the strike call abortive, even foolish. But
McMahon repeatedly refused to recognize Googe. McMahon and
Gorman were so determined that they recessed the convention
for two hours and scoured New York City for Norman Thomas,
the famous Socialist who was known to favor a strike. Upon
his arrival, Thomas delivered a rousing speech, exhorting the
workers to strike, thus producing the desired unanimity. The
strike was called for September 3, Labor Day.

Late summer 1934 found Georgia in the midst of a hotly contested gubernatorial campaign. Governor Eugene Talmadge,
"the wild man from Sugar Creek," was seeking a second two-
year term as the state's chief executive. He had previously
served three consecutive terms as state agriculture commissioner and was extremely popular in the vast rural regions of
Georgia. His opponent, Superior Court Judge Claude Pittman
of Cartersville, was a political novice.

In view of the staggering needs facing Georgia during these

dark days of the depression, Talmadge's simplistic three-
point platform was incredible. He advocated the creation of
the office of lieutenant governor, a four-year term for governor, and payment of the state debt without raising taxes.
Beyond this, Talmadge was saying to the people "that all that
was needed to solve their problems was Ol' Gene -- Ol' Gene
and FDR, that is."[26] Throughout the campaign, Talmadge tried
to associate himself with Roosevelt. His detractors were not
convinced; and Pittman charged repeatedly that Talmadge, who
would not agree to the NRA wage scale for highway workers,
was obstinately blocking the New Deal in Georgia.[27]

Organized labor supported Pittman during the campaign, charging that Talmadge "has failed completely to grasp the fundamental principles of the Roosevelt recovery program."[28]
J. Sid Tiller, president of the Georgia Federation of Labor,
issued a formal statement declaring that "Governor Talmadge
and the State Highway Department are imposing conditions of
virtual peonage upon the workers of Georgia."[29] He called on
fair-minded citizens to save labor from being forced to the
verge of starvation wages.[30] Tiller felt that the action by
the executive committee was taken reluctantly and only after
a personal conference with the governor in which he plainly
announced his opposition to President Roosevelt's recovery
program. Tiller said, "Governor Talmadge is not in sympathy
with the New Deal; his is the reactionary viewpoint of the
advocates of the old deal, which was based on long hours and
low wages."[31] Tiller pointed out that Talmadge had proven
his opposition to the recovery program by his handling of
federal funds sent to Georgia to relieve human suffering.
Instead of attempting to relieve distress, Talmadge used these
funds to depress wages and lengthen hours of labor. He and
his agents acted so flagrantly in setting the wage scale at
five cents an hour in the rural counties of Georgia that federal authorities removed control of these funds from
Talmadge's office.[32]

The Central Labor Union of Augusta and the Columbus Central
Labor Union both concurred unanimously with the action by the
Georgia Federation of Labor, condemning Talmadge for his attitude toward labor and the NRA.[33] The Macon Federation of
Trades issued a separate statement condemning Talmadge's
stand against the NRA as "inexcusable and unpatriotic." The
Macon declaration held Talmadge's position "a brazen one"
which, together with his approval of the deplorable highway
wage scale, stamped his official approval upon chiseling contractors and other violators of NRA codes.[34]

Eugene Talmadge was, indeed, a genuine reactionary -- a vicious racist with a bizarre, flamboyant personality.
Talmadge was the quintessential Southern demagogue. His political strength lay primarily in the rural regions of
Georgia, which held inordinate voting strength due to

Georgia's county-unit system (the Neill Primary Act of 1917).
This system gave each of Georgia's 159 counties two votes for
each representative it had in the General Assembly. In this
way, three tiny counties had the power to nullify the vote of
giant Fulton County (Atlanta); the popular vote was effectively disenfranchised.[35] The candidate with the greatest
following in the rural areas was a certain winner in any
election.

Talmadge knew that his electoral strength lay with his rural
constituents, "the wool-hat boys"; and he courted them assid-
uously. But Talmadge also received warm support from a large
section of Georgia's urban business community. Atlanta bankers and corporation executives soon learned that he was
"safe." He favored a balanced budget, a low tax rate, and
not much public regulation of private enterprise.[36] Talmadge
tended to view unions as conspiracies and had little real
sympathy for organized labor.

Talmadge's bedrock conservatism led him to oppose the NRA on
philosophical grounds. He felt the federal government was
giving too much free money to those who did not deserve it;
he believed, along with most Georgians, that poverty was
still a sign of moral weakness. But the heart of his opposition to the NRA was based on more practical considerations.
Patronage was critical to political success in Georgia, where
local politicians in very small counties controlled crucial
block votes. Election administration was extremely lax in
some Georgia counties and overtly corrupt in others.[37] There
was no secret ballot in Georgia in the 1930s, and local voters were easily intimidated. Talmadge considered it vital
that all favors come from him. But he had no control over
the vast sums of federal money being poured into Georgia's
rural counties under the auspices of the NRA, and he was des-
perately afraid that his power base would be eroded.[38]

Talmadge later became an outspoken critic of the NRA and made
vicious and outrageous public slurs about Roosevelt's physical disability. Talmadge's meanness was legendary. But in
1934, his criticism of the president was still private. Publicly, Talmadge praised Roosevelt and castigated his enemies
for trying to drive a wedge between him and the president.
In an August campaign speech at Thomson, Georgia, Talmadge
said:

> They tried to beat me by saying that I was not fair
> with organized labor, when all labor, organized and
> unorganized, knows that Gene Talmadge is the best
> friend they have. Now they want to beat me by saying
> I'm against Roosevelt. I don't blame them for trying
> because the leaders of the opposition wish mighty hard
> that they had a Roosevelt with his sunny smile and
> heartening voice to run against Talmadge. But they

haven't got him. In Georgia it's not Roosevelt
against Talmadge; it's Roosevelt and Talmadge.[39]

The governor felt that the State Federation of Labor's indictment of him was unfair, and he repeated that he was "labor's
best friend."[40] In a signed article in his own newspaper,
The Statesman, Talmadge pointed out that it was in response
to a charge by the Georgia Federation of Labor that he had
fired the entire five-man Public Service Commission for ne-
glecting its duty in the reduction of utility rates. The
governor said the new commission, handpicked by him, had
taken many actions benefiting labor: they had reduced light
and power rates, telephone rates, bus and truck rates, and
railroad passenger rates, and eliminated the surcharge on
Pullman fares in Georgia. Talmadge suggested that the reduced light and power rates had resulted in the purchase of
millions of dollars worth of new appliances and had created
installation and service jobs for thousands of Georgia workers. The reduced telephone rates had resulted in thousands
of new installations and in many miles of additional wiring
and resultant additional work for the laboring man. He
claimed that the reduced passenger rates and the elimination
of the Pullman surcharge had brought the railroads many new
passengers and forced them to put on more trains, thus creating employment for the men who worked the roadbeds or otherwise assisted in moving the trains.[41]

Talmadge made much of the fact that he had never called out
troops to quell a strike. He said:

> Early this year Judge James Maddox, of Macon, and the
> sheriff of Floyd County called upon me to send troops
> to Rome, where a strike was in progress at the stove
> works. Instead of sending troops, I sent Mr. A. Steve
> Nance, President of the Atlanta Federation of Labor,
> and Adjutant General, Mr. Lindley Camp, instructing
> Mr. Camp not to go to Rome in uniform. On the report
> of these two gentlemen, I did not call out the troops.[42]

In an August campaign speech at Dalton, Talmadge said, "I resent anyone on earth saying that they are closer to labor, or
a better friend to labor, than I. I am a laborer myself.
You can look at my hands, and the color of my skin, and tell
it."[43] Laboring men in Bainbridge had given him his famous
red suspenders.[44] However, he maintained his opposition to
the NRA minimum wage of forty cents an hour for highway construction work, saying,

> It isn't right, it isn't fair, and it isn't honest
> for the State Highway Department, or any other depart-
> ment of the State of Georgia, to assess a minimum wage
> higher than the average citizen receives who pays
> taxes. Why isn't it fair? What is the minimum scale

of wages paid to the people in Georgia who make those
beautiful bedspreads and tapestries that line the
highways in this section of the State? Do these white
women receive 40¢ per hour for that gruelling, tedious
work? Yet, some of the opposition wants the State of
Georgia to pay a boy who drives a truck, or a negro
who rolls a wheelbarrow, a minimum of 40¢ per hour,
when a hard working white woman in the cotton field,
right beside the road where they are, is picking cotton from sunup to sundown. If you put a minimum of
40¢ per hour on picking cotton this year in Georgia,
the present price of lint and seed would not pay the
pick bill.[45]

Organized labor was not convinced. Noting Talmadge's claims
regarding various rate reductions, J. Sid Tiller responded,
"We remind the Governor that workers receiving wages in accord with his publicly announced policies are financially unable to benefit by these rate reductions."[46] Some of
Talmadge's measures, ostensibly undertaken to benefit the
"little man," were actually of great value to the moneyed interest in the state. His dramatic ouster of the Public Service Commission to obtain a reduction in utility rates was
followed by a lowering of the ad valorem tax which more than
compensated the utilities for the rate reduction. His
vaunted reduction of license tag costs to three dollars -- a
major campaign plank during his first run for the governorship -- profited trucking and bus companies infinitely more
than the owners of jalopies.[47]

Although Talmadge had received some labor endorsements, his
relations with organized labor were quite poor on the eve of
the general textile strike. Talmadge had been scheduled to
speak in Macon's Central City Park on Labor Day, September 3,
also the day the strike was to begin; but the Macon Federation of Trades revoked the invitation and returned to the
governor a check for twenty dollars which he had sent to be
used for an advertisement for his appearance. In withdrawing
the invitation, the federation cited Talmadge's recently expressed attitude toward the NRA.[48]

Labor relations had deteriorated badly in Georgia's textile
mills during the summer of 1934, and violence broke out weeks
before the official strike was declared. A strike at Columbus had closed the Georgia Webbing and Tape Company in mid-
July. When the mill attempted to reopen on August 10, a
picket line surrounded the plant. In a scuffle between
strikers and some workers attempting to leave the factory
after work, W. R. Sanders, a thirty-year-old textile worker,
was killed. Sanders was a member of Local 1605 of the United
Textile Workers of America. E. B. Newberry, secretary of the
local textile union, sent a telegram to President Thomas F.
McMahon of the UTW asking for help, saying that the union had

been frustrated in its attempt to employ counsel in Columbus
because "the reputable attorneys whom we sought to engage
were either connected with the manufacturers or had other excuses." The telegram further stated that the "city police
are planning to pin the murder on one of our boys, and we
have 32 eye-witnesses to the tragedy."[49]

On Thursday, August 30, four days before the official strike
call, violence erupted at the Payne Mill in Macon when pickets clashed with workers attempting to enter the gates. One
woman was allegedly struck with a blackjack. The next day
minor disturbances occurred when forty or fifty pickets,
mostly women, crowded onto the railroad tracks and delayed a
switch train for over an hour. The train included several
cars loaded with finished products from the mill. County officers had to remove the pickets forcibly before the train
could leave. Another scuffle occurred in Macon the same day
at the Bibb Number 2 plant when a group of strikers blocked
nonsympathizers from entering, but police quickly stopped the
disorder. Shortly after the last disorder, J. Ralph Gay, an
organizer for the UTW, addressed the pickets and urged them
to use "peaceful persuasion." He told the workers they had
no right to use force to prevent nonsympathizers from entering the mill. Gay warned the workers against violence and
charged mill executives might "plant" men to create disorders
which would be blamed on the union.[50] This charge had some
basis in fact and would be repeated by union leaders throughout the strike.

Anticipating that not more than 10 to 15 percent of the workers would strike, Southern mill owners arrogantly refused to
participate in a desperate final drive by the federal government to avoid the walkout. The owners consequently were
astounded when UTW strike leader Francis Gorman's brilliantly
orchestrated communications network brought out 400,000 textile workers representing nearly 70 percent of all those normally employed in the entire industry.[51] It was the largest
strike ever directed by American labor.[52]

Labor Day was not generally observed as a mill holiday in the
South, and the strike became effective a day earlier there
than it did in the nation as a whole. The union claimed that
100,000 workers were striking on Monday, September 3. Union
and employer claims as to the number idle varied considerably
throughout the strike, and little confidence can be placed on
the figures given by either side. The Associated Press, however, made continuous surveys throughout the strike, and
their figures may be regarded as generally reliable. On September 14, Associated Press reported that 44,480 of Georgia's
60,000 textile workers (75 percent) were idled by the
strike.[53]

Undoubtedly, the desperate economic plight and deplorable

working conditions were primarily responsible for the surprisingly large walkout, but Gorman's "sealed orders" and creative
use of the "flying squadron" also helped. The "sealed orders"
may have been pure hokum, but "flying squadrons" played a real
and dramatic part in the strike. On the morning the strike
began, wherever a mill that had been previously unionized
struck, the union men and women were in their Fords and Chev-
rolets within a matter of minutes and on their way to the
nearest nonunion town.[54] "Thundering into a mill town, several hundred strong, the pickets would jump out of their cars,
parade before the local plant, call on its workers to walk
out, close it if possible and, then, in a few moments disap-
pear, to appear again a few miles further on."[55]

The attitude of the manufacturers insured that the strike
would be laden with violence. The Cotton Textile Institute
described the strike as an "open challenge to law and order,"
claiming it resulted from illegal intimidation.[56] Accordingly, the owners saw fit to take the law into their own
hands. W. D. Anderson, president of the Bibb Manufacturing
Company and the Southern Textile Manufacturers Association,
hired the notorious "Red Demon," Pearl L. Bergoff, a New York-
based strikebreaker. Bergoff promptly dispatched 800 thugs
to Georgia, armed with clubs, tear gas, hand grenades, revolv-
ers, and shotguns. Similar action by owners around the
county bore fruit; sixteen textile workers died before the
strike ended.[57]

George L. Googe, Southern representative for the American
Federation of Labor, who had initially opposed the strike,
constantly admonished the workers to refrain from violence.
He asked the strikers to conduct themselves so as to win the
admiration of the public. Nevertheless, W. D. Anderson publicly referred to Googe as a "terrorizer,"[58] and he called
the strikers "outlaws."[59]

Only minor and sporadic violence occurred in Georgia during
the first two days of the strike. Fourteen people were
arrested in Macon on Tuesday, September 4, as fist fights
broke out on the picket lines surrounding the local mills.
Seventeen arrests were made at the Porterdale mill on the
same day as strikers attempted to prevent a train from entering the plant. Clubs were wielded in a fight at the Cedartown plant, and six women and two men were arrested on
charges of rioting.

N. B. Murphy, mayor of Trion and vice-president of the Trion
Mills, telegraphed Governor Talmadge requesting National
Guard troops; but the governor refused. Murphy charged that
the majority of workers at his plant and those at nearby Sum-
merville wanted to work, but pickets were preventing them
from reporting. Talmadge replied, "the sheriff of your
county has authority to deputize as many citizens over 21

years old as he deems necessary to maintain order. Please inform him of your situation. I am sure he can take care of it."[60]

Talmadge had made a well-publicized campaign promise to "never use the troops to break up a strike";[61] and with the primary election only one week away, he was taking no chances. At this point, approximately half of Georgia's textile workers were out on strike.

On Wednesday, September 5, two men, a strike sympathizer and a deputy sheriff, were killed and over a score injured in a two-hour gun battle between workers and special deputy sheriffs at the Trion Cotton Mills in North Georgia. The mill was being guarded by forty-six "special deputies" at the time of the shootings. Jim Parrish, a local deputy, blamed the whole incident on outsiders from Rome who, he claimed, attempted to disarm some of the special deputies. W. E. Hawkins, a local strike sympathizer, stated that the deputies opened fire on his group while the men were emerging from their car in front of the mill.[62] Another Georgian was killed on the same day in front of the Enterprise Mill at Augusta. Leon Carroll, a striker in the picket lines, was mortally wounded by three shots to the chest and abdomen. Two other pickets were also seriously injured by shots from the gun of policeman Floyd Baird. Baird had charged into the picket line to make an arrest after being hit by a brick thrown by one of the strikers. Numerous arrests occurred throughout the day at the Enterprise and Sibley mills in Augusta.

Riotous clashes at Macon and Columbus led the Bibb Manufacturing Company to close its plants across the state. At Bibb Mill Number 2 in Macon, pickets flipped an automobile on its side as company officials attempted to enter the plant. Shots were fired from inside the car, but no one was injured. Police said they found two pistols in the car. W. D. Anderson's stern visage appeared on the front page of the Atlanta newspapers the next day with a story describing his request to Governor Talmadge for troops.[63] Mill officials in Newnan also requested troops, as did the sheriffs of Hall and Polk counties. Still Talmadge refused. Speaking to textile workers at Columbus, Talmadge said, "You folks just keep cool and calm and I feel there will be no disturbances."[64] The primary was still five days off.

The tempo of the violence subsided during the weekend, but random clashes continued to occur throughout the state. All mills in the Atlanta area were closed, and Police Chief T. O. Sturdivant cited Communist influence. Mill officials and local authorities in Griffin and Cartersville added their names to the list of those requesting troops to curb local disorders associated with the strike.

On Wednesday, September 12, Eugene Talmadge was reelected in
a landslide vote, carrying 155 of the state's 159 counties.
Almost immediately, Talmadge mobilized all 4,000 Georgia National Guardsmen and declared martial law "in all sections of
the state where rebellion or violence or insurrection is
going on that local authorities are unable to handle."[65] It
was rumored that Cason Calloway, textile baron and Talmadge
contributor, phoned the governor saying that the situation
was uncontrollable and requesting National Guard troops.[66]

It was the largest peacetime mobilization of troops in the
state's history. Troops suddenly appeared in Columbus,
Porterdale, Barnesville, Griffin, Social Circle, Rome, Macon,
Aragon, and Cartersville. Thousands of Georgians were
arrested. Talmadge explained that martial law was in force
in all areas where National Guard companies were on duty and
that military courts were provided for prisoners arrested by
the guard. Talmadge declared that military authorities on
the scene could suspend civil courts and, if necessary, the
writ of habeas corpus.

Adjutant General Lindley Camp met a "flying squadron" of
pickets near Newnan with a military "flying squadron" of his
own composed of eight automobiles, each containing heavily
armed guardsmen. Wholesale arrests followed, and Talmadge
ordered the construction of an internment camp (soon termed a
"concentration camp" by the press) at Fort McPherson in
Atlanta to receive those arrested. Commenting on General
Camp's action, Talmadge said, "Lindley Camp has captured the
'flying squadron' and is on his way to Atlanta with it."[67]

The establishment of this concentration camp marked a prece-
dent in the history of American labor struggles. One hundred
twenty-six pickets, sixteen of whom were women, were incar-
cerated behind a tall, barbed wire enclosure near the spot
where Germans were interned during World War I. Georgia
strike leader S. A. Hollihan charged that "Hitlerism" had
come to America. General Camp was adamant in his determination to keep the strikers interned for the duration of the
strike; he declared they were officially awaiting trial by
court-martial.

The camp was clean, however, and the prisoners were well
treated. The women, most in their late teens and early twenties, remained cheerful. Etta Mae Zimmerman, one of the girl
prisoners interviewed in the camp, said, "We feel more hon-
ored to go out with the National Guard than with the scabs."
Miss Zimmerman and all of the other pickets were Georgians
from Hogansville, only a short distance from Newnan, where
they were arrested, thus rendering somewhat silly Talmadge's
claim that the troops were necessary to combat out-of-state
agitators. Mrs. Maude Granger, another prisoner from Hogansville, was quoted as saying, "We got up at 2 o'clock this

morning to go over to Newnan for picket duty. We were just
peacefully picketing. We're tired and a little hungry but we
are still union -- 100%."[68]

Mrs. Granger, a woman of about twenty, said they were not
having a bad time at all. "The troops have been mighty nice
to us. We've closed 14 mills already, and not a lick struck
on anybody."[69]

Explaining his actions, Governor Talmadge said, "The state
troops are being stationed at mills to protect lives. That
means they are there to protect both the strikers and those
who want to work."[70] But this attempt at evenhandedness was
a charade. It became obvious that the mill owners had the
governor's ear when he said, "I have looked into this situation and found that the mills are already paying the NRA wage
scale. In other words, the mills and the parties who wish to
continue working in the mills are following the provisions of
the National Recovery Act."[71] It was an outrageous lie.
Strike leaders insisted that there had been no trouble in
Georgia for several days prior to Talmadge's sudden deploy-
ment of troops immediately after the primary election. On
September 15, after the troops had already been activated,
armed thugs murdered another union member near the mill at
Aragon, Georgia.[72]

When UTW organizer J. Ralph Gay, for no apparent reason, was
arrested in Macon and held incommunicado under $75,000 bond,
and strike leaders in Augusta and Columbus were arrested at
the same time, union men charged collusion between Talmadge
and the mill owners. National strike leader Francis Gorman
branded Talmadge an "arch enemy of labor," asserting in a
telegram that the governor had proven this by "using the
armed forces of your state to drive men back into starvation
conditions and absolute subservience to mill owners. Your
troops have destroyed civil rights and made a mockery of your
own state laws."[73]

It looked as if all was lost, as starvation and intimidation
took their toll, and workers began drifting back into the
mills in increasing numbers. The Winant Board, appointed by
President Roosevelt to investigate the strike, issued a report that was equivocal at best in regard to labor's position.
However, in a last minute bit of resourcefulness, Gorman
chose to call the acceptance of the Winant report an "overwhelming victory" and called off the strike.

Notwithstanding Gorman's imaginative conclusion, the strike
had been an unmitigated disaster for Georgia's textile workers. Few strikers and no union men were rehired, as called
for in the agreement terminating the strike. Four men were
dead, and state labor organization in the textile industry
was in shambles.

The strike ended with militiamen brutally beating a fifth
worker to death in front of his family when he moved too
slowly when ordered from the Calloway Mill property. Talmadge
was not liable in a criminal sense for the perpetration of
any violence; but by late fall of 1934, it was apparent that
he had personally broken the back of the unions in Georgia.[74]

In retrospect, the attempted implementation of New Deal labor
policy in Southern mill communities was bound to cause
trouble. The cultural composition of the mill towns and the
legal reality of Section 7(a) of the National Recovery Act
made conflict inevitable. It was the volatile personality of
Eugene Talmadge that gave the textile strike in Georgia its
unique drama. The militia was activated in other Southern
states; but Talmadge's duplicity regarding his intentions
prior to the primary election, and the brutality and flamboy-
ance with which he suppressed the strike immediately afterward, was unprecedented. His chicanery was endless. Once
the strike was effectively broken, he reverted to a public
posture of fairness to both sides. Talmadge publicly in-
structed General Camp to prevent the owners from evicting
strikers from company housing (privately, he did nothing to
prevent it), and he dramatically ordered the strikebreaker
Pearl Bergoff and his thugs out of the state. Georgia textile workers were not fooled: they knew where Talmadge's
real loyalty lay, but the damage had already been done.

Notes

1 Jack Blicksilver, Cotton Manufacturing in the Southeast: A Historical Analysis (Atlanta, 1959), 98-99.

2 U.S., Bureau of Labor Statistics, Cotton Textile Industry, 1870-1945 (Washington, D.C., 1946), 4.

3 James V. Hodges, New Deal Labor Policy and the Southern Cotton Textile Industry, 1933-1936 (Ph.D. diss., Vanderbilt University, 1963), 16.

4 W. J. Cash, The Mind of the South (New York, 1941), 171-85.

5 Ibid.

6 Blicksilver, Cotton Manufacturing in the Southeast, 5.

7 Textile Bulletin, May 12, 1930.

8 Blicksilver, Cotton Manufacturing in the Southeast, 100.

9 Report of the Board of Inquiry for the Textile Industry, Labor Information Bulletin (Washington, D.C., 1934), 4-6.

10 Hodges, New Deal Labor Policy, 158.

11 Ibid., 167.

12 New York Times, June 20, 1933.

13 U.S., Bureau of Labor Statistics, General Textile Strike, 1934 (Washington, D.C., 1935).

14 Daily News Record, July 11, 1933.

15 Ibid., July 12, 1933.

16 Hodges, New Deal Labor Policy, 194.

17 New York Times, October 19, 1933.

18 Textile Bulletin, October 26, 1933.

19 H. E. Michl, The Textile Industries: An Economic Analysis (Washington, D.C., 1938), 126.

20 Monthly Labor Review, October 1934, 1019.

21 George Brown Tindall, The Emergence of the New South, 1913-1945 (Baton Rouge, 1967), 509-12.

22 John Wesley Kennedy, The General Strike in the Textile Industry, 1934 (M.A. thesis, Duke University, 1947), 19.

23 U.S., Bureau of Labor Statistics, Cotton Textile Industry, 2.

24 U.S., National Recovery Administration, Release 5514 (Washington, D.C., June 4, 1934).

25 U.S., Bureau of Labor Statistics, Cotton Textile Industry, 3.

26 William Anderson, The Wild Man from Sugar Creek (Baton Rouge, 1975), 107-108.

27 Hapeville (Ga.) Statesman, August 7, 1934.

28 Columbus (Ga.) Enquirer, August 1, 1934.

29 Ibid.

30 Atlanta Constitution, August 31, 1934.

31 Ibid.

32 Ibid.

33 Columbus (Ga.) Enquirer, August 2 and 3, 1934.

34 Anderson, The Wild Man from Sugar Creek, 16.

35 V. O. Key, Southern Politics in State and Nation (New York, 1949), 119.

36 Ibid., 116.

37 Ibid., 123.

[38] Michael S. Holmes, The New Deal in Georgia (Westport, Conn., 1975), 28.

[39] Hapeville (Ga.) Statesman, August 14, 1934.

[40] Ibid., July 31, 1934.

[41] Ibid.

[42] Ibid.

[43] Ibid., August 7, 1934.

[44] Anderson, The Wild Man from Sugar Creek, 108.

[45] Hapeville (Ga.) Statesman, August 7, 1934.

[46] Columbus (Ga.) Enquirer, August 1, 1934.

[47] Key, Southern Politics, 116-17.

[48] Columbus (Ga.) Enquirer, August 10, 1934.

[49] Ibid., August 14, 1934.

[50] New York Times, September 1, 1934.

[51] Ibid., September 9, 1934.

[52] Ibid., September 2, 1934.

[53] Kennedy, The General Strike in the Textile Industry, 48.

[54] "Here Comes Gorman," New Republic 80 (October 3, 1934), 212.

[55] Kennedy, The General Strike in the Textile Industry, 52.

[56] New Republic 80 (September 19, 1934), 141.

[57] "Here Comes Gorman," New Republic, 213.

[58] Atlanta Constitution, September 2, 1934.

[59] Columbus (Ga.) Enquirer, September 3, 1934.

[60] Ibid., September 5, 1934.

[61] Anderson, The Wild Man from Sugar Creek, 110.

[62] Columbus (Ga.) Enquirer, September 6, 1934.

[63] Atlanta Constitution, September 6, 1934.

[64] Columbus (Ga.) _Enquirer_, September 6, 1934.

[65] _New York Times_, September 18, 1934.

[66] Anderson, _The Wild Man from Sugar Creek_, 110.

[67] _New York Times_, September 18, 1934.

[68] Atlanta _Constitution_, September 18, 1934.

[69] Ibid.

[70] Ibid.

[71] Hapeville (Ga.) _Statesman_, September 18, 1934.

[72] Kennedy, _The General Strike in the Textile Industry_, 58.

[73] Columbus (Ga.) _Enquirer_, September 19, 1934.

[74] Anderson, _The Wild Man from Sugar Creek_, 111.

PAC to COPE:
Thirty-Two Years of Southern Labor in Politics
Daniel A. Powell

A BRIEF HISTORICAL BACKGROUND

Liberal Democratic losses in the 1942 elections, the enactment of the Smith-Connally Anti-Labor Act the following year,
and uncertain prospects in the forthcoming 1944 elections motivated the executive board of the Congress of Industrial
Organizations (CIO) to establish the Political Action Committee (PAC) on July 7, 1943. Sidney Hillman, president of the
Amalgamated Clothing Workers, was named chairman and director
of the new organization. A few months later, delegates to
the annual CIO convention enthusiastically endorsed the creation of PAC and budgeted $700,000 (later magnified to
$7,000,000 by the press) to provide for its operating costs.
By early 1944 state PACs, as well as city and county units,
had been established by CIO state, city, and county councils
in most Southern states.

George S. Mitchell, the first PAC Southern regional director,
supervised political activities in nine Southern states.*
Mitchell left the PAC shortly after the 1944 elections and
was temporarily replaced by Paul R. Christopher. I began
work with PAC in the South in December 1945 and became PAC
Southern director in July 1946, with the responsibility for
eleven Southern states.

Although the Democratic party regained some of its midterm
losses in the 1944 general elections, two years later the Republicans won a conservative majority in Congress when the
Democrats and PAC outside the South suffered massive defeats
in the general election. As a result, PAC's reputation

---

* Carl A. McPeak was assigned Texas, and W. A. Hollaway had
  Arkansas in his region.

declined precipitantly; and some larger unions drastically reduced their contributions to PAC. Forced to adopt economy
measures, PAC temporarily suspended its field staff operation,
moved its national office from New York to Washington, and reduced its office staff. Adding to its problems during this
very difficult year, PAC's director, Sidney Hillman, died un-
expectedly on July 10, 1946. He was replaced by Assistant
Director Jack Kroll.

CIO national unions resumed their financial support of PAC
after the passage of the Taft-Hartley Act in 1947. Thereafter, full field operations were resumed; and some national
unions created PAC departments headed by full-time directors,
while others assigned staff representatives to work under the
direction of the national PAC and its regional directors.

The passage of Taft-Hartley also forced the AFL to reconsider
its political program. As a result, Labor's League for
Political Education (LLPE) was established in 1948 with
Joseph D. Keenan, secretary of the International Brotherhood
of Electrical Workers, as director. Keenan resigned in 1953
and was replaced by James L. McDevitt, president of the Pennsylvania State Federation of Labor.

By the end of 1948, LLPE units had been established by most
Southern states and city federations, and these committees
were active in the 1948 Southern primaries and in the general
election. In 1954, the LLPE expanded its national staff to
include regional directors to stimulate and supervise its
field activities. At that time Charles Houk, secretary-
treasurer of the Tennessee State Federation of Labor, was appointed LLPE Southern director.

The PAC and LLPE were consolidated at the time of the AFL-CIO
merger in December 1955, creating the Committee on Political
Education (COPE). Kroll and McDevitt were appointed codirec-
tors of COPE.** Resulting from the consolidation of PAC and
LLPE, the field staff was doubled; and the eleven-state
Southern region was reorganized into two areas.

*Attitudes of the Press, the Union Membership,
and the Politicians toward PAC*

Although organized labor in the United States had been actively involved in politics as early as 1828, when the Philadelphia Mechanics Union of Trade Associations founded the
Working Men's Party of Philadelphia, and as recently as 1936,

---

** After the retirement of Kroll in 1957 and the death of
   McDevitt in 1963, Deputy Director Al Barkan became COPE
   director.

when the AFL and CIO (then the Committee for Industrial Organization) supported Franklin D. Roosevelt's campaign for a
second term, the CIO's announcement of the formation of the
Political Action Committee in July 1943 was greeted by scream-
ing headlines suggesting that the American labor movement was
making its first terrible venture into politics.

Joseph Gaer, who analyzes the founding of PAC in The First
Round, writes:

> For months it was impossible to pick up any metropol-
> itan newspapers from Portland, Maine to Portland,
> Oregon without encountering some item about the Polit-
> ical Action Committee. Practically every columnist
> and radio commentator had his say about PAC in general,
> and its Chairman Sidney Hillman in particular. All the
> large circulation weeklies, from Collier's and the
> Saturday Evening Post to Time and Newsweek, considered
> it of sufficient importance to open their pages to a
> discussion of PAC and its meaning. Within the space
> of two months Life magazine devoted two full pages of
> photographs to PAC.

Most of the conservative Southern press tried to outdo the
national press in creating hysteria over the imminent take-
over of the South and the nation by a gigantic Communist-
inspired monster, the CIO-PAC.

Texas congressman Martin Dies, chairman of the House Un-
American Activities Committee, was one of the leaders of the
attempted "red smear" of the PAC. In his biography of Sidney
Hillman, Matthew Josephson concludes:

> He [Dies] rushed forth with a large 215-page report
> on PAC which charged (under congressional immunity)
> that Sidney Hillman aspired to become the Red Chief
> of America in place of Mr. Earl Browder.... it was
> alleged he [Hillman] was building up the CIO-PAC by
> entering into a coalition with the Communists.... a
> terrible power of slander was lodged in the hands of
> Mr. Dies.

Widespread allegations also appeared in some plants and in
various Southern newspapers that PAC was going to round up
the workers like cattle, herd them to the polls, and vote
them for the PAC-endorsed, Communistic, "nigger-loving" candidates.

What effect these widely saturated lies had on CIO members,
their families, and their friends is difficult to assess; but
it is safe to say that such falsehoods and allegations did
not endear PAC to a majority of rank-and-file white members,
whose conservative, Bible-belt environment made them

particularly susceptible to this propaganda. Perhaps the
most effective charge was that union members were going to be
forced to vote for the PAC candidates. Even today it is not
uncommon to hear a rank-and-file member declare defiantly:
"COPE is not going to tell me how to vote."

Among Black members, the effects of the antiunion propaganda
were negligible. Negroes have never put much trust in the
conservative white Southern press, and most Blacks knew that
those who sympathized with or tried to help them usually were
labeled "Communists" or "nigger-lovers."

To counter the slanderous allegations and to explain the purposes and goals of PAC, more than 85 million pieces of literature were printed and distributed by PAC in 1944. More than
15 million pieces of this literature went into the South.

As the years passed, the slanderous attacks on PAC became
fewer and weaker. After the AFL-CIO merger, COPE seemed to
acquire a respectability which PAC was never quite able to
achieve. Today, in my opinion, a vast majority of union members accept COPE as the essential political arm of labor,
even though they may not always agree with or support the
COPE endorsements.

From the beginning the politicians saw PAC as a source of
money, campaign workers, and votes. Most of them wanted PAC
support, but they wanted it as quietly as possible. Jim
Folsom, running for governor of Alabama in 1946, was the only
major candidate in the South I can recall who wanted a public
endorsement from PAC in that year. In the 1949 Virginia
gubernatorial primary, United States Senator Harry Byrd
charged the secretly endorsed PAC candidate with having CIO
support. Two nights later, our candidate went on statewide
radio to deny he had PAC or CIO support. The broadcast was
paid for in part by PAC money. Occasionally some unscrupu-
lous candidate, while seeking PAC covert support, would suggest that we publicly endorse his opponent.

The fear of a public endorsement by labor had diminished by
the mid-1950s; and a few years thereafter, most Southern candidates seeking the support of COPE felt comfortable with a
public endorsement. Today, I know of no Southern state where
COPE does not announce or release to the public its endorsement of candidates.

Effects of the Race Issue on PAC and COPE

The exploitation of the race issue in the South between 1944
and 1970 divided the labor movement, retarded union organization of workers, and seriously impaired the political efforts
of PAC and COPE. No other issue during this period was so

detrimental to the unions and their programs.

The use of the Negro as a political issue reemerged in the
South before the close of World War II. A temporary Fair Employment Practices Commission (FEPC) had been established
during the war to discourage discrimination in employment,
and efforts were soon undertaken to create a permanent FEPC.
When, in addition to the controversy over FEPC, the United
States Supreme Court outlawed the white primary in 1944, the
issue assumed a predominant position in Southern politics.
Events in the following years fanned the issue into a white
heat:

1948
  The Democratic National Convention walkout over the
  adoption of the FEPC platform plank and the subsequent
  birth of the Dixiecrat party.

1950
  The United States Supreme Court decision outlawing
  segregated education in colleges at the graduate and
  professional levels.

1954
  The United States Supreme Court decision banning segregation in public schools.

1955
  Dr. Martin Luther King's Montgomery, Alabama, bus boycott.

1957
  Little Rock, Arkansas, Central High School desegrega-
  tion controversy.

1960
  Beginning of the sit-ins.

1962
  University of Mississippi Riot.

1963
  The Birmingham "Mother's Day Riot."

1964
  Passage of the Civil Rights Act.

1965
  Passage of the Voting Rights Act.

1968
  Assassination of Dr. Martin Luther King.

By the 1946 primaries, the race issue had permeated many of
the gubernatorial, United States senatorial, and congressional
district elections. In Alabama, Handy Ellis charged that Jim
Folsom's election as governor would mean "the complete destruction of our segregation laws."

In Georgia, Eugene Talmadge won the 1946 gubernatorial primary on a white supremacy platform. Warning against his opponent's nomination, Talmadge charged in his newspaper, The
Statesman, on June 13, 1946: "Negro Solicitors will try
white people before Negro Judges and white men and white
women prisoners will be subject to the orders of Negro Sheriffs and their Negro jailers." Table 1 contains a list of
those candidates whose defeats are at least partially attributable to the race issue.

Table 1. Candidates injured by the race issue

Name	Office	State	Year
Luther Patrick	U.S. Rep.	Ala.	1946
Helen Mankin	U.S. Rep.	Ga.	1946
Ned Carmack	U.S. Senate	Tenn.	1946
Martin Hutchinson	U.S. Senate	Va.	1946
Homer Rainey	Governor	Tex.	1946
M. E. Thompson	Governor	Ga.	1948
Frances P. Miller	Governor	Va.	1949
Claude Pepper	U.S. Senate	Fla.	1950
Frank Graham	U.S. Senate	N.C.	1950
Hugo Sims	U.S. Rep.	S.C.	1950
Morris Abram	U.S. Rep.	Ga.	1954
Thurmond Chatham	U.S. Rep.	N.C.	1956
Charles B. Dean	U.S. Rep.	N.C.	1956
Brooks Hayes	U.S. Rep.	Ark.	1958
Ryan DeGraffenried	Governor	Ala.	1962
Frank Smith	U.S. Rep.	Miss.	1962
Richard Preyer	Governor	N.C.	1964
Ellis Arnall	Governor	Ga.	1966
Carl Elliott	Governor	Ala.	1966
George Grider	U.S. Rep.	Tenn.	1966
LeRoy Collins	U.S. Senate	Fla.	1968
William Anderson	U.S. Rep.	Tenn.	1972
Jeff LaCaze	U.S. Rep.	La.	1975

Since union members are a cross section of the community, we
had Klansmen, White Citizen Council members, and unorganized
racists in our local unions. Sometimes they created racial
incidents and divisions within the unions. In more extreme
cases, local unions withdrew from the national union or state

and city labor councils. Some locals refused to participate
in PAC and COPE activities, and occasionally a local union or
city-county labor council endorsed a segregationist candidate
against PAC or COPE endorsed candidates. To retard the collection of voluntary PAC and COPE dollars, allegations were
spread among white workers that these dollars were later contributed to NAACP, SNCC, CORE, or whatever civil rights organization happened to be in the headlines.

Since neither PAC nor COPE supported white supremacy candidates, many of the labor-endorsed candidates were targets for
racial attacks by their conservative, segregationist opponents. Such attacks frequently reduced the union vote for
our candidates. An example is provided by North Carolina
United States Senator Frank Graham, a lifelong friend of
organized labor. Graham lost a majority of the union vote to
an antiunion cotton mill owner, Willis Smith, whose principal
campaign issue was that Graham favored integrated schools.
Similarly, Senator Claude Pepper of Florida had an almost 100
percent prolabor voting record, but he lost enough union
votes in middle and North Florida in 1950 to defeat his bid
for reelection. Pepper was identified as a FEPC supporter.
United States Representative James Morrison, the only Louisiana congressman to vote against Taft-Hartley and a long-time
friend of unions, lost a majority of union voters in 1966 and
his congressional seat when the voters believed racial
charges against him.

The introduction of the race issue by those who desired to
maintain the status quo in the South, especially regarding
trade unionism, frustrated PAC and COPE's efforts to focus
the attention of the voters on the authentic issues of the
period -- the economic and social conditions of the South and
its people. Had the political campaigns during these twenty-
six years been contested on real issues, PAC and COPE would
have been more successful.

By 1972, the issue of race had receded to the extent that it
was no longer a major factor in Southern elections. To be
sure, the race issue could still result in the defeat of a
candidate in a close statewide or congressional district
election, but it had lost much of its vote-getting power.

The symbolic requiem for Negrophobia in Southern politics
came last fall in Mississippi when Democratic gubernatorial
candidate Cliff Finch campaigned for black votes with the
public endorsement of black leaders Charles Evers and Aaron
Henry. Former Mississippi Governor Ross Barnett, reportedly,
narrowly avoided choking to death when he learned that Finch
had appointed civil rights activists Dick Gregory and Charles
Evers as colonels on the governor's staff.

BENEFITS OF THE AFL-CIO MERGER

Perhaps no single factor was more beneficial to organized
labor's political program in the South than the AFL-CIO
merger in 1955. The merger proved beneficial in several ways:
(1) it increased the numerical base for an effective political
program, (2) it expanded the financial base for operations,
(3) it eliminated much of the political division and competition between the AFL and CIO which previously had hampered
political efforts in some areas, and (4) it provided a
stronger and more permanent base for the political action
program than had formerly existed in either the AFL or the
CIO.

Two years before the 1955 merger, the AFL had a total membership of 991,000 in eleven Southern states, more than double
the CIO's 373,000. By the time of the merger, the total membership of the new AFL-CIO exceeded 1,400,000. The expanded
membership resulting from the merger increased the potential
political strength of COPE far beyond that of either PAC or
LLPE.

Due to the lack of money prior to the merger, only seven of
the eleven CIO state councils had full-time executive secretaries or presidents; and there were some AFL state federations that did not have full-time officers. In none of these
states were any of the full-time executive secretaries or
presidents assigned full time to PAC or LLPE. Two years
after the merger, every state AFL-CIO except one had a full-
time officer; and all but two states had two or more full-
time officers. Today all these states have a state COPE director, and six of the eleven have full-time COPE women's
activities directors.

The merger brought an end to much of the hostility that had
existed between rival unions, particularly the building
trades and a few of the larger CIO industrial unions. By having both groups as participants in COPE, we began to get more
unity and support behind COPE-endorsed candidates and fewer
competing endorsements from various unions and trade groups
with the AFL-CIO.

The entire national PAC operation had been financed by contributions from the treasuries of the national and international
unions and individual voluntary contributions of CIO members
collected by the unions. No staff salaries, travel, or operational expenses were paid from the CIO treasury. The amounts
the unions contributed fluctuated from year to year, and operations had to be curtailed or expanded accordingly. Under
the merger the national COPE staff salaries, travel, office,
and routine operational expenses were paid from the AFL-CIO
treasury. Such special national programs of COPE as registration and get-out-the-vote are still financed from

contributions from national and international union treasuries, and all money contributed to candidates for federal
office is from voluntary two-dollar contributions by individual union members. By 1970, fifteen years after merger,
COPE participants, activities, endorsements, candidates, contributions, and operational expenditures have increased more
than tenfold from 1956; and they continue to expand at an
even more rapid rate.

COPE STATE PROGRAMS OF PROGRESS

In 1960, with the assistance of Alabama Council officers, I
formulated and wrote the prospectus for the Alabama Labor
Council's Program of Progress. This was an explicitly
planned, long-range political action-public relations-
legislative program to achieve enactment of a ten-point state
legislative agenda. The overall Program of Progress was
financed by a dedicated assessment of $1 per member per year,
payable 8 1/3 cents per month.

Within five years, every Southern state except one (as well
as several states outside the South) had adopted similar Programs of Progress and, in so doing, doubled, or more than
doubled, the per capita tax which the local unions paid to
the state councils. Mississippi, Arkansas, and Virginia
adopted dedicated assessments of $1.50 per member per year
(12 1/2 cents per month) to finance their Programs of Progress. As a result of these programs, by 1965 the South had a
higher per capita tax for AFL-CIO state councils than any
other section of the nation.

By conservative calculation, it is my estimate that since
adoption of these Programs of Progress in the early 1960s,
ten Southern states have received in excess of $13 million
from the dedicated assessments. Of this, approximately $7 to
$8 million probably has gone into COPE gubernatorial and
state legislative campaigns in these states in the last
eleven to fifteen years. As a result, five of these ten
states today have state minimum wage laws; and some of the
Southern states have workmen's compensation and unemployment
insurance laws among the best in the nation.

THE DEFEATS AND THE VICTORIES

As could be expected in the most conservative section of the
nation (especially considering the type of candidates PAC and
COPE have supported), our political defeats have outnumbered
our victories. Most labor-endorsed candidates were liberals,
usually without sufficient money to finance their campaigns;
many were political novices with little or no organization and
very low name recognition. Indeed, it is surprising that we

did not have more defeats than we did. Table 2 reflects some
of our more memorable defeats because of the caliber of the
candidate; the campaign tactics employed; the time, effort,
and money PAC or COPE put into the election; or a combination
of these factors. In each of these defeats, if the candidate
had not had PAC or COPE support, he undoubtedly would have
lost by a much larger margin.

Table 2. Defeated PAC and COPE candidates

Name	Office	State	Year
Homer Rainey	Governor	Tex.	1946
Frances P. Miller	Governor	Va.	1949
Claude Pepper	U.S. Senate	Fla.	1950
Frank P. Graham	U.S. Senate	N.C.	1950
Morris Abram	U.S. Rep.	Ga.	1954
Ross Bass	U.S. Senate	Tenn.	1966
George Grider	U.S. Rep.	Tenn.	1966
LeRoy Collins	U.S. Senate	Fla.	1968
Ralph Yarborough	U.S. Senate	Tex.	1970
Albert Gore	U.S. Senate	Tenn.	1970

Among our victories, the one for which PAC probably deserves
the most credit was the 1946 election in Georgia of Henderson
Lanham over United States Representative M. C. Tarver, who
had been in Congress for twenty-two years. Early in 1946, a
tabulation of CIO membership by congressional districts revealed that we had a good chance in Georgia's seventh district to defeat an ultraconservative, antilabor congressman.
For the next six months we concentrated our efforts to build
PAC organization in this district. After talking to a number
of potential candidates, we decided that Solicitor General
Lanham of the Rome Judicial Circuit would be the strongest
candidate in the Democratic primary, which was then tanta-
mount to election in the district. However, Lanham was reluctant to run, and it took several weeks to persuade him to
make the race. PAC contributed nearly a third of his campaign funds, furnished five full-time campaign workers together with approximately twenty-five part-time volunteers,
and provided all his sign-and-sound cars and most of his campaign literature and placards. His campaign was concentrated
in those counties where CIO membership was the determining
force. Our members united behind Lanham, and we defeated
Tarver by almost two to one in county unit votes. Less than
a year later, Congressman Lanham cast the only vote in the
Georgia delegation against the Taft-Hartley Bill.

Estes Kefauver's nomination for United States Senator in

Tennessee in the 1948 Democratic primary would not have been
achieved, in my opinion, without the support of PAC. Kefauver's margin of victory was smaller than the probable number
of CIO members who voted for him. We were always able to at-
tain a high degree of unity behind Kefauver among union members. Table 3 provides a list of other victories pleasant to
remember and for which PAC and COPE deserve a good share of
credit.

Table 3. PAC and COPE victories

Name	Office	State	Years
Claude Pepper	U.S. Senate	Fla.	1944
Lister Hill	U.S. Senate	Ala.	1944, 1962
Olin Johnson	U.S. Senate	S.C.	1944, 1950, 1962
Albert Raines	U.S. Rep.	Ala.	1944, 1946
John Sparkman	U.S. Senate	Ala.	1946, 1954, 1972
James Folsom	Governor	Ala.	1946, 1954
Kerr Scott	Governor and U.S. Senate	N.C.	1948, 1954
Gordon Browning	Governor	Tenn.	1948
Russell Long	U.S. Senate	La.	1948
Frank Clement	Governor	Tenn.	1952, 1954
Albert Gore	U.S. Senate	Tenn.	1952, 1958, 1964
Ross Bass	U.S. Rep. and U.S. Senate	Tenn.	1954, 1964
Earl Long	Governor	La.	1956
Ralph Yarborough	U.S. Senate	Tex.	1957
Terry Sanford	Governor	N.C.	1960
Richard Fulton	U.S. Rep.	Tenn.	1962
George Grider	U.S. Rep.	Tenn.	1964
Robert Eckhart	U.S. Rep.	Tex.	1966
William Anderson	U.S. Rep.	Tenn.	1968
William Fulbright	U.S. Senate	Ark.	1968
Lawton Chiles	U.S. Senate	Fla.	1970
Barbara Jordan	U.S. Rep.	Tex.	1972
Andrew Young	U.S. Rep.	Ga.	1972
Harold Ford	U.S. Rep.	Tenn.	1974
Ray Blanton	Governor	Tenn.	1974
Cliff Finch	Governor	Miss.	1975

AN EVALUATION OF PAC AND COPE ON SOUTHERN POLITICS

It is difficult to evaluate the impact of PAC and COPE on
Southern politics. Today we have more misnamed state "right-
to-work" laws than we had when we began PAC in the South in
1944; but we also have more state minimum wage laws, better

workmen's compensation, better unemployment insurance, and more job safety legislation. While we do not have as many strikes today, we also do not have as many National Guardsmen, state highway patrolmen, sheriffs' deputies, and city police breaking our picket lines and slugging our pickets. Today most of our members earn higher wages, live in better houses, wear better clothes, and have more education than in 1944. Many today are more concerned about inflation than unemployment.

COPE has become more respectable and a little more conservative than was PAC. And since the Vietnam war, we have not been as popular on college and university campuses as we once were. But we still remain the largest, strongest, and most meaningful force in America for social and economic change. The issues that COPE deals with today are pretty much the same that PAC confronted thirty-two years ago: more jobs and less unemployment, health care for the masses of citizens, more housing, price controls, consumer protection, fair taxation, better schools, and more adequate social security benefits.

The voting records of the Southern congressional delegations have not improved significantly; but we do have more friends in city halls, in state legislatures, and in governors' offices than we had in 1944. Moreover, the future appears promising. It is easier to vote now. There are no poll taxes to pay, no long years of residency required, no interpreting the constitution to register to vote; and color discrimination is almost a thing of the past. The voting machines are faster and more honest than were the paper ballots. As a consequence, more union members vote today and are probably better informed when they go to the polls. But the basic job of political action remains the same: get the members registered to vote, inform them on the issues and the candidates, and encourage them to vote on election day.

Today we have vastly improved techniques, and we have more and better political organization than existed thirty-two years ago (as do our political enemies). We have developed our political action training seminars; we have perfected telephone bank skills to effectively contact our members; and now, with data processing, we can electronically check our voter registration and precinct membership, add members' telephone numbers, and keep on computer tape for instant use complete membership political data.

We now have the tools; and if we use them well and wisely, we can produce the bountiful South we visioned in 1944. Perhaps in another ten or twenty years we can better evaluate the impact of PAC and COPE on the South and its people.

Comment

A synopsis of the remarks by Wayne Flynt, Samford University, Birmingham, Alabama.

John Allen's paper on the 1934 textile strike is interesting and important, primarily for the questions it raises. Many of the central issues invite further consideration. First, have historians underestimated the importance of women in Southern labor? Despite their reputation as "hard to organize," the involvement of women in riots in Cedartown and Atlanta suggests that they could have been a greater asset to the Southern labor movement than generally recognized. Another possibility raised by Allen's paper involves a larger controversy of New Deal historiography. Although the National Industrial Recovery Act provided, in many cases, a tremendous impetus to labor and enjoyed enthusiastic rank-and-file support, the textile codes had an adverse effect on the 1934 textile strike. Was the National Recovery Administration savior or bane to America's labor movement? Finally, Allen and other labor historians might pursue new directions from questions raised in this paper. A more careful examination of labor's support for Eugene Talmadge might expose a revealing horizontal cleavage among Georgia's unionists. Furthermore, exploration through oral history might answer many of the unsolved problems involving this particular strike and Southern labor history as well. If Allen had interviewed surviving strike leaders, in addition to his research in traditional sources, a more complete account would have emerged.

Daniel Powell's study of PAC and COPE is essentially a narrative account of "what happened" when organized labor jumped into Southern politics. Equally important, and perhaps more interesting, would be a description of "how it happened." How did PAC and COPE deal with the race issue in states where labor was deeply divided? How did labor decide on endorsements? What influence did the rank and file exercise in such decisions, and how did the public media influence the final determination?

Two of Powell's major conclusions need further study. First,
has the issue of race disappeared from Southern politics, as
Powell suggests, or is it only temporarily dormant? For instance, how does one explain the support of Alabama's building trade unions for George Wallace? Furthermore, the rise
of urban Republicanism in the South largely stems from disen-
chantment with the increasingly liberal Democratic party.
Second, have PAC and COPE been as successful as Powell claims?
Perhaps labor's success has been its dirge. Workers have become so affluent that many have lost any sense of class consciousness. The union member frequently looks beyond his
days as a worker to becoming an entrepreneur. Ironically,
personal success leads him to abandon labor politics and em-
brace social conservatism and new political affiliations.
Despite some residual attachment to labor ideals, vertical
mobility has produced a new kind of unionist in a new labor
movement.

Appendix

<u>Thursday, April 1</u>

Registration
Labor Films
Exhibits

Welcome
William M. Suttles, Georgia State University
George Busbee, Governor of Georgia
Martha True, Georgia State AFL-CIO

1. <u>What is "Southern" Labor</u>?

Panel: Claude Ramsay, Mississippi AFL-CIO
F. Ray Marshall, University of Texas
Philip Taft, Brown University
Howard Henson, Laborers' International Union

2. <u>Textile Organizing in the Twentieth Century</u>

Presiding: Everett Dean, Southern Co-Director (retired),
United Textile Workers of America

"Textile Unionism in the Piedmont, 1901-1934"
Dennis R. Nolan, University of South Carolina
"Unionism in the Southern Textile Industry: An Overview"
Bruce Raynor, Textile Workers Union of America

Comment: Joseph Jacobs, labor attorney (Atlanta)
Anna Weinstock, Federal Mediation and Conciliation Service (retired)

3. Antiunion Violence in the Southern Coal Fields

    Presiding: Richard Straw, Williams College

    "The Strategies of the United Mine Workers in Organizing"
      John P. David, West Virginia Institute of Technology
    "The Mingo War: Labor Violence in the Southern West
      Virginia Coal Fields, 1919-1922"
      Daniel P. Jordan, Virginia Commonwealth University

    Comment: John W. Hevener, Ohio State University, Lima
              Oliver Singleton, AFL-CIO Regional Director
                (retired)

4. Labor in the Oil Fields

    Presiding: Aaron Schloss, Oil, Chemical and Atomic
                Workers International Union

    "The Texas-Louisiana Oil Field Strike of 1917"
      James C. Maroney, Lee College
    "CIO Oil Workers Organizing Campaign in Texas, 1942-1943"
      Clyde Johnson, Organizer (retired)

    Comment: Charles H. Martin, University of Alabama,
                Gadsden Program
              Aaron Schloss, Oil, Chemical and Atomic Workers
                International Union

    Labor Awards Banquet -- Hyatt Regency Hotel

                        Friday, April 2

5. Radicalism in the South

    Presiding: Donald G. Sofchalk, Mankato State University

    "The Left Looks South: The 'Southern Strategy' of Amer-
      ican Radicals during the Great Depression"
      John S. Rosenberg, Princeton University
    "Radical Unionism in Arkansas, 1930s"
      Stephen F. Strausberg, University of Arkansas

    Comment: Myles Falls Horton, Highland Research and
                Education Center
              Dan T. Carter, Emory University
              Emanual Muravchik, Jewish Labor Committee

6. <u>Blacks in the Southern Labor Movement</u>

    Panel: E. T. Kehrer, AFL-CIO Civil Rights Department
             Ernest Rice McKinney, A. Philip Randolph Institute
             Vera Rony, University of New York at Stony Brook
             Lamond Godwin, National Rural Center

7. <u>Operation Dixie</u>

    Presiding: Jim Sala, AFL-CIO Region V

    "An Editor in Operation Dixie"
      Lon Vallery, Glass Bottle Blowers Association
    "Textile Workers in Operation Dixie"
      Paul Richards, University of Wisconsin

    Comment: Henry W. Berger, Washington University,
            St. Louis

8. <u>Knights of Labor in the South</u>

    Presiding: H. L. Mitchell, Cofounder, Southern Tenant
            Farmers Union

    "Knights of Labor: Internal Dissensions of the Southern
      Order"
      Melton A. McLaurin, University of South Alabama
    "The Struggle to Unionize West Virginia Coal: The Par-
      ticipation of Black Mine Workers in the Knights of
      Labor and the United Mine Workers, 1886-1903"
      Stephen Brier, American Labor History Series, WGBH

    Comment: Herbert Gutman, City College of New York

9. <u>Obstacles to Organizing in the Southern Textile Industry</u>

    Presiding: James A. Hodges, College of Wooster

    "The Role of Religion in Discouraging Textile Workers
      from Joining the Union in Gastonia"
      Donald W. Shriver, Union Theological Seminary
    "Industry and Community Resistance to Southern Textile
      Organizing, 1937-1939"
      Joseph Y. Garrison, Georgia State University

    Comment: Scott M. Hoyman, Textile Workers Union of
            America
            Roy Whitmire, Southern Co-Director (retired),
            United Textile Workers of America

10. Teacher Unionism

     Presiding: Neil Betten, Florida State University

     "Florida Teachers Strike of 1968"
       Kathleen Lyons, Florida Bicentennial Commission
     "Since 1968"
       Delos L. Carroll, University of South Florida

     Comment: Richard Batchelder, Florida Education Associa-
                 tion United
               Wayne Urban, Georgia State University

11. Southern Labor Songs

     Joe Glazer, Labor's Troubadour

12. Southern Labor History Conference Business Meeting

     Presiding: David B. Gracy II, Georgia State University

                      Saturday, April 3

13. Women in Organized Labor

     Panel: Martha True, Georgia State AFL-CIO
             Eula McGill, Amalgamated Clothing Workers
             Linda Matthews, Emory University
             Mary Bennett, Duval Teachers Association
             Gloria T. Johnson, International Union of
               Electrical Workers

14. Unionization of the West Virginia Coal Fields

     Presiding: Barney Weeks, Alabama Labor Council

     "Frank Keeney Is Our Leader, We Shall Not Be Moved"
       David A. Corbin, University of Maryland
     "The Struggle Against the Law to Organize the Coal
       Fields of West Virginia"
       Richard D. Lunt, Rochester Institute of Technology

     Comment: Warren R. Van Tine, Ohio State University
               Oliver Singleton, AFL-CIO Regional Director
                 (retired)

15. <u>Transit Workers</u>

    Presiding: James Deaton, Jacksonville AFL-CIO Council

    "Public Opinion in the New Orleans Street Railway Strike
       of 1929-1930"
    Gerald Carpenter, Tulane University
    "Atlanta Transit Strike, 1949-1950"
    James W. May, Jr., Peachtree High School, Atlanta

    Comment: Jack Blicksilver, Georgia State University
              C. J. Jacobs, Atlanta Transit Union

16. Southern Politics and Southern Labor

    Presiding: William G. Whittaker, Staff, United States
                House of Representatives

    "Eugene Talmadge and the 1934 Textile Strike"
    John Allen, Peachtree High School, Atlanta
    "PAC to COPE: Thirty-Two Years of Southern Labor and
       Politics"
    Daniel A. Powell, Director, COPE, Area V

    Comment: Wayne Flynt, Samford University
              Stanton Smith, AFL-CIO (retired)

Index

Aderholt, O. F., Chief of Police, Gastonia (N.C.), 60

Adkins, Oscar F., Sheriff, Marion (N.C.), 62

Agricultural Adjustment Act, 227

Akin, Morris, 182

Alabama State Council of Textile Workers, strike called by, 229

Allen, John, 222-23, 256

Amalgamated Association of Street and Electric Railway Employees of America, strike against New Orleans transit system, 192; boycott of New Orleans transit system, 192-93; diverse groups support transit strikers, 195-98; New Orleans unions supporting strike, 203 n 13; New Orleans organizations supporting strike, 204 n 22

Amalgamated Association of Street, Electric Railway and Motor Coach Employees of America, goals of strike, 208-15; negotiations with Georgia Power Company, 1946-1948, 208-209; negotiations in 1949, 209-10; pension plan proposed, 210-211; pressure on union from power structure, 211-13; refusal to cooperate with strike investigator from citizens' committee, 213-14; capitulation to community and company pressure, 215; sale of transit company, 216; union membership, 217 n 1

Amalgamated Clothing Workers, campaign for eight-hour day, 54

American Civil Liberties Union, 140 n 104

American Federation of Full Fashioned Hosiery Workers, 57, 74 n 35

American Federation of Labor, abandoned Southern textile workers, 54; promised assistance to United Textile Workers for 1928 organizing campaign, 57; indifferent toward Elizabethton strikers, 58; supported 1930 Southern campaign, 64-65; struggle between craft and industrial unions, 65; 1930 Danville strike, 66-68; attack on United Mine Workers, 103; exploited race issue in oil industry, 176; established Labor's League for

Taft-Hartley Act, effect on
transit negotiations, 209;
stimulated CIO support for
Political Action Committee,
245; mentioned, 250, 253
Talmadge, Governor Eugene
(Ga.), opposition to New
Deal measures, 229-31; re-
fused troops before elec-
tion, 236; mobilized Na-
tional Guard after elec-
tion, 237; set up intern-
ment camp, 237; exploited
race issue, 249; mentioned,
222, 235-36, 238, 239, 256
Tarver, Congressman M. C.
(Ga.), veteran politician
defeated by Political Ac-
tion Committee candidate,
253
Taylor, W. B., director, Oil
Workers Organizing Commit-
tee, 183, 186, 187
Tennessee Federation of
Labor, 58
Testerman, Cabell, mayor,
Matewan (W.Va.), 107, 108
Tetlow, Percey, 151
Texas State Federation of
Labor, 163
Textile industry, political
influence in South, 85-86;
mill village, 87; and the
worker, 87-88
Textile worker, self-image,
87-88; influx of blacks,
88-89; wages, 91
Textile Workers Organizing
Committee, 68
Textile Workers Union, strike
of 1951, 81; and J. P.
Stevens Corporation, 82-83;
and Wellman Industries,
84-85; and Henderson (N.C.)
strike, 86; and Delta
Knitting Mills, 90; at
Cone Mills, 93; at Canton
(Ga.), 94; mentioned, 92,
95
Theophile, George J., 193
Thomas, M. A., 6
Thomas, Norman, comment on
Marion (N.C.) strike, 64;

blamed AFL for Danville
defeat, 67; mentioned, 151,
229
Thomas, R. J., 185
Thurmond, Senator Strom
(S.C.), 85
Tiller, T. Sid, president,
Georgia Federation of
Labor, 230, 233
Trombley, Bill, negotiator
for Oil Workers Interna-
tional Union, 179
Twine, Ewart, black orga-
nizer, Oil Workers Organizing Committee, 180; threatened, 181; mentioned, 185,
186, 187

United Mine Workers, Dis-
trict 17 founded, 29; in
Flat Top region, 28-30,
41 n 25; racial attitudes,
31; full-time organizer
sent to Flat Top, 34; Simmon's Creek strike, 34-35;
post-World War I problems,
103; West Virginia membership, 104; and first march
on Logan, 106-107; in
Mingo County, 107-10; second march on Logan, 110-12;
organizational framework
in West Virginia, 113;
miner complaints in Mingo-
Logan, 114; enjoined by
courts during Mingo War,
115-16; tactics used
against operators, 116-18;
effects of Mingo War on,
118-19; financial aid to
miners from, 136 n 74; and
the Socialist Party, 143 n
129; attempt to end 1912-
1913 strike, 145; collapse
in West Virginia, 149; attack on Frank Keeney, 151;
mentioned, 27, 102, 105,
106, 120, 130 n 30, 132 n
39, 44, 136 n 72, 139 n
104, 141 n 113, 146, 147,
150, 162, 175
United States Conciliation
Service, established during

About the Editors

Gary M Fink, associate professor of history at Georgia State University in Atlanta, specializes in labor and United States history. He has written articles for such journals as the *Industrial and Labor Relations Review*, the *Journal of Interdisciplinary History*, and the *Missouri Historical Review*. His previous books include *The Search for Political Order: The Political Behavior of the Missouri Labor Movement, 1890-1940*; *Biographical Dictionary of American Labor Leaders* (Greenwood Press, 1974) and *State Labor Proceedings: AFL, CIO and AFL-CIO Conventions, 1885-1974, in the AFL-CIO Library* (Greenwood Press, 1975). His *Labor Unions*, a volume in the Greenwood Encyclopedia of American Institutions, was published by Greenwood Press in 1977.

Merl E. Reed, professor of history at Georgia State University in Atlanta, specializes in United States labor, economic, and urban history. He has written articles for such journals as the *Journal of Southern History, Labor History, American Archivist*, and the *Journal of Negro History*. His former books include *New Orleans and the Railroads, The Struggle for Commercial Empire, 1830-60*. He is presently working on a study of the Fair Employment Practices Committee, 1941-1946.